Church and Theology

Church and Theology

~

Essays in Memory of
Carl J. Peter

edited by Peter C. Phan

The Catholic University of America Press
Washington, D.C.

Library of Congress Cataloging-in-Publication Data
Church and theology : essays in memory of Carl J. Peter / edited by
Peter C. Phan.
    p.   cm.
Includes bibliographical references and index.
Contents: Carl Joseph Peter in memoriam / Robert Trisco — The
contribution of Carl J. Peter, theologian / Richard J. Dillon —
Theologians in the Church / Joseph A. Komonchak — The collegiality
debate / Patrick Granfield — Differences about infallibility — too
significant to be brushed aside as inconsequential / John T. Ford —
Justification by faith and ecclesial communion / Eric W. Gritsch —
Justification by faith / Stephen J. Duffy — Contrition with tears / David
N. Power— Eschatology / Peter C. Phan.
    1. Peter, Carl J.   2. Theology, Doctrinal—20th century.   3. Catholic
Church—Doctrines.   I. Peter, Carl J.   II. Phan, Peter C., 1943–   .
BX1751.2.C495   1994
230'.2—dc20
93-41316
ISBN 0-8132-0798-3 (alk. paper)

Contents

CONTENTS

Foreword

Upon hearing the news of the death of my friend Carl Peter in August 1991, I was deeply grief-stricken. Instinctively there arose before my eyes images and memories of our many encounters and common projects. In and through them I came to know and treasure him as an endearing person and loyal companion as well as a competent theologian and committed pastor.

Our paths crossed in multiple ways. What brought us together was first of all our common academic discipline, namely, dogmatic theology. We became personally acquainted with each other in the International Theological Commission. A fruit of this acquaintance was my visiting professorship at The Catholic University of America in the fall semester of 1983. In his capacity as dean of the School of Religious Studies, Carl had extended me the invitation. The time in Washington was for me very stimulating. He was solicitous, with touching care, to make my stay as pleasant and profitable as possible. Thereafter we remained in brief but regular contact with each other. In the summer semester of 1986 Carl was in turn a guest professor at the Catholic Theological Faculty at the Eberhard-Karl University in Tübingen. At more or less regular intervals we met each other in Rome as members of the International Theological Commission. At these meetings Carl proved himself to be my valuable and committed dialogue partner.

Carl Peter developed a theology firmly anchored in the life of the Church. Even though he suffered in many ways because of the Church, he loved her. The religious formation he received from his parents as well as his studies in Rome, and above all his pastoral activities, enabled this love to grow and mature. As a professor of theology, Carl knew that one could draw the attention of the theological world to oneself if one held fringe positions, but he was also convinced that the Church would not be truly served thereby except in the rarest of cases. His theology was and is Church theology, though in no way could he be characterized as a "corporate" or "court" theologian. In this he was very much an American: honest and above all fair. Both quantitatively and qualitatively, Carl's publications never originated in an ivory tower. On the contrary, they were shaped by his pastoral care as well as by his collaboration in many Church and academic commissions and boards. In these societies his nuanced and balanced opinions were held in high esteem. In particular, he was again and again consulted by the American bishops as a trusted adviser.

Carl Peter's commitment to the ecumenical cause was guided by similar interests. Here too this is evident not only in his many scholarly publications on ecumenical issues but also in his activities in connection with ecumenical associations. From 1967 to 1972 he was a member of the Bilateral Ecumenical Consultation for Dialogue between the Roman Catholic Church and the Presbyterian/Reformed Churches; from 1969 to 1970, a Roman Catholic Observer to the Department of Faith and Order in the National Council of Churches; from 1971 to 1972, an appointed member of the Commission on Faith and Order. Also in the ecumenical context Carl and I had many opportunities to come into contact.

One outstanding event in which our paths crossed again was the Extraordinary Synod of Bishops in the fall of 1985 in Rome. Carl Peter had already been a *peritus* in the 1971 and 1983 synods. In 1985 the task of theological secretary was assigned to me. Early on the idea came to us to hold during the long Roman siestas (the best institution Rome has ever founded!), parallel to the official synod, a sort of "Robbers' Synod" in which we theologians discussed among ourselves the texts of the official commissions. The relator of the synod, Cardinal Daneels, was extremely interested in these consultations. As always, Carl was very committed to them.

It was always a joy for me to meet Carl. Were I to describe his personality in a single sentence I would simply and merely say: He was quite a guy and a good sport. I particularly appreciate his loyalty and devotion to those who were close to his heart. In his way of seeing things and dealing with them, there shone unmistakably his German-American background, in particular his wonderful blend of affability and American pragmatism. He scorned, and rightly so, the myth of German professors, but he knew how to appreciate their scholarly thoroughness, and in this respect in no way was he their inferior. Lastly, and most profoundly, he was a man and a priest of childlike piety.

I rejoice over the fact that this volume has been planned to honor Carl Peter. It provides an excellent insight into the life and work of this important man and introduces readers to the central themes of his theology. I sincerely thank all those who have contributed to the realization of this book and wish it a wide and favorable reception to perpetuate Carl Peter's memory.

BISHOP WALTER KASPER
(translated from the German by Peter C. Phan)

Introduction

It would not be inappropriate, I suppose, to introduce this volume in memory of Carl Peter with a personal anecdote. In the morning of Monday, August 19, 1991, I met Carl at the faculty mailboxes in the Theology Department. We briefly swapped stories about our summer activities. Carl told me he had enjoyed teaching in the summer school at St. John's University in Collegeville, Minnesota. Then I reminded him that I had written him a note earlier asking him to come to one of the classes in my seminar for incoming doctoral students and talk about the nature and tasks of systematic theology. Carl said that on the day I had asked him to lecture he would have to be at a Lutheran-Catholic Dialogue meeting. However, due to budget constraints there was a possibility that the meeting would be canceled. In that case, he said, he would love to comply with my request. Sometime that evening Carl died.

The conversation would not have been anything more than a friendly chit-chat with no particular significance except for the fact that in retrospect it reveals three characteristics of Carl Peter: his love for teaching, his interest in ecumenical unity, and his generosity toward colleagues and students. These traits can readily be acknowledged by those who had the good fortune to know Carl.

Carl Peter had not yet reached the age when professors are usually honored with festschrifts by students and friends. Shortly after his death, it occurred to me that such a posthumous homage is the least The Catholic University of America could do to pay the enormous debt it owed him and to perpetuate his memory. In planning this commemorative volume for Carl Peter I had two things in mind. The essays should deal with theological themes that lay close to Carl's heart and on which he had produced significant writings, and the contributors should be chosen from among those who knew him personally.

The foreword and the first two essays give us insights into the life, work, and theology of Carl Peter. Bishop Walter Kasper eulogized his friend as theologian, ecumenist, and churchman. Robert Trisco paints a portrait of Carl against the background of his family and his manifold activities both inside and outside The Catholic University of America. Richard Dillon evaluates Carl's theological achievements in three areas: faith in search of understanding (theological method), faith in search of hope (eschatology), and faith in search of consensus (ecumenical dialogue).

The title of this volume, *Church and Theology*, not only recalls Carl Peter's double life long love—Carl was quintessentially a theologian in the service of the Church to which he was intensely loyal—but also serves as the leitmotif of the remaining seven essays. In one way or another they all touch upon important aspects of the relationship between theology and church life.

Joseph Komonchak argues for a *concrete* understanding of the mutuality between church and world and within this ecclesiology discusses both the function of theology as a public discourse and the role of theologians *in* (not *and*) the Church (not the magisterium). Patrick Granfield presents the current discussion on one of the important issues of post-Vatican II ecclesiology, namely, episcopal collegiality, especially as it is exercised in the synod of bishops and episcopal conferences. From his analysis it is clear that episcopal collegiality is a unique, complex, and processive reality, not to be modeled on other social structures. Starting with a discussion of Carl Peter's writings on papal infallibility, John Ford moves on to evaluate the U.S. Lutheran–Roman Catholic Dialogue's common statement, *Teaching Authority and Infallibility in the Church*, and offers a critical *tour d'horizon* of current literature on papal infallibility, commonly recognized as one of the most intractable obstacles to ecumenical unity. Ford concludes by outlining some outstanding issues for a theology of infallibility, such as the questions of *jus divinum*, doctrinal development, and the "reception" of noninfallible teachings.

Eric Gritsch focuses on another common statement of the U.S. Lutheran-Roman Catholic Dialogue, *Justification by Faith.* After a survey of the history of the theology of justification in both the Roman Catholic and Lutheran Churches, he assesses the common statement in the light of that theology. He concludes by urging that agreement among the churches should not be limited to doctrinal matters but should be extended to worship, to "pulpit and altar fellowship." Stephen Duffy essays a contemporary theology of justification, a much-neglected theme in current Roman Catholic theology, by retrieving the insights of Girolamo Seripando's "double justice" theory, John Henry Newman's *Lectures on the Doctrine of Justification*, and Paul Tillich's notions of existential alienation and doubt. Duffy argues that these insights provide a much-needed corrective to current anthropologies that overemphasize the person's agency and freedom to the eclipse of his creatureliness, vulnerability, and communal history.

David Power studies the practice of expressing sorrow for one's sins by means of compunction, often accompanied by tears, common in early penitential liturgies, from canonical penance to tariff penance to medieval devotional literature. He then attempts to retrieve this practice for contemporary life on the basis of the concept of God's holiness. Peter Phan uses the recent document of the International Theological Commission entitled "Current Questions on Eschatology" as a springboard to assess contemporary theology of the "Last Things," especially of such issues as the intermediate state, reincarnation, and *apocatastasis.* He then explores new approaches to this central (but not last) theme of Christian theology that listen to other religious traditions; promote liberation for the poor and the oppressed because of race, class, and gender; and attend to the integrity of the whole creation.

A man averse to adulation, Carl Peter, I suspect, would have been ill at ease with this, albeit modest, homage to him. But he would, I am no less certain, enjoy immensely the theological discussions this book will spawn, even though he might not agree with every position espoused by contributors to this volume, and would say so without beating around the bush, peremptorily, stentoriously. That was the Carl Peter we knew and loved. May he live forever with God and in our memory.

PETER C. PHAN

PART I

Carl Peter

A Portrait

1

~

Carl Joseph Peter
In Memoriam

ROBERT TRISCO

When Carl Joseph Peter was found dead in his quarters in Curley Hall on the campus of The Catholic University of America on the morning of August 20, 1991, at the age of fifty-nine, he was mourned not only because he had been expected to live for many more years but also because he was prevented by this relatively early death from making many more contributions to theology and the Church. Yet in his rather short life he had already accomplished far more than most priest-scholars accomplish in a career of normal length. Theologians will judge his scholarship; in this essay the main events of his six decades will be sketched.

When he was buried alongside his mother and father in a cemetery in Omaha, he was returned to the soil from which he had sprung and in which he had struck deep roots. If knowledge of one's family background is always necessary for an adequate understanding of mentality and outlook, this requirement is especially compelling in the case of Carl Peter, who was so proud of, and loyal to, his grandparents, parents, and siblings. His paternal grandfather, the patriarch of the family, Valentine Joseph Peter, who lived until 1960, emigrated from a town in Franconia with his parents and two sisters at the age of fourteen in 1889 and settled in Rock Island, Illinois. Since his father was ill and died three years after arriving in the United

3

States, Valentine had to work to support his mother and sisters and could not attend high school, though he did go to night school. Eventually he was employed by a German-language newspaper, and soon he came to learn every aspect of the newspaper publishing business and printing trade. In 1897, at the age of twenty-two, he went to Peoria to work as a city editor of *Die tägliche Sonne*, while continuing to study history, government, and world affairs. Six years later, with his savings and borrowed money, he bought the failing *Volkszeitung* at a sheriff's auction in Rock Island; he thus became the youngest publisher of any paper in Illinois. As German-speaking immigrants continued to flock to the United States, the number of potential buyers or readers of newspapers such as his increased. In that setting of almost limitless opportunities and boundless expectations Valentine Peter thought of expanding his business. In 1907 he bought the Westliche Presse in Omaha and purchased a weekly newspaper, which he renamed the *Omaha Tribune* and converted into a daily. Shortly afterwards he purchased two other German newspapers and consolidated them into the *Omaha Daily Tribune*, which was German in all but name; it was the only daily German paper in the states of Nebraska and Iowa. While satisfying his readers' needs for various kinds of information, he also tried to smooth their transition to American ways.

After the outbreak of World War I the German-speaking immigrants were even more eager for news from their homelands, and Valentine Peter bought out small papers in other Nebraska cities or towns. While his business was thus thriving, the public opinion of large segments of the English-speaking population turned against Germany. As a publisher and editor, Peter was even more subject to the suspicion, prejudice, and hostility of native Americans than most German immigrants, and his sons, who delivered the papers, were jeered and even physically assaulted. He had advocated nonintervention in the European conflict, but after Congress declared war on the Central Powers, he wrote editorials in support of Liberty Loan bonds. In spite of constant harassment, he never missed a publication date, while many other German papers succumbed. After the war he undertook further expansion; in the 1920s and 1930s he purchased and incorporated into the Peter enterprise German newspapers in a dozen states; eventually he acquired a total of seventeen German-language newspapers.

Through his newspaper empire Valentine Peter influenced public opinion over a large area. In politics he was a staunch Republican. He greatly admired Theodore Roosevelt and adopted his ideal of a "Square Deal" for every American. In his editorials he regularly supported Republican candidates such as Warren Harding and Calvin Coolidge. After the war he worked with many organizations to collect money for the relief of starving people in Europe; he was appointed to the committee to aid the hungry and represented especially the German-speaking sections of the Continent. In this way he became acquainted with Herbert Hoover, whom he esteemed so highly that he endorsed him even against the Catholic Democratic candidate Alfred E. Smith in the presidential election of 1928. He was also familiar with many lesser politicians and businessmen in the Middle West. He supported women's suffrage and strove to revitalize German clubs, singing societies, and other social organizations after the war.

Valentine Peter did not limit his interests to newspaper publishing. In 1922 he was appointed the Nebraska representative for the German consulate and for the Austrian consul general. He also founded a travel bureau which arranged passage to Europe and even tours for both immigrants and native Americans.

In 1905 Valentine Peter married Margareta Reese of Davenport, and eventually they had twelve children. Their eldest child, born in 1906, was named Carl (after Carl Schurz, whom Valentine admired). He graduated from the Creighton University School of Law in 1928 and helped his father manage their businesses. Willing to take calculated risks, he was gifted with prudence, ability, and vision. In 1929 he married Anne Marie Schinker, who was born in Omaha in 1905. She was the daughter of Michael Edward Schinker and Mary Catherine Mergen. The Schinker family had emigrated from Alsace-Lorraine in 1887; they first settled in Bettendorf, Iowa, and then moved to Nodaway County in northwestern Missouri before reaching Omaha in 1904. Michael was a boilermaker for the Union Pacific Railroad. Anne Marie was secretary to the vice president of Paxton Gallagher Company from 1923 to 1931.

Carl Peter died of a heart attack in 1960 at the age of fifty-four. Thereafter their son, the younger Carl, who, like his father, was the eldest child in the family, felt a special responsibility for his mother.

Mrs. Peter was active in several fields. She was a Red Cross volunteer for more than thirty years as well as a hospital volunteer. She was a member of religious societies. In her political affiliation she was a member of the Friends of the Republican Party of Nebraska from 1961 on, and in the business sphere she was a member of the boards of directors of several family companies. She died as a result of a domestic accident in 1982.

Father Carl Peter was then left as the head of the family. He had two brothers, James B. (born in 1933) and Valentine J. (born in 1934), and one sister, Mary Anne (born in 1941). James received a B.S. degree from Creighton University, an M.D. degree from St. Louis University, and a Ph.D. degree from the University of Minnesota. He became a professor of medicine in the University of California at Los Angeles, specializing in rheumatology, and director of Clinical Immunology Laboratories in Santa Monica. In 1976 he founded Specialty Laboratories, Inc., in Los Angeles, which became the largest single provider of diagnostic and prognostic testing in the country. Dr. James Peter is also a prolific author of scientific articles on medical and biochemical subjects.

Valentine followed Carl as a seminarian at the North American College in Rome. He received a B.A. degree in philosophy and a license in sacred theology from the Pontifical Gregorian University and was ordained a priest for the Archdiocese of Omaha in 1959. Later he earned a doctorate in canon law from the Lateran University and a doctorate in theology from the University of St. Thomas Aquinas. After teaching in a seminary, a college, and Creighton University, holding various offices in the archdiocesan matrimonial tribunal, and serving on several civic and ecclesiastical committees and boards, he was appointed executive director of Boys Town in 1985.

Mary Anne obtained an M.A. degree from Creighton University and married an officer in the United States Air Force, Robert Hohman. She came to be the closest to Carl geographically, for she and her family lived in Alexandria, Virginia, both soon after he took up residence in Washington and again in his last years.

An indication of Carl's pride in his family is the fact that after his own name first appeared in *The American Catholic Who's Who*, he saw to it that the next edition would contain entries also for his mother and his two brothers, as can be seen in the edition for 1980–81 (the last one ever published).

Carl was born in Omaha in the depths of the Great Depression on April 4, 1932. Starting in kindergarten at the young age of four, he attended the grammar school of Holy Cross Parish in that city, where he was taught by the Sisters of Mercy of the Union; the pastor was the Reverend John L. Paschang, who became Bishop of Grand Island in 1951. After sailing through the eight grades, he went to Creighton University Preparatory School. These first four years of Jesuit education were later to be continued in Rome. Following the example of his uncle Paul F. Peter, who was less than ten years older than he, Carl felt a vocation to the diocesan priesthood. For his first two years of college Archbishop Gerald T. Bergan sent him to the Seminary of the Immaculate Conception, conducted by the Benedictines of Conception Abbey in western Missouri. Although his education was cramped by the deficiencies then common to institutions of that kind, he cultivated his mind through copious reading. There he was introduced to the liturgical movement, which increased his appreciation of the Mass and the Divine Office.

Having proved himself to be ready to study philosophy intensively, Carl was next sent to Rome by Archbishop Bergan, who was himself an alumnus of the North American College. While a large group of new students crossed the Atlantic together on the southern route, Carl sailed alone on the *Queen Mary* and benefited from the solitude to read Toynbee and to study Italian. On September 14, 1951, he was officially enrolled in the college, which had been refurbished and reopened in 1948 by the rector, Bishop Martin J. O'Connor, at the original address on the Via dell'Umiltà; it remained there until 1953, when it was moved to the grand new building on the Janiculum. Among his successive spiritual directors were the distinguished Jesuit and former rector of the Pontifical Gregorian University, Vincent A. McCormick (a substitute for one year, 1952–53), and Frederick W. Freking, who in 1957 became Bishop of Salina. At the college Carl became acquainted with students from many American dioceses and formed friendships that were to last a lifetime. Through daily walks with his *camerata* he came to appreciate the monuments, ruins, churches, and museums of the Eternal City, and through occasional presence at papal ceremonies and audiences he developed a respectful affection for the august pontiff, Pius XII, whose great encyclicals he studied and whose tireless labors for peace and postwar moral reconstruction he admired. The periodic electoral campaigns, conducted with mass rallies in squares and marches in streets, with raucous loudspeakers attached to automobiles and garish posters affixed to the walls of buildings, kept him aware of the perduring danger of a communist seizure of political power.

Such distractions, however, did not prevent Carl from concentrating his attention on his studies. As a seminarian at the North American College, he was admitted to the Faculty of Philosophy of the Pontifical Gregorian University, which was located across a square from the rear entrance of his residence. Just as the college broadened his view of the Church in the United States, so the university expanded his knowledge of the universal Church through his contact with teachers and students from many different countries, especially Europeans, and with members of many different religious orders. To mention some of his Jesuit professors suggests the schools of thought to which he was introduced: René Arnou, Frederick C. Copleston, Joseph de Finance, Georges Delannoye, Eduard des Places, Paolo Dezza, Peter Hoenen, Vittorio Marcozzi, Francesco Morandini, Alois Naber, Francis O'Farrell, Filippo Selvaggi, and Gustav Wetter. Under the direction of this international group of scholars Carl obtained such high grades at the end of his first year that toward the end of his third semester in January, 1953, he was chosen to defend selected theses in a public disputation. Later that year, for the excellence with which he earned his very first degree, the baccalaureate in philosophy, he was awarded a *benemerenti* gold medal by Pope Pius XII. While his classmates in philosophy at the North American College were content with that degree and moved on to theology, Carl secured his archbishop's consent to take a third year of philosophy, and received the licentiate's degree, again *summa cum laude*, in 1954. His thesis was entitled "Instrumentalism and the Philosophy of John Dewey."

In the autumn of 1954 Carl entered upon the program in theology at the Gregorian University with no less avidity than he had shown for philosophy. Here too the international Jesuit faculty was comprised of some outstanding experts; his professors (those in biblical studies, canon law, church history, and other auxiliary disciplines not included) were Juan B. Alfaro, Zoltan Alszeghy, Charles Boyer, Giuseppe Filograssi, Maurizio Flick, Josef Fuchs, Clement I. Fuerst, Francis Furlong, Mauricio Gordillo, Edwin F. Healy, Franziskus Hürth, Bernard Lonergan, Hermann Schmidt, Francis Sullivan, Sebastian Tromp, Karel Truhlar, William A. Van Roo, Henri Vignon, John Wright, and Timóteo Zapelena. Carl always esteemed his Jesuit professors highly, because they were devoted to teaching and writing, lived simply, and set a praiseworthy example for their students. In due course he was awarded the baccalaureate in sacred theology in 1956 and the license in 1958, both *summa cum laude*. Meanwhile, having been appointed sacristan in his class, Carl, along with five classmates, was ordained to the priesthood in the summer between his third and fourth years of theology instead of the following December with the rest of the class; the ordination was conferred by the Vicegerent of Rome, Archbishop Luigi Traglia (later the Cardinal Vicar of Rome), on July 14, 1957, in the historic church of Santa Sabina on the Aventine.

Having completed his education for the priesthood in July, 1958, Father Peter returned to his archdiocese and was appointed assistant pastor of St. Patrick's Church in Fremont, Nebraska, and dean of studies in Archbishop Bergan Catholic High School in the same city. After two years filled with such pastoral and educational experience he was invited by Archbishop O'Connor (recently promoted to a higher titular see) to return to the North American College as an assistant vice-rector and repetitor for four years. Hence, with the permission and blessing of Archbishop Bergan, Father Peter left the Archdiocese of Omaha, as it turned out, never to have another assignment in it, though he subsequently lent his assistance to various parishes during vacation periods and maintained his contacts with the clergy.

His new work with the seminarians on the Janiculan Hill was designed to allow him time to pursue graduate studies simultaneously. Since he already held licentiate's degrees in both philosophy and theology, he decided, with his characteristic industry and diligence, to undertake doctoral programs in both disciplines. Continuing his theological studies at the Gregorian University, he wrote under the direction of Father Alfaro a 307-page dissertation, which was approved also by Father Lonergan as reader. He defended it in a public oral examination in 1962 and by invitation published it in 1964 in the prestigious series Analecta Gregoriana under the title, *Participated Eternity in the Vision of God: A Study of the Opinion of Thomas Aquinas and His Commentators on the Duration of the Acts of Glory.* Meanwhile, he fulfilled the requirements for the doctorate in philosophy in the University of St. Thomas Aquinas (formerly called the Angelicum), writing a briefer dissertation entitled *The Doctrine of Thomas Aquinas Regarding Eviternity in the Rational Soul and Separated Substances,* also published in 1964. These were to be the only books he would ever publish.

Besides immersing himself in medieval Scholasticism, especially Thomism, and contemporary neo-scholasticism, especially neo-Thomism, Father Peter also learned much about the mid-twentieth-century Church. By Archbishop O'Connor, who, besides the rectorship, held an office in the Holy See, he was instructed in ecclesiastical etiquette and acquainted with some of the personalities and practices of the Roman Curia. He witnessed at close range first the proximate preparations for the Second Vatican Council and then its first two periods. At the American College he was often at table not only with the archbishop, who was also engaged in drafting the *schemata*, but also with American cardinals and other dignitaries who were intimately involved in conciliar affairs. Hence, he could understand the background and thinking that explained decisions of the pope and of the assembled bishops of the world. Such familiarity with the mind of the highest teaching and governing authority was, of course, a distinct advantage for Father Peter in his future work.

Leaving Rome in the middle of the council, Father Peter was appointed on September 1, 1964, assistant professor in the School of Sacred Theology of The Catholic University of America and took up residence in two small, spartan rooms in historic Caldwell Hall. For the purpose of this essay it will be convenient to follow his teaching career to the end and then to take up his activities outside the University. Over the years he offered courses on creation, grace, Christian anthropology, the Trinity, faith, and Christian eschatology, and he conducted graduate seminars on "Quests of Jesus," "Ministry in the New Testament and the Primitive Church," "The Council of Trent and Ecumenism," "Theories of Dogmatic Development," "Comparative Medieval Eschatology," and "Nature and Grace." He enjoyed lecturing and also preaching, speaking with self-assurance and conviction. Meanwhile, he wrote articles—nine for the *New Catholic Encyclopedia*, which was being edited at The Catholic University of America and was published in 1967—as well as book reviews and read scholarly papers at conferences.

In 1967 Father Peter was promoted to the rank of associate professor of dogmatic theology, and in the following year he was elected the faculty representative of the Ecclesiastical Schools to the university's Board of Trustees. The latter was a delicate position at the time when some of his colleagues had signed a statement dissenting from Pope Paul VI's teaching on artificial birth control in the encyclical *Humanae Vitae*. Not only had Dr. Peter not signed the statement, but he publicly took "serious exception" to it, defending the Holy Father's right "to teach with authority and thus to assist Catholics in the formation of their consciences." Four years later he received final promotion to the rank of ordinary professor of systematic theology. His rise through the academic ranks was rapid; to be an ordinary professor at the age of forty was exceptional, especially for one burdened with so many obligations outside the university.

In 1973, through a major reorganization of academic units, the School of Religious Studies was established, and the former School of Sacred Theology was reduced to the level of a department within it. Upon the recommendation of his colleagues Professor Peter was appointed the second chairman of this new Department of Theology in 1975 and served from May of that year to August 1977. Having demonstrated his administrative ability, he was then appointed the second dean of the School of Religious Studies, succeeding the Reverend Colman Barry, O.S.B. After another consultation of the faculty four years later Dean Peter was reappointed, but he declined to be considered for a third term in 1985. He resumed full-time teaching and at the beginning of his last academic year was given the Shakespeare Caldwell-Duval Chair in Theology.

As dean, Father Peter strove to develop the school in several ways. He worked to build up the faculty and to increase the salaries, even giving bonuses to deserving lay teachers at Christmas. He secured funds to support students coming from the Third World. When the Catholic Daughters of the Americas resolved to endow a chair for American Catholic history as a memorial of the bicentennial of the American Revolution, he skillfully encouraged them to fulfill their commitment. He lavished courtesies on one of the visiting professors in that chair, Dr. Annabelle M. Melville, who was a liberal benefactor, according to her means, of the Department of Church History. In 1981 he personally wrote a proposal to the Lilly Endowment for a grant of $5,000 to seek ways of increasing the school's endowment funds. After the money was granted, he was able to pursue his appeal to Mrs. Gertrude Pardieck Hubbard of Richmond, Indiana, who eventually bequeathed approximately $1.3 million to establish an endowment fund that would provide scholarships for the brightest doctoral candidates and awards for distinguished faculty. Since Theological College was part of the school's budget, the dean had a measure of financial

responsibility for that seminary, too. *Ex officio* he was a member
of the university's Academic Senate and during those eight
years was also a member of the Committee on Academic Affairs
of the Board of Trustees; from 1978 to 1981, he was chairman
of the Senate's Committee on Honorary Degrees. (In 1990 he
again became a member of that committee.) In his management of the school he was often authoritarian; in a sharp dispute with the Department of Church History over the chair-
manship, for example, he appointed himself acting chairman
for the year 1979–80 (and even included this office in his *curri-
culum vitae*). It became evident that steps would eventually be
taken to remove the Reverend Charles Curran from the faculty
and then the dean would be squeezed between the ecclesiastical authorities and some of the faculty and students. It was not
surprising, therefore, that Dean Peter did not seek a third term.

As the Curran case wrought ever more grievous harm to the
university, Father Peter thought of undertaking a project of
personal research under the title "Academic Freedom in Catholic Theology and The Catholic University of America: A Case
Study (1967–89) with Implications." After obtaining modest
amounts from the university's Faculty Research Fund, he submitted proposals to the Association of Theological Schools in
the United States and Canada and to the Lilly Endowment. In
1990 he received $5,000 from the former and $20,586 from the
latter. Having taken a leave of absence for the year 1990–91, he
collected relevant materials, even documents not previously
available, for example, from the American Association of University Professors. He was still working on an envisioned book
when he died, but his brother Valentine has asserted that the
work will be finished.

In his last few years Father Peter also procured support for
particular collections in the University Library. After he wrote
a proposal jointly with the director of libraries, Adele Chwalek,
and with the curator of Rare Books and Special Collections,
Carolyn T. Lee, Our Sunday Visitor Foundation in March 1988
granted $25,000 for cataloguing, preserving, and bringing
to the attention of scholars a large collection of Catholic
Americana in the form of pamphlets (numbering more than

eight thousand) that had been given to the University. A year later, by means of a proposal written jointly with Miss Chwalek and the head of the library division for religious studies, Bruce Miller, he obtained $50,000 and in May 1990, $75,000 for the preservation and restoration of the canon law library as well as for the microfilming of deteriorating canon law periodicals. Finally, he persuaded the fund named in memory of his mother, the Anne Marie Schinker Peter Fund, to grant $60,000 for the preservation and restoration of rare books in Mullen Memorial Library, and he obtained other grants from the president and secretary-treasurer of Specialty Laboratories, Inc. Obviously, his interest in the entire School of Religious Studies did not decline once he left the deanship. In the same spirit he also consented in 1988 to serve on the editorial committee of The Catholic University of America Press.

Outside the university Father Peter was no less busy than within. So fond was he of teaching that he even devoted half of his summer vacation to that work for many years. From 1970 to 1989, with the exception of 1976–85 (when he was departmental chairman and dean), he was visiting professor of systematic theology in the Graduate School of St. John's University, Collegeville, Minnesota, every summer. In the summer of 1974 he also held a research fellowship in the Institute for Ecumenical and Cultural Research in Collegeville. In keeping with an exchange agreement between Catholic University's Department of Theology and Princeton Theological Seminary, he was a visiting lecturer, commuting to New Jersey every week, in the spring semesters of 1974 and 1976.

As a theologian, Father Peter became a member of the Catholic Theological Society of America when he was appointed to the faculty of The Catholic University of America and he read five major papers at its annual meetings within the next decade. From 1966 to 1969 he was chairman of its Committee on Current Problems, and from 1967 to 1969 he was secretary of its Committee for Liaison with the Committee on Doctrine of the National Conference of Catholic Bishops. In June 1970, he was elected vice president of the society, and he succeeded to the presidency for the year 1971–72. Although his younger colleague, Father Curran, had already been president in 1969–70, it was still a high honor for Father Peter to be recognized in this way when he was not yet an ordinary professor or forty years old. At the twenty-seventh annual convention he read a presidential address entitled "Why Catholic Theology Needs Future Talk Today," later published in the proceedings for 1972. Afterwards he became chairman of the Committee on Publications. At the thirtieth annual convention he was presented with the John Courtney Murray Award for distinguished achievement in theology for 1975; in the citation he was described as "a working theologian . . . who teaches effectively, studies intensively, writes significantly, dialogues sensitively, gives of his talents generously, and, in a special way, has contributed more than most to the life and growth of the Society itself." He was said to do all these things consistently and exceedingly well. With regard to his teaching he was praised for his "clarity, precision and depth of insight into the complexities of the dogmatic tracts from creation to the eschaton." Mention was also made of "his current plans for a series of volumes in systematics in the Roman Catholic tradition" that was to begin "with a treatise on Christology." Regrettably, these plans were never realized.

The citation also stated that Father Peter enjoyed "the respect and confidence of the Roman Catholic Bishops and of Protestant scholars as well." Indeed, his service both to individual bishops and to the episcopal conference had begun early and was to continue throughout his life. In 1967 he was chosen by the National Conference's Committee on Ecumenical and Interreligious Affairs to take part in the dialogue between the Catholic Church and the Presbyterian/Reformed churches in the United States. Although he served faithfully for five years, he never considered these discussions to be sufficiently serious or profound. He was pleased, therefore, in 1972, to be appointed a member of the Roman Catholic-Lutheran Bilateral Consultation in the United States, and he remained a member until he died. In this way he acquired an ever deeper knowledge of the writings of the Reformers and of the Catholic theologians of the sixteenth century and of the Council of Trent. In spite of the labor required in preparation for and in participation in the frequent meetings of this group, he derived great satisfaction both from the discussions and from the consensus statements adopted. Moreover, in 1969–70, he was appointed a Catholic observer (one of three) to the Department of Faith and Order in the National Council of Churches. Lastly, in 1986 he became a member of the Washington Chapter of the Roman Catholic-American Jewish Committee Dialogue.

Father Peter further assisted the American hierarchy at meetings of the Synod of Bishops in Rome. In 1971 he was a *peritus* for the five episcopal delegates from the United States to the third general assembly, at which one of the topics was the ministerial priesthood. In regard to the question of celibacy he advocated an experiment of married priests. When this suggestion was rejected, he returned home in a state of long-protracted perturbation. This disillusionment notwithstanding, in 1983 he was again invited to be the *peritus* of the American episcopal delegates to the sixth general assembly of the Synod of Bishops, the theme of which was "Reconciliation and Penance in the Mission of the Church." He was also appointed by Pope John Paul II an *adjutor Secretarii Specialis*. Since he had written several articles on the sacrament of penance, confession, and general absolution, he was well qualified to advise the bishops and this time was satisfied with the outcome. Finally, he was the *peritus* for the president of the National Conference of Catholic Bishops, Bishop James W. Malone, at the second extraordinary assembly of the Synod of Bishops, held in 1985 to commemorate the twentieth anniversary of the conclusion of the Second Vatican Council. In the following year Father Peter was appointed a theological adviser to the National Conference's Committee on Doctrine, and he was still serving in that capacity at the time of his death.

Father Peter's ecumenical work, however, was not limited to his participation in bilateral dialogues as a representative of the National Conference. He was also invited by the National Council of Churches to be a member of its National Faith and Order Colloquium from 1970 to 1973, was named a member of the Interdenominational Study Group on Intercommunion for the Department of Faith and Order in 1970–71, and was appointed a member of the Commission on Faith and Order in 1971–72.

Even before the papal appointment for the 1983 Synod of Bishops mentioned above, Father Peter had been appointed by the Holy Father in 1980 to the International Theological Commission for a five-year term, and in 1986 he was reappointed for another quinquennium. When he joined the Commission, the only other American among the thirty members was the biblical scholar Barnabas Mary Ahern, C.P. In the annual meetings held in Rome he was associated with prominent theologians from many countries, such as Walter Kasper, formerly a professor in the University of Tübingen and now Bishop of Rottenburg-Stuttgart, who became a good friend of Father Peter and at his invitation came to The Catholic University of America as a visiting professor in the fall term of 1983. Father Peter was a member of the Commission's subcommittee that prepared the report on "Penance and Reconciliation" in 1984. Finally, in the year of his death Father Peter was serving the Pontifical Council for the Promotion of the Unity of Christians as a member of a three-man American team appointed to evaluate certain sections of the statement *Lehrverurteilungen—kirchentrennend?* which had been published by a Joint Ecumenical Commission of Catholics and Protestants in Germany. In all his service both to the American bishops' conference and to the Holy See, Father Peter's primary object was not to please his superiors but to promote the cause of truth as he perceived it: *amicus Plato, amicus Cato, sed magis amica veritas.*

As Father Peter became known outside The Catholic University of America for his administrative expertise, he was asked to share his wisdom and skills with other institutions. From 1976 to 1985 he was a trustee of the Pontifical College Josephinum, the seminary in Worthington, Ohio. In 1988 he was elected to the Board of Trustees of Saint Mary's Seminary and University in Baltimore. As dean of the School of Religious Studies he was *ex officio* a member of the Board of Trustees of the Washington Theological Consortium; he was chairman of its executive committee during his last two years as dean (1983–85). Finally, he was a member of the executive committee of the International Conference of Catholic Theological Institutions, and he was the host for the Second General Assembly of that Conference, which was held on the campus of The Catholic University of America in August 1986, and was attended by sixty-nine delegates from five continents.

The large number of positions or bodies to which Father Peter was elected or appointed indicated the height and extent of his professional reputation. In addition, he was honored formally in several ways. As early as 1972 he was the first recipient of the Distinguished Alumnus Award of the Alumni Association of the North American College, an organization to which he was, ironically, not conspicuously loyal. Six years later Creighton University conferred on him the degree of Doctor of Divinity *honoris causa*. Honorary membership in Phi Beta Kappa was granted to him in 1985, and only two years before his death he was elected to the Catholic Commission on Intellectual and Cultural Affairs.

Unaffected by such honors, Father Peter never lost his "common touch." Although he had eaten at the Pope's table, he liked the company of ordinary, upright people, such as Anne M. Wolf (1905–1987), the secretary for many years in the editorial office of *The Catholic Historical Review* and the executive office of the American Catholic Historical Association, a woman of firm faith, strong will, frank speech, decisive action, and devotion to duty—in many ways like himself in character. At her urging he had become a life member of the association, and in her memory he established a fund and contributed four-fifths of its endowment. He was remarkably loyal to friends who he thought had been treated unjustly, and by the same token implacably hostile to those who had presumably wronged them. He maintained a close interest in his nephews, nieces, and more distant younger cousins. To the elderly he was particularly considerate and thus endeared himself to Monsignor John Tracy Ellis in his final years. With his quick wit and keen sense of humor he was, when he wished to be, a vivacious conversationalist. At the same time he seemed to his peers to be afraid of appearing to curry favor or to observe merely conventional norms out of human respect; thus he often scrawled notes in a way that the recipients could regard as slighting when proper usage would have prescribed some formality.

Although he was highly cultured, he had simple tastes and hobbies. He lived frugally, squandering no money on the furnishing or decorating of his quarters. He owned a small automobile, a Ford Escort, without such conveniences as cruise control (in spite of the long distances that he drove between Washington and Nebraska or Minnesota in the summer). He dressed plainly but always wore proper clerical attire in the classroom and the office. He liked to cultivate a vegetable garden and even to cook some favorite old dishes. Although he appreciated classical music, he seldom attended concerts or operas, much less plays. Once he left his student days behind, he rarely traveled as a tourist and never outside the United States and Europe, but he did sometimes accompany his brothers, sister-in-law, and other relatives on a vacation in the American West or on a visit to some previously unseen place such as Prague.

Another trait of Father Peter's character was his material generosity, which can be affirmed with certainty but cannot be measured with precision until his personal papers are deposited in some manuscript collection. He demanded as high a fee for lectures and other professional services as in his estimation the institution or individual inviting or requesting could afford, but then he often directed that the honorarium be paid directly to some charitable cause he designated. Similarly, he meticulously kept detailed records of expenses in order to be able to make and justify the greatest possible itemized deductions when he would file his income tax returns, but again his purpose was to hand over less to the federal and local governments and thus to have more to donate to worthy beneficiaries. Knowing that his money was being wisely spent to advance religion or learning or to relieve poverty or suffering was reward enough for him. The charitable bequests that he made in his last will and testament have not yet been disclosed.

In appearance Father Peter, while retaining much of his dark hair, increased in girth over the years. He did not deny his hearty appetite and took little exercise. Walking, as he did in the earlier years in Washington with Monsignor Joseph N. Moody, and swimming were his main forms of physical exertion. He was subject to extreme, abrupt mood swings that occasionally disconcerted his table companions. His wonted energy and apparent health concealed how badly diseased his heart and coronary arteries had become.

Hence, he succumbed at once to the massive heart attack that struck him down on the very day on which he was to fly to Germany for a brief vacation with his brother James and some members of the latter's family. His suitcase was ready, his passport valid, his traveler's checks purchased, his airplane seat reserved. But his bags were also packed in a figurative sense for the longer journey on which he was suddenly summoned to set out. He has left behind a trunk full of benefits for others—the seminarians, many of them now priests, and graduate students whom he taught, the institutions and individuals he improved, and the writings that the contributors to this volume have examined and evaluated.

Ipse dux clarus fuit et magister,
exhibens sacrae documenta vitae
ac Deo semper satagens placere
pectore mundo.

(From the Hymn at Lauds for the Common of Pastors)

2

~

The Contribution of
Carl J. Peter, Theologian

RICHARD J. DILLON

Accuracy and understatement are both unlikely when you attempt to gauge the impact that Roman ecclesiastical training might have had on a young middle-American of pious German stock and ordination-vintage 1957. Blend into this picture such "bread-basket" virtues as fierce personal and institutional loyalty, self-taxing integrity, and prickly independence, and you get the complex mixture that both promoted and limited the professional career of Carl J. Peter, theologian.

One cannot possibly assess that career without granting full weight to his unusually long cultivation in Rome: seven years as seminarian (because he started in mid-college), then four years as vice-rector and repetitor at the North American College. All of the Rome years were spent under the tutelage of the Most Reverend Martin J. O'Connor—not a theologian, to be sure, but a considerably stronger influence on CJP than most theologians would prove to be. Archbishop O'Connor is remembered by generations of "Roman-American ecclesiastics" as an unrivaled master and tutor of "romanità," that delicately cured system of cautious diplomacy and social correctness under which ecclesiastical careers are launched and held aloft. CJP himself was too encumbered by critical intelligence to use the system successfully; but its strictures against the unguarded

21

word and the uncontrollable "spin" left their definite impression on the way he lived and taught, including the way he wrote. Not that careerism was his passion either, for he knew well that scholarship and high office do not go together in the American church. It was with his native sensitivity and rigorous sense of responsibility that the incessant cautions of "romanità" found a natural and influential partnership.

On balance, the effect of this conditioning was by no means negative. For one thing, it entered a personal profile in which intellectual acuity and honesty outweighed it by far. But furthermore, it probably accounted for the moderation and craving for the middle ground which made CJP an outstanding ecumenist as well as a successful academic administrator. People always knew where he stood; indeed, they also knew that where he stood was safely within the dimensions of what the situation warranted. His "centrist" instincts kept him in an often painful struggle to keep "left" and "right" wings of the church communicating with each other.[1] The pressure on anyone standing in that breach must have grown especially intense during his two-term service on the Pope's International Theological Commission (1980–90). Unfortunately, the veil of curial secrecy over most of the commission's proceedings leaves us only guessing as to the influence for moderation and fairness he managed to wield in the many neuralgic issues which came on the agenda during his tenure.

One speaks more venturesomely of the "downside" of CJP's "centrism." One of his graduate students put it to him boldly:

1. An example of the delicate, sometimes downright acrobatic balancing which this involved can be seen in "Rendering an Account of Hope: A Joint Task of Theologians and Bishops," *Chicago Studies* 17 (1978): 159–67, where CJP argues against G. Lindbeck for the coherence of the ecclesiology and eschatology of *Lumen Gentium* (Vat. II): "The Council was not afraid to say *both-and* in contexts where a more obvious logic suggested *either-or*" (162). He was inclined to lay the blame for the current "crisis" in Roman Catholic teaching more on the governed than the governors, the "widespread attitude of take-your-pick among the dogmas" rather than the episcopal distrust of theologians which Lindbeck had alleged. Nevertheless, CJP saw some of the truth in the latter suggestion which has imposed itself more and more through subsequent events: trust between the two ranks of church teachers, he wrote, is not as lacking as some would have it, but neither is it "as widespread as it must be if Roman Catholics wish to render an effective, credible account of their hope" (167).

"Are you holding the center, or straddling the fence?" Again, it was not the careerist's guile but the faithful servant's tender conscience which kept him listening to both sides. His need to register the fact that he held both ears open sometimes burdens his published prose with qualifications and appositions which do little to clarify the argument. Moreover, his attempts to wed the old and the new in theology, like the "scribe-become-disciple" in Matt. 13:52, have also occasionally drawn colleagues' criticism of a simplistic bridge-building.[2] Most inconclusive and most unavoidable, however, is the question why his prodigious intelligence and expository skills never produced a book-length theological treatise after the two Roman dissertations. He promised such a treatise on "a contemporary systematics of belief" early in his career,[3] but it never appeared. Instead of this kind of work, which would have put his celebrated course-content and elegantly structured exposition to fruitful use far beyond his classroom, we have a slew of short to medium-sized articles, about one hundred twenty-five during a quarter-century, ranging over the breadth of his specialty with critical mass in the three areas designated for this review. His lavish generosity in time devoted to students may account for the sidelining of book-authorship, but only partially. A few of the six-score articles might have been fused into a book in less time than the next few articles took. Was it his inability to say "no" to any but theoretical queries, meaning that nearly everyone who wanted a publishable lecture or book review got one? That, too, is a partial explanation at best. There was probably also a certain inhibition before the inhumanly perfect balancing act that any lengthy treatise bearing his name would have to be. His conditioned scruples about unguarded words and their damaging "spin"—pastorally, of course, not politically—might have made the project of a full-length treatise, inevitably destined for classroom or parochial use, altogether too daunting.

2. See "A Roman Catholic Contribution to the Quest of a Credible Eschatology," *Proceedings of the Catholic Theological Society of America* (hereafter *Proceedings*) 29 (1974): 255–71, especially the critique of C. E. Braaten (276–77). We shall discuss this exchange in the second part of this paper.
3. "Does Faith Call for the Church?" *Proceedings* 25 (1970): 192 (with n. 13).

I said this last consideration was the most venturesome, but as one who knew CJP well, I wager it is true. Nor is it a mere moot issue, for the painful struggle to be perfectly evenhanded and respectful of all truth-claims has to be understood for what it was: the doubled-edged blade of his theologizing, which both exquisitely trained and occasionally inhibited the hand that wielded it. We shall find this combination of fine-tuned fairness and occasional handicap in the three areas where we claim to have found the critical mass of his publications: (1) the theologian's franchise: *fides quaerens intellectum*; (2) the theologian's ultimate service: *spes quaerens intellectum*; and (3) *this* theologian's fondest aspiration: *intellectus quaerens consensum*—the ecumenical contribution.

1. Fides Quaerens Intellectum

The 1974 issue of the yearbook of the North American College, *Roman Echoes*,[4] includes in its wide-ranging retrospect on the institution's recent history and alumni a two-page feature which tells us volumes about our subject. There, surrounded by photos of several redoubtables of the Gregorian University faculty of the *dopoguerra*, stands an admirable statement by CJP: "I Stand in Debt to Them." With geysers of nostalgia for every other feature of Roman seminary life spouting on either side, his statement humbly and gratefully recalls his professors:

They influenced students by the simplicity of their life-style, their priestly dedication, and their commitment to scholarship. I know I stand in debt to them for most of what was beneficial in my own priestly and theological formation.

Two generations of students at The Catholic University of America, and legions more from the summer sessions at St. John's in Minnesota, would testify in unison that he lived up straight

---

4. *Roman Echoes of the North America College: An Historical Collection from the Life and Experience of Its Recent Years* (Rome, 1974), unpaginated. The occasion seems to have been the twenty-fifth anniversary of the publication. The college celebrated its centenary year in 1959.

to the model he had found in those cavernous *aule* above the Piazza della Pilotta. But there is more in the yearbook statement. He venerates the professors for having required that he familiarize himself "with a system of thought that was very influential in later Roman Catholic tradition"—classical Thomism, presumably. But then, with characteristic, guarded candor:

> To be sure, I have not always found that system adequate to meet the intellectual challenges I have had to face subsequently. But what the Gregorian did offer was an opportunity to acquire a foundation for later theologizing that would still be disciplined while becoming more open to different insights and remaining faithful to the Roman Catholic tradition.

CJP's ambivalence concerning hard and fast methodologies, even that of the modern transcendental Thomism he learned via Bernard Lonergan at "the Greg," is an abiding feature of his theologizing which made room for greater pastoral accountability and ecumenical sensitivity. He clearly admired Lonergan and claimed the transcendental method diversely practiced by him and Karl Rahner as the one he sooner recurred to than any other, ". . . and not, I think, simply because I tire of searching. It seems to help me, just by being what it is, to relate what and why I believe as a Christian to why and what I think I ought to believe just by being human."[5] Here are the two basic loci of theology which he would valiantly struggle to keep in a balanced relationship: faith's tradition, what one shares with other Christian believers, and human experience, what one shares with others as human beings.[6] A further ideal of our theologian emerges as he admits his misgivings over the tendency of transcendental method to tyrannize the exposition of doctrine:

5. "A Shift to the Human Subject in Roman Catholic Theology," *Communio* 6 (1979): 72.
6. "A Shift," 57. Cf. also "Does Faith Call for the Church?" 192–93; "Christian Eschatology and a Theology of Exceptions: Part 2," in *Wisdom and Knowledge: Festschrift for Joseph Papin*, ed. Joseph Armenti (St. Meinrad: St. Meinrad Press, 1976), 285–87; "Metaphysical Finalism or Christian Eschatology?" *The Thomist* 38 (1973): 140; and application to training for priestly ministry in "Faith, Ministry, and the Role of Philosophy in the Training of Future Priests," *Proceedings of the American Catholic Philosophical Association* 44 (1970): 249–60, esp. 255–56.

Still the way they [Rahner and Lonergan] suggest that theology should be done makes Christian faith in the Roman Catholic tradition credible as commitment (*fides qua*) and as conviction (*fides quae*). In fact I know of no other method that makes that faith look like so intellectually responsible and attractive an option.[7]

Every student CJP ever taught will remember this anvil insistence of his: theology is *fides quaerens intellectum*, and there is no incompatibility between Christian faith and critical intelligence.[8] To show that faith is reasonable fulfills the theologian's basic responsibility to the church. To theologize without a clear intellectual method, on the other hand, is to indulge in "stream-of-consciousness" or "free-association-of-ideas" discourse,[9] which is basically incommunicable and so fails the test of real nourishment for church and society. (No reader will have much difficulty, however, in remembering contemporary theological discourse of this kind.)[10] CJP credits Bernard

7. "A Shift," 70.
8. "I think the interplay of both is found in good Christian theologizing" ("A Roman Catholic Contribution," 271). "A religious creed that permanently refuses to be questioned as to the why and wherefore of its pretensions cannot long or rightly expect to claim the allegiance of intelligent men and women. . . . Faith resting solely on faith and refusing even to consider its presuppositions is lacking what is required to make it credible to human minds and hearts" ("Catholicism and the Presence of the Living God," *American Ecclesiastical Review* 158 [1968]: 330). For CJP insisting on the compatibility against distancing the two, *pace* Barth (and Pannenberg), see "A Roman Catholic Contribution," 260. For Thomas Aquinas as CJP's model in this respect, see "A Roman Catholic Contribution," 263; and "Metaphysical Finalism," 137–38. See also "Doctrine and the Future: Some Suggestions," in *Toward Vatican III: The Work That Needs to be Done*, ed. D. Tracy, J. B. Metz, and H. Küng (New York: Seabury, 1978), 45–54, taking as its banner sentence the message sent by the fathers of the Second Vatican Council ("Nuntii quibusdam hominum ordinibus dati," *Acta Apostolicae Sedis* 58 [1966]: 12): "Ayez confiance dans la foi, cette grande amie de l'intelligence" (cf. *The Documents of Vatican II*, ed. W. M. Abbott [New York: America Press, 1966], 731).
9. "A Shift," 58. Cf. "Christian Eschatology and a Theology of Exceptions: Part 1," in *Transcendence and Immanence: Festschrift in Honor of Joseph Papin*, (St. Meinrad: Abbey Press 1972), 144: a word-game "one plays . . . at will and with *ad hoc* rules"—the cynic's view of theology which is all too frequently validated!
10. A reader who schools himself or herself in CJP's courtly style can find among his more than one hundred book reviews muted indications of where he found a work belonging to this genre. One instance in which he was unusually explicit was in his defense of Trent's norms for sacramental confession against a 1968 book by F. J. Heggen ("Renewal of Penance and the Problem of God," *Theological Studies* 30 [1969]: 492).

Lonergan's book, *Method in Theology* (1972), with combatting a trend of current theology away from accountability to rational method:

No one convinced of the importance of reason should fail to pay tribute to this work's author for one thing. He has made a decided effort to reverse the flight of theology from rationality. . . . Theology is a cognitional enterprise and has hope of surviving and flourishing only if it seeks to live by its nature, which involves the structure basic to human knowing and choosing."[11]

Transcendental method,[12] because it takes careful stock of the human subject who believes and craves understanding, and because it draws upon modern philosophy's engagement—not to say obsession—with the act of knowing, appears to forge the best connection between Christian tradition and the modern experience. The weaknesses of the method—its apriorism, its occasionally pretentious intellectualism, and its tendency to ignore the effects of the fall on human acts of cognition[13]—kept CJP aloof from the cheerleading one got used to hearing among the epigones of Lonergan and Rahner.

One aspect of Lonergan's procedure in *Method in Theology* that CJP emphatically did not disown is the candid admission that one's personal faith formatively influences the method of theologizing. If Langdon Gilkey criticized Lonergan for this,[14] CJP stands by him in it. In the formula, *fides quaerens intellectum*, he is not afraid to acknowledge that faith plays the prior

11. "A Word on Behalf of Method in Theology," *The Thomist* 37 (1973): 609.

12. CJP offers a lucid exposition of the method in "A Shift," 60–62, such as we missed in "A Word on Behalf." He specifies two main reasons why the method is called "transcendental": (1) because the postulated cognitional pattern is thought to be a priori, pregiven, innate—not one acquired by observation but the precondition of any kind of intellectual knowledge; (2) because in the operations which that pattern makes possible and unifies, "there is always a pointing and straining beyond the presently known and grasped." "Experience, understanding, judging, and reasoning involve a transcendental dimension because while they occur, the human subject finds present to itself an even greater unknown that has not been properly experienced, understood, affirmed, or subjected to the canons of logic." That "known unknown" is "the horizon within which all knowing occurs" ("A Shift," 62).

13. "A Shift," 70–72.

14. "A Word on Behalf," 610. Cf. also "A Shift," 69.

role, initiating and carefully monitoring its give-and-take with reason.[15] Lonergan's adherence to the doctrine of Vatican I on the compatibility of faith and reason included his insistence on the permanent validity of such doctrinal statements for the human contexts to which they were originally addressed.[16] They will always remain valid and true, CJP explains, as responses to the specific questions they were originally intended to answer. "Subsequent development occurs when new or different questions arise, . . . [but *not*] by challenging the old answers as so inadequate that they are false responses to the original questions."[17] This consensus, which was even then under attack from restive theologians like Hans Küng, got its support from transcendental method, specifically the "circularity" it found in the noetic process between the knower's vantage point and the judgments that can be reached. Lonergan's method found "what one would expect to find in the subjectivity of a believer committed to the permanent truth of certain basic positions of Christianity, not least of all about Jesus."

15. Here again, Aquinas is the model: he had *faith* as a Christian which positively influenced the answers he found about right and wrong, truth and falsehood, reality and appearance, life, death, the hereafter, and so on. But he approached these same issues in other ways; he walked these avenues in light of a *reason* possessed by other human beings without his religious conviction and its perspectives. His approach set up a "mutual relation" between the two sources of enlightenment, *reason* and *faith*, "with each at once clarifying and being clarified by the other" ("Metaphysical Finalism," 140). An interesting hermeneutical model applying the faith-reason partnership to contemporary social problems, but in the sequence choice-faith/hope-understanding, rather than the reverse, is given in "The Church—Can It Help Man Move Forward?" in *The Church and Human Society at the Threshold of the Third Millennium* (Villanova, 1975), 135–57, esp. 142–44.

16. "A Shift," 66–69; "A Word on Behalf," 610. Besides Lonergan's *Method in Theology* (New York: Herder & Herder, 1972), see his *Doctrinal Pluralism* (Milwaukee: Marquette University Press, 1971), 46: "What God reveals, what the church infallibly declares, is true. What is true, is permanent. The meaning it had in its own context can never truthfully be denied." Seconding this view, CJP writes: "Let it be clear that I too accept and appreciate the doctrine about doctrine in *Dei Filius* of Vatican I. In holding to it, I find all sorts of reasons that suggest to me I am proceeding with intellectual responsibility and not blindly or whimsically" ("A Shift," 67).

17. "A Shift," 68. See n. 24 below, concerning CJP's endorsement of Karl Rahner's appraisal of Chalcedon along these lines.

This is often the case when one relates one's basic positions to one's basic method or methods. The circularity as such invalidates neither the position nor the method.[18]

CJP's disappointment with Lonergan was in the latter's failure to apply his method to specific doctrines (other than the Vatican I "doctrine about doctrine"). He was preoccupied, as are not a few of his disciples, with showing "what operations are to be performed in the theological enterprise" rather than with affecting "the content that results when one performs those operations."[19] Karl Rahner, on the other hand, had shown the way to enlist transcendental method in the struggle to understand doctrines considered infallible by virtue of papal or conciliar declaration, though currently found by some to be incompatible with modern historical or cultural understanding. One of these was magisterial "infallibility" itself, over which Küng and Rahner had reached their "Working Agreement to Disagree" in 1973.[20]

CJP contributed his first paper published by the Lutheran-Catholic dialogue on this dispute, and his endorsement of Rahner's position demonstrated the staunch, centrist Catholic

18. "A Shift," 69.
19. "A Shift," 66. This sizeable difference in concentrations surfaces between CJP and another Lonergan student, David Tracy, when the latter had criticized the widely publicized "Hartford Appeal for Theological Affirmation" of 1975, an interconfessional statement warning against debilitating concessions by Christian theologians to contemporary secular culture. CJP, who had signed the statement "gladly" along with twenty-three other academicians and church people, contributed a survey of Roman Catholic reactions to it in the volume, *Against the World For the World*, edited by the organizers, Peter Berger and Richard Neuhaus (New York: Seabury, 1976); see "A Creative Alienation: *Hartford* and the Future of Roman Catholic Thought," 78–98. Tracy claimed that "Hartford" had mistaken the role of theologians; it is for churches to proclaim affirmations and negations (beliefs), but not for theologians, who should rather deal with evidence and argumentation. CJP's reaction is no surprise: "Which propositions do and do not call for affirmation by the Christian is a matter this writer would prefer to see theologians help determine instead of simply leaving the task to the churches. Where would the churches, whatever their structures, look to get the answers . . . ?" (91; cf. Tracy, "To Be a Theologian," *Worldview* [June 1975]: 40–41).
20. See *America*, 7 July 1973, 10–11, and CJP, "A Rahner-Küng Debate and Ecumenical Possibilities," in *Teaching Authority and Infallibility in the Church: Lutherans and Catholics in Dialogue VI*, ed. P. Empie, T. A. Murphy, and J. Burgess (Minneapolis: Augsburg, 1980), 159–62, 325–26.

30   RICHARD J. DILLON

viewpoint which the Lutheran partners could rely on hearing from him. He held with Rahner that the doctrines of Vatican I and II on the infallible teaching authority of the Church are binding on Roman Catholic believers "with the proviso that both need to be interpreted to see how they help express the gospel in the situation of the present day."²¹ *Mysterium Ecclesiae* (1973), the Holy See's "defense of Catholic doctrine on the Church against certain errors of the present day," warned that one could not, as a Catholic, deny the possibility of infallible statements. It did concede to theologians, however—in due subordination to their superiors in the hierarchy—a dialogical role in the magisterium, specifically "in dealing with the historical conditioning of the human words in which God's Word has been expressed over the centuries."²² CJP considered this an important provision. By thus admitting some historical conditioning of dogmatic expressions, the statement "left room for further investigation of what the infallibility asserted by Vatican Councils I and II may mean in a broadened cultural and Christian horizon."²³ For such further investigation, "transcendental method appears, at least in my opinion, to be the most promising philosophical theory to warrant the conviction that time-conditioned language can express infallible truth."²⁴ He an-

21. "A Rahner-Küng Debate," 165.
22. Ibid., 163, citing the U.S. Catholic Conference edition of the declaration, 8. CJP was less than satisfied by the argumentative content of the declaration. "As to the explanations that *Mysterium Ecclesiae* gives for the position it takes on infallibility, there is something left to be desired. At times being convinced is simply not enough; a teacher has to try to be convincing, especially when offering supposed grounds for a conviction" (165). Persuasion is a very basic teacher's art which he prized but with which "official" church teachers often seem to dispense.
23. "A Rahner-Küng Debate," 166. The adjoining sentence here is vintage CJP: "As to the *theological* dispute regarding infallibility, it may be around for a good while, especially since Roman Catholics can and do live their faith in a way that is directly affected very little by this controversy."
24. Ibid., 165. Rahner was an ally in demonstrating this conviction also in regard to the christological dogma of the Council of Chalcedon, which typified dogmatic definitions in being both "an end and a beginning": "it expresses a truth that will stand the test of time (an end) but that gives rise to further questions and inquiry (a beginning)" ("Jesus Christ and Dogma: Karl Rahner and Chalcedon," *Chicago Studies* 26 [1987]: 318). This perspective guards against both extremes on doctrinal statements: the traditionalists, who consider that they need only be repeated and inquiry beyond them is superfluous; and the "pick-and-choose" Catholics, who decide for themselves on dogmas to be considered too

ticipated that people on both sides of the Lutheran-Catholic barricade would be unhappy with his position, and he will hardly have guessed incorrectly. The discomfort of the embattled centrist did not befall him unawares.

Although he found such occasions for recourse to the transcendental method for understanding doctrinal statements in context, CJP appears to have become more at home with *positive theology* than speculative. As his years went forward and the work of the Lutheran-Catholic Dialogues engaged and fascinated him all the more, he concentrated on producing the kind of intense textual study of classical theological testimonies which would be his special legacy to the dialogues. A zest for this kind of work, which is not everybody's favorite, was already in evidence in his doctoral dissertations, both on the exotic subject of creaturely participation in God's eternity as taught by St. Thomas Aquinas.[25] Just as astonishing as the self-discipline required to produce such studies is the rigorously consistent and thorough hearing which CJP accords his witnesses. One thinks of the dissertations when examining later published essays on the decree on justification in the Council of Trent,[26] Trent and the Lutheran confessions,[27] or the contest

---

time-conditioned to express any divine truth today. Chalcedon, for example, in solemnly defining Jesus Christ's "one and the same" relation to the second person of the Godhead, left his human history and salvific mediation unspoken, hence in danger of being forgotten. Though one always returns to the Chalcedon statement for the truth about Christ's identity succinctly stated, one also never stops trying to get beyond the formula so as to do justice to the New Testament's christological statements "from below," such as Phil. 2:6–11 (ibid., 323). Chalcedon may therefore be incomplete and inadequate, but it is not erroneous; and analogies can be drawn to the Rahner-Küng controversy on infallibility (ibid., 324). The Rahner essay discussed here by CJP is in Rahner's *Theological Investigations* I (Baltimore: Helicon, 1961), 149–200.

25. *Participated Eternity in the Vision of God,* Analecta Gregoriana, 142, Series Facultatis Theologicae, sect. B, no. 45 (Rome: Gregorian University Press, 1964); and *The Doctrine of Thomas Aquinas Regarding Eviternity in the Rational Soul and Separated Substances* (1964).

26. "The Decree on Justification in the Council of Trent," in *Justification by Faith: Lutherans and Catholics in Dialogue VII,* ed. H. G. Anderson, T. A. Murphy, and J. A. Burgess (Minneapolis: Augsburg, 1985), 218–29, 361–65.

27. "The Office of Bishop and the *Jus Divinum*: Trent and the Lutheran Confessions," *Cristianesimo nella Storia* 8 (1987): 93–113. Most recently off the press is the laconic study of "The Communion of Saints in the Final Days of the Council of Trent," contributed to the difficult phase of the Lutheran-Catholic dialogues

between Luther and Cajetan over indulgences.[28] The style of argument is always the same: painstaking thoroughness in representing a position, with editorializing held to a barely audible minimum. The value of such expositions as working papers in the charged atmosphere of inter-confessional exchange undoubtedly accounts for the satisfaction and broad appreciation which CJP obtained in that arena (to be taken up in section 3 below).

Given the focus of his graduate training, however, CJP did not attempt to extend this kind of exegetical inquiry to the Bible, although he strongly maintained the primacy of the biblical witness to revelation and the final accountability of theology and church to that witness.[29] Interestingly enough, he had a premonition of struggles he would later have a part in—discussed already—when he issued a familiar (and largely futile) plea for cooperation between exegetes and systematicians, saying that hermeneutical sensitivity on the part of the exegete must be matched by greater accountability to the sources among systematicians; and thus the latter might reexamine what might be the valid meaning of "irreformable doctrine" in an age that is "only too aware of the relativity of any language form." "Closed, complete, permanently valid systems" to

---

which was still underway when he attended his last session (see H. G. Anderson et al., eds., *The One Mediator, the Saints, and Mary: Lutherans and Catholics in Dialogue VIII* [Minneapolis: Augsburg, 1992], 219–33, 377–79).

28. "The Church's Treasures (*Thesauri Ecclesiae*) Then and Now," *Theological Studies* 47 (1986): 251–72.

29. "The Role of the Bible in Roman Catholic Theology," *Interpretation* 25 (1971): 87–94, esp. 88: citing the declaration of Vatican II that the teaching office of the Church is not to be above but bound by God's word, especially the Scriptures (*Dei Verbum*, II, 10), which are "the soul of sacred theology," CJP avers that the assertion about theology was "more the setting of a goal than a statement of fact," and it occasioned an examination of professional conscience by many Roman Catholic systematicians. The present author's impression is that the examination of conscience never proceeded very far, especially in the United States and in the Lonergan school. Cf. similar assertions of the primary scriptural norm by CJP in "Faith, Ministry, and the Place of Philosophy," 256–58. A certain ambivalence toward the short-lived biblical "conversion" of some Catholic theologians in the wake of Vatican II surfaces in a later essay: "Perhaps it says something of Roman Catholic scholars that they could be undergoing such a conversion intellectually so close to the time when Death-of-God theology would germinate as a reaction to biblicism in American Protestant circles" ("Metaphysical Finalism," 133).

which any problem can be referred for solution are "excluded in a world which recognizes the unavoidable historical conditioning of the systematizer."[30] The exegetes, for their part, must not evade questions raised by the faith that seeks understanding, such as *why* the given books should have the normative authority that they claim, or how to avoid confusing biblical images with the reality to which they point or the truth they convey.[31] Scripture scholars should remember the disasters of the past when such matters of fundamental hermeneutics were deeded to the dogmatists. Both guilds should communicate so as to show that "Christian believing is an option capable of being subjected to critical analysis in which its freely embraced foundation stands up well under scrutiny without thereby becoming conclusively established."[32]

The last is such a typical CJP sentence, straining to express all necessary qualifications and arguing for a rational unity in theological endeavors which irresistibly go asunder. The lack of collaboration among theologians, and between them and the magisterium, caused him real discomfort. It redounds to the widespread failure of magisterial statements to *persuade* the public (see note 22 above), and so to the increasing incomprehension and antagonism with which statements of "the teaching of the church" are greeted by the secular information-media. When the church thus fails to address "faith seeking understanding," it fails to live up to one of the principal reasons why "faith calls for the church."[33]

After mentioning the disputes over "infallible" teaching and irreformable dogmatic statements, we should not pass over this final question about faith seeking understanding. What about

30. "The Role of the Bible," 93.
31. Cf. "Why Catholic Theology Needs Future Talk Today." *Proceedings* 27 (1972): 150.
32. "The Role of the Bible," 94.
33. "Does Faith Call for the Church?" esp. 193–96. Cf. also "Doctrine and the Future: Some Suggestions," esp. 46: "Believing, teaching, and confessing may be carried out on the basis of the word of God in such a way that both Christians and others are set to thinking about the meaning of life because they want to do so." Imagine if the Roman Catholic Church would "come up with ways of expressing [its] convictions that would more frequently and more spontaneously invite serious thought and reflection." Indeed!

the *freedom* which is indispensable to any intellectual inquiry that would be taken seriously, and most especially that which claims the name of Christian? Here CJP made his mark early in his tenure at The Catholic University of America, possibly with repercussions which lasted until the end of it. He subscribed to the faculty strike in support of a censured colleague in 1967 and recorded a forthright statement of the principle at stake in the dispute:

What is at stake . . . is whether education on the university level is to be taken seriously. If so, an atmosphere of *freedom* must be assured for the serious scholar in his research. . . . History offers ample precedents to warrant the assertion that the cause of truth is not served by the suppression of scientific opinion. The lot of man is not improved by removing from the scene of influence any who think and reflect and subsequently speak and write."[34]

When the theologian's questioning is suppressed or reduced to a minimum, he wrote elsewhere, "a stultified dogmatism" results, and no theologian can achieve anything of significance in such an atmosphere. Theologians must be free to pose questions responsibly, whereas fear of reprisal in one form or another in the past kept many a promising question from being posed.[35]

Already when he wrote these latter sentiments, however, CJP felt that the pendulum had swung far in the opposite direction, toward random and undisciplined questioning which provokes bewilderment and cynicism outside the specialty. He demanded of colleagues, as of himself, that theological questions be raised responsibly and methodically. In his rigorously even-handed way, he was requiring of his colleagues what he wished for in the magisterium: pains taken to *persuade* via responsible and communicable *method* of argument. He had, moreover, a tender conscience about the *admiratio populi* toward scholars of sacred science addressing one another through bullhorns! Perhaps it was the combination of his roles as consultor to the

34. "Statement during Catholic University of America Strike," in *Beyond One Man*, ed. Albert C. Pierce (published by the editor, 1967), 42 (italics mine).
35. "Christian Eschatology and a Theology of Exceptions: Part 1," 145.

Holy See and dean of his school, but he began to view academic freedom for theologians as a more complex issue than it had appeared when he was starting out. When faculty unrest recurred in the 1980s over issues continuous with those of 1967, he was not ready to march.

One can explain only some of the cooling factors which moderated his approach to cases of academic freedom at his university.[36] (He left behind no public utterance to warrant addressing individual cases.) I doubt that his basic principle on the necessity of freedom in the exercise of the theologian's charism had changed; I suppose, as with all others who age and mature, his prudential norms had changed. His high-level administrative and consultative jobs had certainly exercised that combination of innate and school-bred caution mentioned earlier. This much is certain: it was out of fidelity to himself and his sense of mission that he took the stands he did; he courted favor with no one here below.

2. Spes Quaerens Intellectum

Hope, and therefore the quintessential *future*-orientation of all Christian belief, is the pivot of CJP's theology. This means it is the middle term between the first and third segments of this study: faith seeking understanding, and faith seeking ecumenical consensus. It is also the connective tissue one discovers among many of his published works, from early essays on

36. Not the least aspect of the tragedy of his untimely death is the abortive end of the project on which he had embarked after the end of his deanship: a history of the relations between the Holy See and The Catholic University of America in the incendiary sphere of academic freedom. The only published product of this project, which had been assisted by grants from the Association of Theological Schools and the Lilly Foundation, was "The Many Faces of Academic Freedom," *Origins* 20 (1991): 520–24. As the sponsor of the lecture in which that paper was delivered at Fordham University, I well remember the palpable disappointment in the audience when the delivery was concluded. Instead of exploring the lurid details of recent Catholic University faculty strife, which everyone had come to hear, it had been a typically well-researched, rigorously (even stolidly) untemperamental presentation of the *complex* history of academic freedom as a legal issue in the United States. Strictly characteristic of CJP: ever so fair and thorough, and pleasing to neither side!

Christian "future talk" to late ecumenical papers on the inter-
cessory roles of Mary and the saints. Already in 1972, he wrote:
"In my opinion, perhaps the most important role of the theologian today is to ask the right questions with regard to man's
hope; hence the crucial character of eschatology."[37] He was fond
of citing 1 Peter 3:15 as expressing especially the theologian's
trust: "Always be ready to make your defense to anyone who
demands from you an account of the hope that is in you." He
was convinced that the Christian church had to be the "herald
of hope" to motivate the commitments and sacrifices needed
to move humanity toward God's new world, the future that
Jesus named "the Kingdom of God."[38]

a. The "Eschatological Reservation."

Of decisive importance to the tenor of CJP's theologizing,
and indeed of his whole personality, is what exegetes and theologians know as the "eschatological reservation." This is the
necessarily submissive eye to God's future which holds the con-
ceits of human projects and institutions firmly in check. He did
not hesitate to cite the future-relatedness of the Church and all
its expressions, including its doctrinal formulas, as *limitations*
on the claims that can be made for them in the present. The
Church is not identifiable with the future "Kingdom of God,"
he clearly recognized, and it is a fatal mistake for theology to
confuse them. One is the complex action of God fashioning the
future goal of creation ("the Kingdom of God"); the other is
God's historical instrument and herald of that future purpose
(the Church).[39] The nexus between Church and Kingdom is that

37. "Christian Eschatology and a Theology of Exceptions: Part 1," 146.
38. "The Church—Can It Help Man Move Forward?" 148–51; cf. "Rendering an
Account of Hope," 166–67; "Doctrine and the Future: Some Suggestions," 49;
"Why Catholic Theology Needs Future Talk Today," 157–63.
39. "Why Catholic Theology Needs Future Talk Today," 158: "The real distinction between election to the Church and election to God's Kingdom can hardly be
repeated too often. . . . A cry of dismay is still raised when the distinction is made
in some circles. This indicates the deep roots that the contrary view had in the
minds and hearts of at least a notable segment of the Roman Catholic community
in this country. It was renewed contact with biblical studies that led to seeing the
distinction once again." CJP cites W. Pannenberg, *Theology and the Kingdom of God*
(Philadelphia: Westminster, 1969), as making this point with particular effective-

of special instrumentality, involving the preaching of the gospel and the ritual commemoration of the Lord's death "until he comes" (1 Cor. 11:26), both operations of a *human* tradition and institution. With the "all-too-human" come, of course, betrayal and disappointment. And so the Church-Kingdom nexus "is a reality of faith rather than evident reflection of facts."[40] This eschatological perspective on the church fosters "a realistic ecclesiology," he declares, one he finds "Roman Catholic theologians at present less inclined to deny . . . than to neglect. . . ."[41] That is about as close to critical temper as one gets in CJP's writing, but it makes a point that is so very well taken. So much Catholic "ecclesiology," especially that which reflects American "organizational" and "planning" compulsions, gives the impression of self-contemplation and self-analysis, only slightly more sophisticated than the "prayers of the faithful" which invite the Lord's help as "*we* build his kingdom." The fine words of CJP's close friend, Bishop Walter Kasper, strike the American ear as downright heresy:

. . . the Kingdom is totally and exclusively God's doing. It cannot be earned by religious or moral effort, imposed by political struggle, or projected in calculation. We cannot plan for it, organize it, make it or build it, we cannot invent it or imagine it. . . . The Kingdom of God is, notwithstanding all human expectations, opposition, calculations and plans, God's miracle, God's doing, God's lordship in the truest sense of the word.[42]

---

ness. Catholic readers will also remember Richard McBrien, *Do We Need the Church?* (New York: Harper and Row, 1969), and the excellent summation of modern philological and exegetical insights on the formula, "the Kingdom of God," in Walter Kasper, *Jesus the Christ* (New York: Paulist, 1977), 72–88.

40. "Why Catholic Theology Needs Future Talk," 161. Neither the human character nor the sinful state nor the historical nature of the Church "offers grounds in my view for justifying a refusal to accept the Church as more than it can demonstrate itself to be—a special agent or instrument of Christ in promoting the Kingdom of God" (162).

41. Ibid., 163. As an example, he notes that the perspective was by and large ignored in the four papers on the church's mission, including his own, that were presented in the *Proceedings of the Catholic Theological Society of America* of 1970 (vol. 25, with papers by G. Baum, K. McDonnell, R. McBrien, and CJP). It is this writer's impression that slighting the "eschatological reservation" is endemic to Roman Catholic ecclesiology, and the 1970 *Proceedings* were no aberration.

42. *Jesus the Christ*, 81.

Where this crucial understanding is kept in mind, there is not only "realistic ecclesiology," but appropriate creaturely humility and tentativeness in all discourse about God—the very traits one finds in all the theologizing of CJP.

His thoughts about Church and Kingdom are found in his presidential address at the Catholic Theological Society's 1972 convention (see notes 39–41). Besides offering a premier specimen of the clarity and persuasiveness of his writing, the address marks the point of axis between the stages of his thought which we are tracing. On the one hand, it explored the relationship between eschatology and the abiding validity claimed for dogmatic statements, a problem of faith seeking understanding to which we observed his application of transcendental method (section 1). On the other hand, it counterposed the danger of *blasphemy* in denying a positive relationship between the Church and the Kingdom to that of *idolatry* in confusing the two; and this balancing of ecclesiological perils was to furnish the basis of his proposal of a "catholic principle" to counterbalance the "protestant principle" in the Lutheran-Catholic Dialogue on justification (section 3, below).

First of all, the "eschatological reservation" has obvious and serious implications for dogmatic formulations which claim to be infallible truth "that will never need to be contradicted in a changing future for the sake of the gospel."[43] Modern historical consciousness and linguistic analysis weigh in against such claims. Eschatology adds the dimension of the uncharted future, insisting that "any formula with the claim of abiding truth can only be understood in relation to world history, and that means to its own future," which inevitably makes it preliminary and incomplete.[44] God's future, powerful and trustworthy, yet also incalculable, makes everything of the present questionable, and that includes theological statements. "Those defending the adequacy of dogmatic formulae forget this too readily." But then CJP strains for the unfailing balance: "So often do others who argue against the ability of those same for-

---

43. "Why Catholic Theology Needs Future Talk," 164.

44. W. Pannenberg, "Hermeneutics and Universal History," in *History and Hermeneutic* (New York: Harper and Row, 1967), 149, cited with approval by CJP.

mulae to serve as guides that cannot prove fundamentally false in the future or need to be contradicted for the sake of the gospel."[45] As we saw in section 1, historical reason needs a boost from faith to keep us out of the camp of those "others."

CJP's ecclesiological middle-ground is circumscribed by the countervailing dangers of the idolatry which prematurely apotheosizes the Church and the blasphemy which sells it short as the Kingdom's instrument. Here is a shrewd rationale for his "centrism" which he first brought out in the discussion of eschatology.[46] It is sinful both to divinize the all-too-human in the Church and to deny God's active presence where it is bestowed. The Kingdom of God embracing all of creation is still in the future, but "the Church exists to point to that coming victory of God and to do so effectively. Indeed the faith and hope that the promise of God's reign generates . . . are already a foreshadowing of his Kingdom. . . . The consequence is that a close bond must be recognized between the Kingdom of God in the future and the Church in the present."[47] The kingdom's coming is neither the exclusive operation of the Church nor so exclusively God's as to make the Church irrelevant. The one perspective disqualifies the arrogance and presumption which are so common in churchly discourse; the other counteracts the corrosive discouragement to which the rest of us are more susceptible.

b. St. Thomas and the "Theology of Hope."

Rather less successful, in this author's opinion, was CJP's attempt to bond the argument of his doctoral dissertations to the "theology of hope," which was enjoying a very temporary

45. "Why Catholic Theology Needs Future Talk," 165. After sect. 1, we hardly need to identify the adversary here as Hans Küng. For an analogous suggestion concerning moral absolutes in eschatological perspectives, see "Christian Eschatology and a Theology of Exceptions: Part 2," 291–92 with n. 12.

46. "Why Catholic Theology Needs Future-Talk," 158–63. On the two dangers, see also "The Church—Can It Help Man Move Forward?" 148; and then in the discussion of justification, "Justification by Faith and the Need of Another Critical Principle," in *Justification by Faith* (cited in n. 26), 309; also "Justification and the Catholic Principle," *Lutheran Theological Seminary Bulletin* 61 (1981): 25.

47. "Why Catholic Theology Needs Future Talk," 159.

vogue during the years immediately following his graduation from Rome to Washington. In fact, it was very likely the coincidence of his thesis-work and the attention attracted by the early works of Jürgen Moltmann and Wolfhart Pannenberg that suggested the Thomistic version of "spes quaerens intellectum" which was laid before the Catholic Theological Society convention of 1974.[48] Actually, the convention address was a less comprehensive and, to this observer, much less persuasive statement of the case than CJP had published earlier that same year in *The Thomist*.[49] The criticisms made by the two interlocutors (see note 48) indicate that the argument was something less than a rousing success;[50] and in fact it seems not to have been further developed in subsequent publications.

More appropriate here than a rehearsal of the full argument is an analysis of what it was that did not forge conviction. CJP felt he could build a bridge between Thomas's doctrine of "participated eternity" and Moltmann's of a powerful divine future which is mostly discontinuous with past and present and risks leaving the latter all but "God-forsaken."[51] Moltmann's phrase depicting the relationship between the divine promise and existing reality, *inadaequatio rei et intellectus*,[52] had to be a red flag

48. "A Roman Catholic Contribution," 255–71, with criticisms by C. E. Braaten (273–78) and Schuyler Brown (273–78).

49. "Metaphysical Finalism," 125–45.

50. "A Roman Catholic Contribution," 267–71, is presented as a reply to the two critiques which CJP added to the published version of his paper. This section is methodological, in the main, and does not seem to address the more telling criticisms, particularly those put forward by Braaten.

51. On "the god-forsakenness of all things" and "the absence of the Kingdom of God" demonstrated by the Cross of Christ, see J. Moltmann, *Theology of Hope* (New York: Harper and Row, 1967), 223. The criticism of Moltmann by CJP ("A Roman Catholic Contribution," 259; "Metaphysical Finalism," 130–31) reflects the objection made by many against *Theology of Hope*: the word of divine promise seems to be placed in sheer antithesis to all past and present reality, and only what does not yet exist can correspond to the promise (see n. 52). Braaten complained, in response to CJP, that this familiar criticism hung on a single thread of Moltmann's early thought and did not take into account the self-corrections the latter had made in his later book, *The Crucified God*, emphasizing the anticipations of God's future in the historic Christ-event (*Proceedings* 29 [1974]: 275).

52. *Theology of Hope*, 85: "Promise announces the coming of a not yet existing reality from the future of the truth. Its relation to the existing and given reality is that of a specific *inadaequatio rei et intellectus*." See also p. 102 on the structure of promise experienced in ancient Israel.

to any self-respecting Thomist, considering the concerted attack on analogical reasoning which Moltmann mounted to defend the transcendence of the future announced by Jesus' resurrection.[53] CJP, of whose dedication to Aquinas his dissertations left no doubt, backed his quarry into a corner: is the only alternative to collapsing the future into the present to make the present soteriologically void? To this dilemma, which was overstated even in the terms set by *Theology of Hope*,[54] he proposed Thomas's doctrine of creaturely participation in God's eternity as the solution. He felt this concept was a genuine eschatology, and not the "metaphysical finalism" taking all surprise out of the future which Moltmann had claimed in dismissing it.[55] Moreover, in using the concept to understand the radical difference between human life in time and the future beatific vision, Thomas was comparing ideas he had inherited from Augustine, Boethius, and Peter Lombard with the theory of act and potency he had learned from Aristotle. He was thus doing only what Bultmann, Moltmann, and other moderns would attempt: employing good philosophy in a believer's quest for understanding the grounds of *hope* (*spes quaerens intellectum*, Moltmann's own adaptation of Anselm).[56]

In fact, Thomas's recognition of the difference between the time of earthly existence and the sphere of the beatific vision does make a necessary start toward understanding what we hope for. Because even in its present existence the human bears the divine image, it was possible to argue by analogy to a partial similarity between God and creatures in the existence they share hereafter.[57] He applied precisely the idea of *duration* analogously

---

53. *Theology of Hope*, 175–82.
54. And CJP was typically tentative about it: a "seeming" dilemma ("Metaphysical Finalism," 131). He noted that C. E. Braaten had found the same compromise of the New Testament's proleptic eschatology in Moltmann (in *Christ and Counter-Christ* [Philadelphia: Fortress, 1972], 18). For Moltmann's view of the transformation of the present through the proclamation of its future horizon, which is the gospel of the Crucified and Resurrected Lord, see *Theology of Hope*, 329–38.
55. See his essay "Theology as Eschatology," in *The Future of Hope*, ed. F. Herzog (New York: Herder/Seabury, 1970), 13.
56. "Metaphysical Finalism," 137–38. Cf. Moltmann, *Theology of Hope*, 32–36.
57. "Metaphysical Finalism," 138–39.

to God, angels, and humans, and held that the way in which the two creaturely ranks get to share God's own unique eternity can be understood by recourse to the Aristotelian theory of act and potency.[58] The intermediary sphere thus created between time and eternity was known to the medievals as "aevum," and in it angels and humans are drawn by God's grace, not their own powers, into the experience of knowledge and love without succession which Thomas saw as beatific vision.[59] This is "the ultimate perfection of which angels and men are capable in the order of knowledge and love: knowing and loving in a way akin to God's, without *before* or *after* endlessly."[60] CJP stresses—but the act-and-potency schema compromises his point—that this experience of duration-without-succession "is radically different from what both enjoy outside God's gift of himself as ultimate *grace* in his kingdom."[61] Moreover, this ultimate actuation of human potency allows for anticipations of its acts of knowledge and love in earthly human life. In particular, "*charity* is . . . the connection between present and future for Thomas. . . . The kingdom that is to come has a hold on the present and offers a foretaste of itself in Charity. The latter becomes the nexus between this life and that to come."[62]

CJP felt he had held the precarious middle ground here between eschatological dualism and an exclusively "realized eschatology." He thought he had built a bridge between Aquinas

58. Ibid., 141–43, 145; also "A Roman Catholic Contribution," 265.

59. Successive acts of knowledge and love belong to the nature of angels and humans; only God is completely without succession, which is the result of *potency* in other beings. Consequently, both creatures are drawn closer to God's eternity according to the measure of their "unactuated potency" ("Metaphysical Finalism," 142, 143). "Participated eternity is the duration of an act that completely exhausts the potency of its subject for immediate knowledge and love of God; that is, its subject is open to no greater perfection" (*Participated Eternity in the Vision of God*, 32; cf. also pp. 103, 107).

60. "Metaphysical Finalism," 143 (italics his).

61. Ibid. (italics mine). See also *Participated Eternity*, 31–34, for the emphasis on God's grace as the indispensable agency of this ultimate perfection for both angels and humans. CJP needed to bring out this part of the argument in his Catholic Theological Society exchange with Braaten and Brown ("A Roman Catholic Contribution"), whereas there, but for an allusion to "amazing grace to man in the present" (266), it is hardly aired.

62. "Metaphysical Finalism," 144 (italics mine). A radical dualism between future and present is thus avoided, says CJP, without collapsing the future into the present (cf. also 141).

and the "theologians of hope," but it is not difficult to see why the latter would not be won over. Only a few years after the 1974 Catholic Theological Society debate, two other Catholic theologians, G. Greshake of Vienna and G. Lohfink of Tübingen, published essays which explored the same terrain, though they surprisingly made no mention of CJP's work.[63] Their evaluation of Thomas's position showed just the degree of critical distance that CJP had not been able to gain, either in his dissertations or, less understandably, in the later essays. For example: (1) Lohfink thought the "aevum" concept was a helpful, even necessary gambit for moving eschatology out of the rigid alternative between time and eternity. Understanding of "aevum" gained nothing, however, from speculative analogies with the angels or the act-potency scheme; in these, Thomas was unable to rise above his time. The phenomenology of earthly existence in time is the only solid ground on which to arrive at what "aevum" might involve.[64] (2) Greshake confirms what we had reason to fear when act and potency came into the discussion: that the transcendence and gratuity of the Kingdom of God were put at grave risk. Under the dualism of body and soul which persists in Thomas's thought, immortality naturally accrues to the soul as a subsisting spiritual entity. According to a syllogism that further muddies the water, the existence of the soul outside the body cannot go on in perpetuum because it is "contra naturam."[65] The logic seems (videtur) to lead to the necessity of the resurrection of the body, and Thomas only meets this problem through last-minute theological scruple. The problem, like not a few others, comes from the legacy of Greek anthropology.[66]

63. *Naherwartung, Auferstehung, Unsterblichkeit: Untersuchungen zur christlichen Eschatologie*, Quaestiones Disputatae 71, 5th ed. (Freiburg: Herder, 1982).
64. Lohfink, "Zur Möglichkeit christlicher Naherwartung," in *Naherwartung* 38–81; here, 64–67. It is interesting that J. Ratzinger rejected the application of "aevum" to Christian eschatology on the basis of the unviable analogy with angels; see his *Eschatologie—Tod und ewiges Leben* (Regensburg: Pustet, 1977), 150–52, and the reply of Lohfink in "Das Zeitproblem und die Vollendung der Welt," in *Naherwartung*, 131–55; here, 145–47.
65. *Summa contra gentiles* IV, ch. 79.
66. G. Greshake, "Das Verhältnis 'Unsterblichkeit der Seele' und 'Auferstehung des Leibes' in problemgeschichtlicher Sicht," in *Naherwartung*, 82–120; here, 95–96.

It is not that CJP overlooked the problem which "partici-pated eternity in the rational soul" raised by seeming to make bodily resurrection "an afterthought or anticlimax."[67] He in-cluded in his dissertation the apparently wavering views of Thomas on whether bodily resurrection "brings the blessed any intensive increase of glory."[68] Thomas clearly thought that, de-spite the "unnatural" condition of the human soul outside the body, the soul was capable of *perfect* beatitude in the separated existence it has between the moments of death and the general resurrection. He declared it "obviously false" to deny that "the soul can have beatitude without the body." To avoid making bodily resurrection otiose altogether, he took the usual way out: he posited a distinction between essential and existential perfections of the beatified soul and claimed that reunion with the body pertained only to the latter.[69] The conundrum for the person wishing to stand with Thomas on the middle ground between metaphysical finalism and transcendent eschatology seems thus to be quite formidable.[70]

CJP knew well these *non liquets* in Thomas's position, but he did not see the compromise of Christian eschatology in them that others have seen. Nor did he recognize any obstruction of Thomas's potential contribution to the modern "theology of

67. "Metaphysical Finalism," 131, identifies this as the error of substituting metaphysical finalism for authentic eschatology.

68. *Participated Eternity*, 273–80: the commentary on the Book of Sentences (*In IV Sent.*) seems to say it does, whereas the *Summa theologiae* seems to exclude any increase by making the beatific vision "one, continuous, and everlasting" (I-II, q. 3, a. 2, ad 4).

69. *Summa theologiae* I-II, q. 4, a. 5. Greshake: "According to Thomas, then, the beatitude of the soul is increased by the body, but that does not keep him from speaking of the *perfect beatitude* of the soul. It is therefore questionable whether the preliminary nature of the soul's beatitude can be pointedly brought out in the writings of high scholasticism . . . " ("Das Verhältnis," 96; italics his).

70. Schuyler Brown's critique of CJP in *Proceedings* 29 (1974): 279–82, deals with the compromise of New Testament eschatology which the Thomistic argu-ment seems to involve; but Brown proceeds entirely too far in the opposite di-rection by overlooking the elements of present foretaste and "earnest" that are present even in the Pauline perspective he emphasizes. I emphatically agree with Brown when he observes: "Luther's distinction between the *theologia crucis* and the *theologia gloriae* seems not to have lost its cautionary importance for Roman Catholic theology." I am not sure, however, that CJP deserved to be a particular target of this caution; cf. "Christian Eschatology and a Theology of Exceptions: Part 2", 288–90; "Why Catholic Theology Needs Future Talk."

hope" in the fact that the latter's notion of faith had "a strong structural dependence on a kind of authority that failed to withstand the onslaughts of critical reason during the Enlightenment."[71] The temperamental factor in his mostly uncritical promotion of the Thomistic eschatology appears where he complains that "too few people take him [Thomas] seriously any more."[72] More than the usual "bridge-building" and "centrist" thinking are at work here, it would seem. This is CJP the dogged loyalist; and Thomas Aquinas was one of the icons of his schooling that resisted even the extremely gentle kind of criticism he might address to other theological witnesses.

c. Mary and the Saints in Eschatological Perspective.

In the mid-1980s, after the Lutheran-Catholic dialogue had registered its important convergences on, but diverging applications of, the doctrine of justification by faith, it identified certain test issues for the application of this "criterion of authenticity for the church's proclamation and practice."[73] Among such obvious problems as means of grace, ecclesiastical structures, and infallibility, the Lutheran partners wondered "whether official teachings on Mary and the cult of the saints, despite protestations to the contrary, do not detract from the principle that Christ alone is to be trusted for salvation because all God's saving gifts come through him alone."[74] To this issue, which has been around since the Reformation and will likely continue to rankle in the foreseeable future,[75] CJP felt it poten-

---

71. C. E. Braaten, *Proceedings* 29 (1974): 277.

72. "Metaphysical Finalism," 132; cf. also p. 145: "This was a medieval who in his own way came very creditably to grips with a problem facing eschatologists of our day as well. For that fact alone he deserves much more serious attention from our contemporaries than he is receiving." In saying "mostly uncritical," I make room for the fact that CJP did acknowledge that Thomas "did not understand the relation between believing faith and critical reflection in terms of historical consciousness. One is obliged to do so after Dilthey" ("A Roman Catholic Contribution," 270).

73. "Justification by Faith: Common Statement," *Justification by Faith* (see n. 26), 57, 69.

74. Ibid., 57.

75. Some of the Reformation background, especially Luther's sharp criticisms in the *Smalcald Articles*, is surveyed by CJP in "The Church's Treasures," esp.

tially soothing to apply the "eschatological" perspectives of
Lumen Gentium, the Second Vatican Council's dogmatic constitution on the Church.[76] He recounted one of the historic con-
tests between conservatives and liberals at the council which
led to a significant victory for the latter: the containment of
the treatment of Mary within that of the Church, hence her
steadfast association with Christ the Redeemer and with the redeemed. Chapters 7 and 8 of *Lumen Gentium* thus deal successively with the saints and Mary, and the connecting link
between them is "the eschatological nature of the pilgrim
church and its union with the heavenly church."[77]

This is a significant adjustment of the perspective we discussed above, under "the eschatological reservation." The
Church is portrayed in the constitution as looking to the future
for its final perfection and the completion of the work God has
already begun with it (VII, 48); but the saints and Mary represent that segment of the Church that is already arrived at its
perfection, hence can function as model, sign of hope fulfilled,
and source of effective intercession for the struggling society of
"wayfarers" (*ecclesia viatorum*). Although an ingredient of future
expectation is retained here and the differences between
present and future are not overlooked,[78] the exiles on earth and
the glorified in heaven are said to "form one church and are
united one to another" in belonging to Christ (VII, 49).[79] This
legitimately blends the perspective of the Deutero-Paulines (Co-

---

270–72. In his 1988 essay, "A Moment of Truth for Lutheran-Catholic Dialogue,"
CJP observes that there are "genuine differences between Lutheran and Roman
Catholic members of the dialogue when it comes to assessing creaturely mediation and cooperation in the ways in which Christ's grace reaches human
beings" (*Origins* 17, no. 31 [1988]: 541). See n. 115 below.

76. "The Saints and Mary in the Eschatology of the Second Vatican Council,"
in *The One Mediator, the Saints, and Mary* (n. 27 above), 295–304, 389–91. This
essay duplicates and enlarges "The Last Things and *Lumen Gentium*," *Chicago Studies* 24 (1985): 225–37.

77. *The Documents of Vatican II*, 78–96; cf. CJP, "The Saints and Mary," 299;
"The Last Things," 231.

78. Cf. "The Saints and Mary," 299–300; "The Last Things," 232–33.

79. "The mystical body of Jesus Christ has bonds linking members on both
sides of the pale of death" ("The Saints and Mary," 301; "The Last Things," 234).
CJP cites this doctrine as the foundation of the practice of offering prayers for the
dead, considering that a third category united in "the one church" is the group
of those who have died "and are being purified" (VII, 49).

lossians, Ephesians) with Paul's own sustained emphasis on the eschatological tension defining Christian existence between the resurrection and the parousia. Deutero-Pauline ecclesiology tended to draw these two christological events into one so that the Church became identified already with the heavenly society of the redeemed.[80] This was part of a New Testament development away from the "temporal tension" inherent in Paul's eschatology, favoring the progressive merger of heavenly and earthly spheres rather than the apocalyptic dualism of present and future. *Lumen Gentium*, like most other utterances of the magisterium, shows a pronounced leaning toward this un-Pauline "apotheosis" of Church, where the Exalted Lord and the Church threaten to become indistinguishable. Here lies an abiding difference between Lutheran and Catholic thought-structures, cloven precisely by divergent *eschatologies*.[81] Unless the small grain of "eschatological reservation" in *Lumen Gentium* can be enriched by the nuanced arguments CJP advanced above (Church-Kingdom difference, and so forth), Lutherans and Catholics are unlikely to chart the common ground for their beliefs about Mary and the saints, or any of the other "mediation" issues.

d. Summation.

By locating the center of gravity of his published thought in *eschatology* rather than the ecclesiology favored by so many Catholic theologians, CJP demonstrated his sensitivity to a root nerve of confessional differences between modern Christians, but also his feeling for exactly where theology comes to grips

80. J. C. Beker, *Paul the Apostle: The Triumph of God in Life and Thought* (Minneapolis: Fortress, 1980), 159–63.

81. Gerhard Forde, "Justification by Faith Alone," in *In Search of Christian Unity*, ed. J. A. Burgess (Minneapolis: Fortress, 1991), 64–76; here, 74–75. Forde, a Lutheran participant in the Dialogue, cites J. Moltmann: "When the universal church excluded Marcion as a heretic, it lost for itself the category of the new. . . . Since then, God's revelation has no longer been proclaimed in terms of the claim of the new and of freedom for the future, but it has been proclaimed by the authority of what is old and always true. No longer is the *incipit vita nova* announced, but instead a *restitutio in integrum*" (*Religion, Revolution, and the Future* [New York: Scribner's, 1969], 14).

with the needs of ordinary people.[82] "Giving an account of our hope" means all three things developed in this section: (a) letting the future discipline the present and put a rein on churchly presumption; (b) finding grounds for hope in the present experience of the baptized; (c) defining the bond which exists between the living and those who have preceded us in death. CJP gave creditable if not uniformly compelling "accounts" in all three areas. We can only hope for a skillful editor willing to forge the scattered essays into a first-rate, book-length *Eschatology*.

3. Intellectus Quaerens Consensum

CJP's appointment to the Lutheran-Roman Catholic Bilateral Ecumenical Consultation in 1972 began a truly remarkable and unpredictable shift in his career as a theologian. When he became a regular participant in dialogues with non-Catholics, his native sensitivity and largesse of spirit began to overrule the narrower reflexes of his training, and he undertook an earnest audition of both the Lutheran voices on the Dialogue and their founding fathers. Most amazing to his students and friends was the scrupulous and sympathetic study he devoted to Martin Luther himself, whose image adorned a T-shirt given him by appreciative Lutheran seminarians at Gettysburg. No one should have been surprised, come to think of it; Luther was simply receiving the treatment anyone could expect from one who took their common faith so seriously.

The agendas included at the beginning of the published volumes of the Lutheran-Catholic Dialogue will show that CJP delivered many more papers than he published.[83] There is a cumu-

---

82. "The Church—Can It Help Man Move Forward?" 151–52: "Many need not only a chance to hope, but a reason for hope . . . if they are to rise above their status quo and exert efforts for others. Christian doctrine, with the powerful tradition it arises from, must engage the world in a give-and-take at precisely this point: challenging people to purify, intensify, and multiply the kind of situation in which God's promise can make its influence felt."

83. Some of the unpublished papers contain broader slices of the Luther-research he contributed to the common statements of the dialogue. An example is

lative and reiterated substance to his Dialogue-related essays, however, which warrants our trust that the essence of his contribution is accessible in the publications.

In 1980, with the Dialogue embarked on its consideration of *justification by faith*, CJP advanced his proposal of a "catholic principle" to complement the criterion of all church preaching and practice which Lutherans posit in justification.[84] He would later admit that "the catholic principle," with its exclusionary confessional sound, was not the best name for what he was advocating;[85] but he continued to insist that his "principle" is a rigorously necessary consequence of taking justification *as criterion* seriously. It is possible that justification *as criterion of all church life* was finally soft-pedaled by the Lutheran Dialogue partners in the interests of a common statement, with the result that CJP's counter-criterion did not win the consideration that it might have.[86] It is curious, in any case, that the

---

"The Centrality of Justification by Faith in the *Smalcald Articles*: A Contemporary Roman Catholic Assessment and Response," which was read at a symposium on the Lutheran Confessions at Concordia Seminary, Fort Wayne, Ind., in January 1987. Correspondence I found in that file indicated CJP expected publication of the paper in the *Concordia Theological Quarterly*, but that seems not to have followed.

84. "Justification and the Catholic Principle" (1981). This paper was delivered outside the Dialogue, at the Martin Luther Colloquium at the Gettysburg seminary in 1980. The discussion following the paper (25–32) is valuable as a source of both the further thoughts of CJP and the predictable reservations of the Lutheran partners. The criteriological weight of justification by faith as the *articulus stantis et cadentis ecclesiae* comes from a famous statement of Luther: " . . . quia isto articulo stante stat Ecclesia, ruente ruit Ecclesia" ("Expositio in Ps 130:4"; WA 40/3:352–53).

85. "Justification by Faith and the Need of Another Critical Principle, " 376, n.2.

86. This is, at any rate, the contention of Gerhard Forde, who confesses disappointment with the common statement precisely because it did not address the criteriological significance of justification *sola fide* ("Justification by Faith Alone"). It spoke of "increasing accord on *criteria* of Christian authenticity" (plural) and accepted "justification as *an* [not *the*!] *articulus stantis et cadentis ecclesiae* protective of the *solus Christus*" (*Justification by Faith*, 70, 73). Similar skepticism concerning the common statement and a more explicit complaint that the Lutherans on the dialogue were too amenable to the other side are expressed in C. E. Braaten, *Justification: The Article by Which the Church Stands or Falls* (Minneapolis: Fortress, 1990), 118–23. Forde names CJP as "one of the happy exceptions to the general reluctance to discuss the issue of the criteriological significance of justification by faith alone" ("Justification by Faith Alone," 69). His earnest listening to Lutheran voices left no doubt that justification was "not just another doctrine or even the first among doctrines," but the *articulus stantis et cadentis ecclesiae*, and he was determined to take this seriously ("A Moment of Truth for Lutheran-Catholic Dialogue," 539; "Justification and the Catholic Principle," 18).

paper advocating "another critical principle" (n. 85) is listed in
the *Justification* volume of the Dialogue as "commissioned by
the dialogue and discussed in a conference telephone call by
the systematic theologians on the dialogue."[87] Was CJP being
more honest with the exigencies of both sides than the majority of the partners wanted to be?

His "Catholic principle," or whatever we should finally call
it, was drawn from Paul Tillich's distinction between "the catholic substance" and "the protestant principle" in Luther's
legacy.[88] The first was "the body of tradition, liturgy, dogma,
and churchmanship developed chiefly by the ancient church"
and embodied for Luther in the Roman church of his day.[89] The
second was the understanding of salvation in terms of the unconditional grace of God by which the sinner is declared *just*
(in the right) without any winning deed on the latter's part,
only the submissive disposition of faith in the redeeming death
of Jesus Christ (*sola fide*).[90] This authentically Pauline view of
salvation as inalienably and unqualifiedly *God's* doing had to
be wielded as a razor-sharp pruning knife against all pretensions of humans and their institutions to deliver salvation on
terms of their own. Since such pretensions can be made in
practically any quarter of church life, the truth of justification
had to be considered *the* criterion of all Christian expression,
working against "a self-absolutizing and consequently demon-

87. *Justification by Faith*, 12. Approval of CJP's Catholic principle came from at least one other Roman Catholic participant in the dialogue, Avery Dulles, S. J., in *The Catholicity of the Church* (Oxford: Clarendon Press, 1985) 6–7.

88. "Justification by Faith and the Need," 305–8. According to Tillich, justifi- cation by grace through faith is the "first and basic expression of the Protestant principle itself" (*Systematic Theology* III [Chicago: University of Chicago Press, 1963], 223); but he was concerned that the protestant principle should not be considered apart from the "catholic substance," without which there would be danger of reducing or eliminating the sacramental mediation of God's Spirit (122). CJP also cites Jaroslav Pelikan, *Obedient Rebels: Catholic Principle and Protestant Prin- ciple in Luther's Reformation* (New York: Harper and Row, 1964).

89. "Justification and the Catholic Principle," 18.

90. One gets both a first-rate introduction to justification as theological topic and a choice specimen of CJP's lucid expository style from his brief article, "Justifi- cation," in *The New Dictionary of Theology*, ed. J. Komonchak et al. (Collegeville: Glazier/Liturgical Press, 1988) 553–55. See also "Sin and Atonement in the Roman Catholic Tradition," in *The Human Condition in the Jewish and Catholic Traditions*, ed. F. E. Greenspahn (Hoboken: Ktav Publishing House, 1986), esp. 129–46, 137–45.

ically distorted church"[91] when the ultimate trust of believers is awarded to any of the church's creations.[92] CJP was quite willing to take this "stand-or-fall" criterion with complete seriousness inasmuch as it is a protection against the idolatry which exchanges God's saving works for human works.[93] But now we recall our discussion of the twin perils of idolatry and blasphemy in appraising church life in section 2a.

Out of a desire to avoid confusing the creaturely with the Creator and to realize that no work of a sinful creature can win God's forgiveness, they [the churches] may regard the sacred as something religiously indifferent or even sinful. To fail to recognize the divine where it is in fact being mediated or embodied because the mediating agency . . . (is) touched by a sin may well involve both insolence and arrogance with regard to the divine. Christian churches need to avoid both idolatry and blasphemy in their attitudes and stances toward the Catholic substance. Justification by faith alone helps as a safeguard against the former; another critical principle is needed to assist in avoiding the latter.[94]

How to formulate this other principle? "Be not so prone to expect sin and abuse that you fail to recognize grace where it is at work."[95] Or elsewhere: "Seek in faith to recognize God's grace in Jesus Christ and through the Holy Spirit, grace that because of the divine promise has been at work, is working yet, and will work in the future in individuals and institutions despite sin and abuse."[96]

A Catholic instinctively recognizes where CJP is coming from. His hackles were raised by the language of "unconditionality" attaching to the Lutheran understanding of justification,

91. Tillich, *Systematic Theology* I (Chicago: University of Chicago Press, 1956), 227.

92. Ibid., 37.

93. "Justification by Faith and the Need," 309: "The criterion of justification by faith alone is an imperative to keep the churches from idolatry." Similarly "Justification and the Catholic Principle," 19: "the Protestant principle" reducible to the first commandment, "No strange gods"!

94. "Justification by Faith and the Need," 309. Cf. also "Justification and the Catholic Principle," 25; "A Roman Catholic Response" (to G. O. Forde), in *In Search of Christian Unity* (n. 81 above), 81–82.

95. "Justification by Faith and the Need," 309.

96. "A Roman Catholic Response," 83.

beginning with Luther's emphasis on "God's unconditional promises in Jesus Christ" as that which all church structures must serve.[97] The language intends to protect *sola gratia*, which is dependent upon *solus Christus*. God justifies because of his promise to do so in Jesus Christ, and not because of even the best efforts or the most exquisite rituals of human supplicants. Jesus Christ is the "sole mediator" of God's saving action, and the principle of justification by faith is "the correlative of the sole mediatorship of Christ. . . . Lutherans believe that this principle has continuing validity, since the tendency of Christians to rely on their own devices rather than on Christ is unabating."[98] But the unconditionality of the divine promise in Christ obviously does not exclude the instrumentality of word and sacrament, CJP declares; these were given to be indefectibly administered by the church, and "their role is unquestionably similar to what in other contexts is that of *conditions*."[99] Might they not be considered at least *subsequent* conditions of God's saving action without making them pretenders to divinity or temptations to works-righteousness? And what then protects our trust in the church's stewardship of these divine gifts? How can the preaching of God's unconditional forgiveness of the sinner through Christ leave intact the listeners' sense of their inherent goodness as God's creatures and the importance of the good things they do by divine grace?[100] These are matters of "the catholic substance" which *sola fide* justification endangers and CJP's companion principle would aim to protect.

97. "Justification by Faith and the Need," 306–7, citing G. Lindbeck, "Article IV and Lutheran/Roman Catholic Dialogue: The Limits of Diversity in the Understanding of Justification," *Lutheran Theological Seminary Bulletin* 61 (1981): 1–15. See also "Justification and the Catholic Principle," 19: CJP is ill-at-ease when the "alone" of "by faith alone" is made equivalent to "unconditionally." Cf. G. O. Forde, "Justification by Faith Alone" (n. 81 above), 67: "To say that justification by faith alone is . . . with Luther . . . the plumb line [*Richtschnur*] by which all teaching is to be measured is therefore already to say that when used as a criterion of judgment it functions hermeneutically . . . to direct and foster the speaking of the unconditional gospel. . . . There is . . . the overriding concern that what is spoken in the church, *at all costs*, be the unconditional gospel."
98. "Justification by Faith: Common Statement," in *Justification by Faith*, 56.
99. "Justification by Faith and the Need," 311 (italics mine).
100. Ibid., 312: "To preach that God's promise has prevented the destruction of the last vestige of the divine image and freedom in the sinner need not lead to an anxious conscience. Nor does any and all reference to human freedom in con-

This promotion of an additional principle reflects Catholic wariness of "using any one doctrine as the absolute principle by which to purify from outside, so to speak, the catholic heritage," and of applying the gospel "without drawing on the full resources available within the church," such as the sacraments and the ordained ministry as well as Scripture and preaching.[101] At the same time, one is not hard-pressed to comprehend the Lutherans' perplexity with CJP's proposal of a principle analogous to justification to reverse, in effect, the latter's thrust. It seems to be a butter knife next to the pruning knife! G. O. Forde is made wary "by the fact that some of those same elements of 'Catholic substance' which Peter wants to safeguard with this new principle are precisely those which justification by faith alone wants to subject to more careful critical examination."[102] Robert Jenson was bothered by the suggestion that "somehow I can tell where the work of God begins and ends." And relishing the pruning metaphor, he added: "If you would just say, 'take as little as you think you can to keep the bush shapely,' that would make sense to me."[103] George Lindbeck, acknowledging that Lutherans work so hard at unmasking works-righteousness that they risk "critiquing away" the church, nevertheless doubts that one can oppose this tendency with a theological principle. "Criticizing catholic substance in the light of justification by faith is in a sense a human task, but the creation of catholic substance is not something human. The refreshment of the Christian tradition is something that cannot be done by a principle. We have to leave it up to God."[104]

And there it stood. CJP's principle did not win a place in the consensual statement of the Dialogue, but he had insisted on focusing the discussion at its nerve-center. Straining the fabric

---

version necessarily reduce itself to works-righteousness." "Reference to human dignity and goodness despite the repeated successes of sin . . . might well lead to a renewed ultimate hope in God and penultimate hope in self as never lacking divine assistance. But that would be preaching influenced by an important critical principle in addition to that of justification by faith" (313).

101. "Common Statement," 56.
102. "Justification by Faith Alone," 70.
103. "Justification and the Catholic Principle," Discussion, 29.
104. Ibid., 30.

at one angle is the unassailable truth of the sole mediation of God's salvation by Jesus Christ, crucified and risen. At the other angle are the "means of grace" ("the catholic substance") and their inevitable human handling. The truth of justification by faith has been so well refined in modern exegetical discussion that serious differences do not persist concerning its more fundamental terms;[105] but the application of this truth as a hard discipline of the human handling required by the "means of grace" will probably remain controverted, especially when it comes to declaring it the "article on which the whole church stands or falls."[106] CJP recalled how Luther had put this non-negotiable principle on the table in the "Smalkald articles" of 1538, having chafed at Melanchthon's "leise treten" (pussy-footing) with Rome in the Augsburg confession.[107] There are times when this kind of forthrightness with what cannot be

---

105. Therefore satisfaction could be expressed over the American Lutheran-Catholic consensus-statement by a European exegete who spells out the points of exegetical convergence that encouraged it; see Karl Kertelge, "Rechtfertigung aus Glauben und Gericht nach den Werken bei Paulus," in his *Grundthemen paulinischer Theologie* (Freiburg: Herder, 1991), 130–47, esp. 143–47. Since exegetes understand Paul's theme in terms of a "new creation," not merely a judicial verdict, and because they understand the human recipient as active rather than passive, old antinomies could be overcome, such as justification vs. sanctification, merely forensic vs. real righteouness, *sola fide* vs. judgment according to works, faith's indicative vs. its imperative, and so forth. Cf. also "Common Statement," 58–73; CJP's "Sin and Atonement in the Roman Catholic Tradition," 139–45.

106. The Dialogue's common statement on justification acknowledged an apparently "irreconcilable" difference here ("Common Statement," 57), and C. E. Braaten comments: "Here lies the core of the difference that explains all the other more obvious differences" (*Justification* [n. 86 above], 9). Regarding the Pauline evidence, recent studies have raised doubts as to whether justification is the central and controlling theologoumenon of the letters, let alone the "canon within the canon" which E. Käsemann and others in Luther's following continue to make it (see Käsemann, *Essays on New Testament Themes* [Chicago: Allenson, 1964], 57–58; *Das Neue Testament als Kanon* [Göttingen: Vandenhoeck und Ruprecht, 1970], 368–69, 405). As the occasional and contingent framing of Paul's arguments becomes better understood, justification appears increasingly as a "theological peak-statement" (Kertelge, *Grundthemen*, 133), but as only one salvation-symbol among several (J. C. Beker, *Paul the Apostle* [n. 80 above], 256–60), very much prompted and conditioned by his contest with Jewish-Christian missionaries and their gospel of law observance plus faith in Jesus as Messiah (cf. A.J.M. Wedderburn, *The Reasons for Romans* [Edinburgh: Clark, 1988], 108–23).

107. "On this article [justification] nothing can be given up or compromised even if heaven, earth, and things that do not last should be destroyed. . . . On this rests all that we teach and live against the Pope, the devil, and the world"

yielded is a sounder policy than stepping gingerly to an ecumenical minuet. "I suspect we are at one of those moments
today," declared CJP, who was certainly not given to the
strategy of the preemptive strike.[108]

His uncharacteristic disposition to pound the table seems to
have been prompted by the apparent stalemate between the
churches' official responses to their theologians in dialogue.
The American Catholic bishops' committee on doctrine re-
sponded to the joint statement on justification in 1984 with a
wholly predictable question which hardly required reading the
theologians' work: how does the ultimate responsibility of the
episcopal college to define what accords with the gospel relate
to *sola fide* justification functioning as the gospel's ultimate criterion?[109] A more extended and careful evaluation came from
the bishops in 1991, in which the validity of the *christological*
consensus reached by the Dialogue was ratified but abiding and
effectively church-divisive differences on its *ecclesiological* consequences were noted.[110] The Lutheran bodies which now com-
pose the Evangelical Lutheran Church in America (ELCA) were
initially dubious about the basic "consensus on the gospel"
which the Dialogue's common statement had asserted;[111] but a

(S.A. II/I; T. G. Tappert, ed., *Book of Concord* [Philadelphia: Fortress, 1978], 292).
C. E. Braaten writes very much in the same spirit in *Justification*.

108. "The Centrality of Justification" (n. 83 above); also "A Moment of
Truth," 539.

109. "Lutheran-Catholic Dialogues: Critique by the Committee on Doctrine of
the National Conference of Catholic Bishops," *Lutheran Quarterly* 1/2 (Summer
1987): 125–36; here, 134. The critique is summarized by CJP in "A Moment of
Truth," 539–40. Other concerns of the committee were: Eucharist as propitiatory
sacrifice, ordained ministry and apostolic succession, papal primacy by divine
law, infallibility, and Marian dogmas—but for the last two items, much as they
might have been in 1538.

110. The Roman Catholic Bishops of the United States, "An Evaluation of the
Lutheran-Catholic Statement *Justification by Faith*," *Lutheran Quarterly* 5 (1991):
63–72; cf. CJP, "A Role Model in an Ecumenical Winter," *Worship* 66 (1992): 2–10;
here, 8–9. This statement endorsed the confession of God's promise and saving
work in Christ as the "ultimate trust" of Christians, but it insisted on the
Church, from whom Christ is never separated, as "penultimate trust," as for example in its teachings on the papacy, purgatory, and the saints. Consensus on
the christological gospel is not enough to warrant full communion between
Catholics and Lutherans because the nexus between "ultimate" and "penultimate" trusts is too tight.

111. See *Justification by Faith*, 74. Cf. the statement of the thirtieth biennial
convention of the Lutheran Church in America (*A Response to Justification by Faith*

recent, as yet unratified report of the Ecumenical Affairs Committee of the ELCA indicates a disposition to accept the "fundamental consensus on the gospel," and also to give affirmative answer to the Dialogue's question whether remaining differences on the doctrine could not be worked out between the two churches in "full communion" with each other.[112] CJP, in one of the last of his publications, saw neither paralysis nor "quick-fix" susceptibility as the upshot of these ecclesiastical responses to the Dialogue.[113] He noted elsewhere, however, that "most observers are not sanguine that communion between Roman Catholics and Lutherans has much of a chance of coming closer during the present pontificate."[114]

Most trying to even the ecumenical optimist is the fact that the differences brought out in the church leaders' responses to the Dialogue are basically the same as those that drove the original wedge in the sixteenth century. The Lutherans reject any compromise of the truth of Christ's unique mediation and criticize "any function, form of worship or piety, office or person that looks like a pretender in this context." The Catholics can tolerate justification as a toothless christological abstraction, but when it comes to a criterion—*the* criterion—of church teaching and practice, they take up cudgels to defend the "means of grace," stressing "the truth of the manifold cooperation to which [Christ's] mediation gives rise as his grace is communicated to those in need of it." CJP concludes: "I sus-

[New York: Dept. for Ecumenical Relations of the L.C.A., 1986]), and the statement of the Interchurch Relations Committee of the American Lutheran Church (*The American Lutheran Church, Thirteenth General Convention: Reports and Actions: Supplement* [Minneapolis: Office of the General Secretary of the A.L.C., 1986], 827–31). CJP discusses these responses in "A Moment of Truth," 540.

112. I depend on CJP for this account of the committee report; see "A Role Model," 7–8.

113. Ibid., 9; cf. "A Moment of Truth," 541.

114. "Mountains Moved by Faith that Hopes," *Word and World* 11, no. 3 (1991): 293. Also noted there is the fact that "not a few members of the Evangelical Lutheran Church in America (ELCA) seem to be wondering (some of them out loud) whether the Spirit of Jesus is not working more effectively in breaking down barriers between them and Anglicans or the Reformed Churches than between them and Rome." CJP cites George Lindbeck, "Reformation Heritage and Christian Unity," *Lutheran Quarterly* 4 (1988): 477–502; John Hotchkin, "Standards for Measuring Ecumenism's Course," *Origins* 20 (1991): 509, 511–14.

pect that we are dealing here with what ecumenists today might call a fundamental difference. I doubt that it will ever be completely eliminated."[115] As his last writings are published amidst the sobering business of the ongoing Lutheran-Catholic Dialogue—indulgences, purgatory, the cult of the saints, Mary, the authority of bishops, ethical teachings, celibacy, the ordination of women—his name holds the honorable memory of one who forthrightly traced the basic fault-line from the beginning by insisting on the right in both perspectives on justification. Was he "holding the middle" in this, or "straddling the fence"? At least with his "model for an ecumenical winter," blind Bartimaeus (Mark 10:46–52), he was training everyone's murky vision on the one and only eventual source of church union.[116]

4. An Admiring Retrospect

In our review of the three closely related topical areas of CJP's published legacy—faith and reason, eschatology, and the Lutheran-Catholic unity agenda—we have been struck repeatedly by qualities of his work which appear with unwavering consistency. First, an unusually magnanimous reception of all truth-claims made it possible to hear out his interlocutors without constant reminders of where he considered them wrong. He always brought the discussion around gradually and gently to his own *prise de position*, and this usually involved generous adaptations of the other party's language and concerns as his own. Moreover, he consistently demonstrated his refined historical sense and acumen, and his respect for the great witnesses of the past to the point of actually *reading* them, not just tossing their names about. He had come to the conviction that "retrieving the past may be part and parcel of ecumenical re-

115. "A Moment of Truth," 541. For the present, his next line remains wistful: "But could such a difference exist in a more united church—could it be a difference within one faith rather than of diverse faiths?"
116. "A Role Model," 2–10; "A Moment of Truth," 541. The posthumous article, "A Role Model," originated in a paper given in July 1991 to the Council of the Lutheran World Federation meeting in Chicago.

sponsibilities in the present."[117] He was intrigued by Harnack's question whether the Western schism would have occurred had Trent's teaching on justification been formulated and applied earlier in the sixteenth century;[118] and yet his own account of the Tridentine decree submitted to the Lutheran-Catholic Dialogue attempted no uncritical syncretism, but only the deferential question whether Lutherans today might "see in the doctrine articulated by Trent on justification a truly Christian understanding of the gospel."[119] A truly astonishing self-discipline kept the exposition of even earth-shaking matters in the same laconic temper and humble submission to all the evidence.

Finally, there was never any doubt that the roots and loyalties of this theologian lay firmly in his Roman Catholic tradition. One sensed he had occasionally to stretch out of joint to keep the Catholic tradition, and the high Scholasticism of his training in particular, from falling out of communion with contemporary academic and ecclesiastical fervors. His veneration of "the catholic substance" kept him from adhering to the fads and fashions, usually named after anointed mentors, which seem to grip systematic theology anew in every generation. He was usually struggling to blend the new into his vision of a *theologia perennis*, as in the problematic instance of the "theology of hope." As a Catholic theologian true to the word's derivation, he usually advocated a "both-and" rather than an "either-or" approach to sacred things, knowing full well that God and the sovereignty of Christ are far greater than stringent human alternatives can encompass. Indeed, his personal largesse influenced his vision of the largesse of God's future Kingdom; and that, in turn, defined the size and strength of the

117. "The Communion of Saints" (n. 27 above), 220; cf. also 233.
118. "Sin and Atonement in the Roman Catholic Tradition," 140–41.
119. "The Decree on Justification in the Council of Trent," in *Justification by Faith*, 228. Similarly "The Communion of Saints," 233: "In this ecumenical age it is up to the sons and daughters of the Reformation to decide whether these developments . . . [of Tridentine teaching in Vatican II] help, hurt, or leave matters unchanged." C. E. Braaten, for one, is disinclined to take comfort from Trent (cf. *Justification*, 104–6, citing the sixteenth-century Lutheran critic of the Council, Martin Chemnitz).

"hope seeking understanding" that controlled his theology from its center.[120]

As some readers knew and others will have gathered, these have been the thoughts of a friend and admirer of Carl Peter. This essay has argued with his legacy very much as one argued with him in person: often though not inevitably in agreement, sometimes chafing at his "centrist" gymnastics or diplomat's inhibitions, but always downright certain that one's sentiments had been thoughtfully heard.

120. The centrality of hope in CJP's theology was highlighted in the citation accompanying the John Courtney Murray Award for distinction in theology, awarded him by the Catholic Theological Society in 1975 (*Proceedings* 30 [1975]: 262–63).

PART II

~

Church and Theology

3

~

Theologians in the Church

JOSEPH A. KOMONCHAK

Most discussions of the topic "Theologians and the Church" tend to focus on the relations of the former with the hierarchy. There are easy explanations of this phenomenon, not least of all the past century and a half of notorious conflicts that come to mind simply by citing representative events and texts—the Munich Congress, the Syllabus of Errors, the First Vatican Council, Modernism, *Pascendi* and *Lamentabili*, the Pontifical Biblical Commission, *"la nouvelle théologie,"* *Humani Generis*, the Second Vatican Council, *Humanae Vitae*, and so on—and the people involved in them—Pius IX, Döllinger, Newman, Rosmini, Loisy, Tyrrell, Pius X, Blondel, Duchesne, Lagrange, Benigni, Garrigou-Lagrange, Batiffol, Bonsirven, Teilhard de Chardin, Pius XII, Chenu, de Lubac, Bouillard, von Balthasar, Congar, Rahner, Leclercq, Murray, John XXIII, Paul VI, John Paul II, Küng, Curran, Schillebeeckx, Boff, and so forth. For all the often considerable differences, at the heart of these conflicts were the competing claims of theologians and of representatives of the Church's magisterium. This history is part of our common consciousness and continues to play a major role in both the intellectual and the emotional framing of the question of the relationship between theologians and the Church.

But the reduction of the relationship between theologians and the Church to that between theologians and the magisterium is as unfortunate as it is understandable. A terminological point is easy to make: at the time of the Second Vatican Council it was considered progress that the identification of "Church" with "hierarchy" was overcome through the recovery of the biblical and traditional (patristic and medieval) referent of the term "Church" to the whole body of believers. The Council's Dogmatic Constitution on the Church, *Lumen Gentium*, reflected this passage in its very structure, when two chapters on the Church as Mystery and as People of God preceded the discussions of hierarchy and laity and a chapter on the common call to holiness preceded the chapter on the religious life. To reduce the Church once again to the hierarchy is a betrayal of the Council's achievement, one that is not entirely avoided by the use of such terms as "the institutional Church," which normally means simply the hierarchy and which is both theologically and sociologically indefensible.

But the point is not merely terminological; it is substantive. For the issues at stake in defining the place and role of theologians in the Church are neither exhausted nor chiefly determined by their relationship to the hierarchy. Consider simply the types of questions that spring to mind if one restates the question in terms that reflect various fuller understandings of the term "Church," as in "Theologians and the Mystery of the Church," "Theologians and the People of God," "Theologians and the Body of Christ," or "Theologians and the Sacrament of Salvation." In any of these formulations, the relationship between theologians and hierarchical magisterium ceases to be central and becomes a question that arises in a larger context which supplies the presuppositions, the principal elements, and the criteria for a description and resolution of the specific question.

Most importantly, concentrating on the relationship between theologians and magisterium tends to set the two bodies in opposition to, or at least in tension with, one another. Each group of people tends to be defined by distinction from the other, with primary emphasis laid upon their distinct rights and responsibilities and with a tendency towards group-bias. Authority and freedom are counterposed. Real or potential conflicts come to the forefront. A sense of their communion in a single enterprise may be given lip service, but it tends to be threatened or dissolved as interest quickly shifts to the management of tension or the resolution of conflict.

I wish to suggest that it is time to overcome this state of affairs, and so I will devote these pages to a consideration of the larger issue. That is why I have not entitled this essay "Theologians *and* the Church," but "Theologians *in* the Church." In doing so, I am not maintaining that theology, in some defensible meaning of the term, may not be practiced outside the Church; I am simply indicating my primary interest here in theology as undertaken within the community of Christian believers. Perhaps I should state from the beginning, leaving the rest of this essay to make the point in detail, that to discuss theology as an enterprise undertaken within the Church is *not* to assume that it makes no universal or public claim. In fact, the demolition of this assumption is one of my primary intentions.

The Church

Both historically and theologically, what we call the Christian Church arose and arises out of the event of Jesus Christ. The Church is the *congregatio fidelium*, the assembly of those who believe that Jesus of Nazareth, who was crucified, has been made both Lord and Christ. This very statement so closely ties the Church and Christ as to suggest a clarification of the first sentence in this paragraph. It is not enough to say that the Church arose and arises out of the event of Jesus Christ: the emergence of the Church, both historically and theologically, is a dimension of the event of Jesus Christ. John Knox was so aware of this as to say something at first very startling: that the emergence of the Church *is* the event of Jesus Christ.[1] The only

1. "The only difference between the world as it was just after the event and the world as it had been just before is that the church was now in existence. A new kind of human community had emerged; a new society had come into being. There was absolutely nothing besides. This new community held and prized vivid memories of the event in which it had begun. It had a new faith; that is, it saw the nature of the world and of God in a new light. It found in its own life the

thing one could point to as different in the world before and after Jesus of Nazareth was the existence of the community of believers. The Church is the difference Jesus of Nazareth has made and makes in human history. Had the Church not arisen, what might count as "the event of Jesus of Nazareth" would have been considerably different from what, both historically and theologically, it did in fact become.

It was in fact through the Church that Jesus of Nazareth became an historic figure, an agent of history. It was Christians who preserved the memory of his mere existence, who remembered his words and his deeds, who proclaimed him to have conquered death and to have become Lord, Messiah, and Savior, who interpreted him as the enfleshment of the very Word of God, who understood their own communal experience as a fellowship in his Spirit that made them members of his very Body, who undertook to bring others into communion with him and with his Father, who invited those to whom they spoke to make him the principle and the criterion of a redirected personal and collective history. The Church made Jesus of Nazareth an historically significant figure.

Once a narrowly eschatological interpretation of his significance faded and Christians settled in for the long haul of history, the scope of Christ's redemptive influence came to be seen also to transcend the boundaries of the Judaism from which Jesus had come and to require the mission to the Gentiles and the effort to evangelize the society and culture of the Greco-Roman world. From then on, the inward necessity, for the sake of the Church's own integrity, to keep alive the memory of Jesus Christ and to proclaim his saving power, has been also an outward engagement with culture and history, and it was always theologically unsound and sociologically naive to think that his significance could be reduced to the sphere of the personal and private or to the dimensions of a sect.

---

grounds—indeed anticipatory fulfillments—of a magnificent hope. But the memory, the faith, and the hope were all its own; they had neither existence nor ground outside the community. Only the church really existed. Except for the church the event had not occurred"; John Knox, *The Early Church and the Coming Great Church* (London: Epworth Press, 1957), 45.

The history of that engagement with history and culture is, of course, as complex and ambiguous as is the history of the encounter of individuals with Christ. More than once, in both histories, the Gospel and its grace did not succeed in completely overcoming ignorance and embedded sinfulness. Compromise and mediocrity have never been rare, which is why *heroic* sanctity is required of candidates for canonization. But as this does not deter the Church from continuing to preach Christ and to call for the conversion of individuals, so the ambiguity of past encounters with culture and history should not suggest that the Church leave off the task of the redemption of the entire human project.

The intrinsic link between concern for the integrity of the Church as the *congregatio fidelium* and commitment to the redemption of history is clear also from a consideration of the process and of the agents of the Church's self-realization. As the Church first arose out of the conviction that Jesus of Nazareth had been raised from the dead, so it continues to arise from the communication and appropriation of the word of life: "What we have seen and heard we proclaim to you so that you too may have fellowship with us, and our fellowship is with the Father and with his Son, Jesus Christ" (1 John 1:3). The witness of one generation of believers evokes the faith of a new generation and this process reproduces, extends, and widens the communion that first came to be out of the event of Easter and Pentecost. Everything else about the Church—its Scriptures, its creeds, its worship and sacraments, its structures, its laws—exists in order to prepare for, to promote, to safeguard, and to articulate in words, deeds, and relationships the distinctive communion that arises out of the witness to and appropriation of the centering grace of God that was in Christ Jesus.[2]

The grounding witness is an invitation to conversion, the *metanoia* which was the urgent goal of Jesus' proclamation of the reign of God (Mark 1:15) and the event whose dramatic character led Paul to compare it to the death and resurrection

2. See Thomas Aquinas on the new Law, *Summa theologiae* Ia-IIae, q. 106.

of Christ and to attribute it to the Spirit of the one who raised Jesus from the dead (cf. Rom. 8:11; cp. 1 Cor. 12:3: "No one can say, 'Jesus is Lord,' except in the Holy Spirit"). The event divides the personal history of the believer into two moments as different from one another as light is from darkness and life from death. A new self emerges, principle of a new life, capable of a new personal history, undertaken as the unfolding of the implications and requirements of the gift given in Christ and appropriated in the Spirit.

In its most dramatic forms, this personal event interrupts a personal life-project, gives it a new energy, and orients it in a new direction. The freedom of God in his mercy encounters the misdirected freedom of a sinner, overwhelms it in love and forgiveness, opens it to a new field of vision and a new realm of possibilities, and introduces it into a new community. Personal conversion is the event in which God intervenes in an individual's project of self-constitution. Descriptions of conversion articulate that self-transforming event in the details that distinguish one life from another, that tell of the misuse of freedom in sin, of the evidences, slight and gradual or dramatic and sudden, by which God has disclosed the possibility of a new self, of the moment of decision when possibility became reality accepted in grateful eagerness. One may speak so generally, but the event is always particular, describable only in terms of quite specific and concrete personal dramas.

Through such events, the Church fulfills its mission of evangelization for the sake of conversion, assuring at the same time that the apostolic fellowship of believers will continue. No one has any difficulty in relating the self-realization of the Church to the transformation of individual self-projects. At one and the same time the lives of individuals are changed by the encounter with the witness to the Gospel, and the communion in Christ that is the heart of the Church is renewed and broadened.

That the renewal of the Church's inner life is also intrinsically related to the collective history of mankind is perhaps less commonly acknowledged. In fact, of course, the spread of the Gospel did bring about considerable alterations in the social and cultural life of the West, but no theory of this transformative role was developed, in part because the sense was lacking that the human race is engaged in a collective self-project in which intelligence and freedom could be exercised for the sake of transforming the physical, economic, social, and cultural conditions in which people live and act. The idea of progress seems to be a modern invention. Unfortunately, it also seems to have emerged at a time when various factors led to the widespread assumption that religion had very little relevance to the task of collective human self-realization in the spheres of science and technology, economics and politics, society and culture. Religion concerned what one did with one's private self. The larger collective self-project could be safely indifferent to the differences among religions and even to those between belief and unbelief.

The Catholic Church consistently opposed this privatizing of religion, which it took to be the mortal sin of what it condemned as "liberalism." But, particularly in the century and a half before the Second Vatican Council, its opposition was so global that "progress, liberalism, and recent civilization" could be lumped together, almost as if they were synonyms, in the last proposition condemned in the Syllabus of Errors. This undifferentiated repudiation became the motivating principle of the construction of a subculture and subsociety which, in part because it appealed so strongly to the social and cultural effects of the Gospel in the formation of Christendom, seemed to offer only a past ideal as the simple substitute for the liberal idea of human progress. So great was the opposition to this idea and so powerful was the drive to create a countervailing, antimodern Catholic identity that, paradoxically and often quite contrary to the intentions of popes and bishops, the self-realization of the Church at times came to be seen, both inside and outside, as a distinct event, occurring in a separate and differentiated sphere of human life and without significance for the collective human self-project. Ironically, the Roman Catholicism of the last two centuries was very modern in its antimodernity.

A classic ecclesiology developed to support this response to modernity. Against the tendency of the modern nation-state to

reduce religious groups to simple voluntary associations ultimately subordinate to its own authority to define society and
culture, theologians and canonists identified and defended the
internal integrity of the Church as a separate, autonomous, and
self-sufficient, and in that sense "perfect," society. Against a
modern trend toward democracy, they stressed the authority of
a hierarchically organized clergy to which they tended to re-
serve all initiative. To ideas and forces that were international
in their appeal and effectiveness, they opposed a universalistic
vision of the Church as a single people governed from a central
headquarters by a sovereign and infallible head in whose hands
lay the direction of an increasingly centralized and uniform
Church polity.

Although this classic ecclesiology was in good part developed
in the service of the modern Catholic response to the ideas
and forces that were shaping the modern world, it showed surprisingly little interest in the Church-world relationship itself.
Apart from occasional appendices, scholia, or corollaria devoted to a rejection of "liberalism," there was only the chapter
on Church and State. Right up to the eve of Vatican II, however, this chapter was devoted to a defense of the Church's
unique rights, still conceived largely in terms of premodern
political circumstances ("the Catholic State") and thought to
be sufficiently guaranteed by institutional negotiations
between the supreme ecclesial and secular authorities (concor-
dats). The larger sphere of Church-world relations that includes
the responsibilities and activities of Christians in the construction of societies and cultures and in the direction of
human history went largely unnoticed in the classical treatises
on the Church.

In this respect the classical modern ecclesiology fell far short
of the vision that modern popes had begun to articulate. Under
Leo XIII but particularly under Pius XI, the emphasis on
Church-State relations began to be supplemented by an appeal
to Catholic organizations and movements to engage themselves
in the effort to win the modern world back to Christ not only
for the sake of the Church's freedom to fulfill its distinctive
spiritual mission for the salvation of souls but also to address

what John Courtney Murray called "the spiritual crisis in the temporal order." The papal support of "Catholic Action," for example, represented an appeal directly to the laity to assume their responsibility for bringing Christian ideas and values to the larger public debate on the character and direction of human history. The Church-world relation, in other words, was not to be settled simply by institutional negotiations between sovereign authorities but required an active participation by lay Christians in the collective self-realization of mankind.

It was this appeal that was to inspire and energize the new thinking and new enterprises that would surprise so many people in the debates that defined the drama of the Second Vatican Council. The decade of the 1930s was crucial to this development. A sense of crisis was nearly universal. Economic depression seemed to confirm the weaknesses of liberal capitalism. The League of Nations collapsed under the weight of revived nationalism. The war fought to make the world safe for democracy was followed by the rise of fascist, Nazist, and communist totalitarianisms. With individualism discredited and collectivism threatening, the moment seemed opportune for Catholics to propose a third alternative based upon a distinctive vision of the relationship between person and community derived from a broadened and deepened sense of the scope of Christ's redemptive work and yet not inspired or directed by nostalgia for a premodern ideal of Christendom.

Thus it was in the 1930s that Jacques Maritain outlined his notion of a new but "profane" Christendom under the historical ideal of pluralistic and democratic regimes, that Christopher Dawson turned his attention to the relationship between religion and culture, that Marie-Dominique Chenu and Yves Congar began to call for an incarnation of the Gospel into modern milieux from which the Church was absent, that Teilhard de Chardin continued to elaborate a cosmic vision of the faith appropriate to the world modern science was revealing, that Henri de Lubac published a book on the social aspects of dogma, that Bernard Lonergan began to sketch a theology of history derived from the Pauline doctrine of the recapitulation of all things in Christ, that John Courtney Murray was imbibing the ideas that would lead him soon to urge upon American Catholics their responsibility for the construction of a Christian culture.

In every one of these cases, an ecclesiology that ignored the Church-world relationship, reduced it to premodern models of Church-State relations, or assigned it principally or even exhaustively to the clergy, was implicitly or explicitly criticized. The reality of "the world," of history, began to come to the forefront and to be included in the drama of the human self-project that defines the hermeneutical context in which to communicate and appropriate the Christian Gospel given *propter nos homines et propter nostram salutem*. This self-project was now understood not merely as the drama of the struggle between sin and grace in an individual's self-realization, but also as including the same dramatic struggle in humanity's collective self-realization. The world was no longer simply the unchanging backdrop against which individual actors played their roles; it was itself the drama that was unfolding. The world was not the stage, but the play itself.

But this understanding of the world as history necessarily entails an altered understanding of the Church. What does it mean now to speak of the Church "in" the world? The preposition is no longer spatial, as if "the world" means simply the physical or even social "place" in which the Church comes to be. The world in its most significant theological sense means now what human beings have made of themselves, for good and for ill; and, since that is never something accomplished once and for all, it means what human beings are now making of themselves and what they are about to make of themselves. That is the world "in" which the Church comes to be. The event of the Church's self-realization is a moment in the world's self-realization; it is one of the possible things which human beings can make of themselves, can do with their freedom. The self-realization of the Church, as the community that results from the communication and appropriation of the Gospel, is an event within, a choice with regard to, the self-realization of humanity.

The Church is also, of course, a *differentiation* within the world's self-realization. This portion of humanity is brought together by the announcement of what God has done in Christ and by the appropriation of that message as the word of life. No other portion of humanity is distinguished by this word and faith, which is what grounds the meaning of the word "world" that associates it with those who either have not yet accepted or have rejected the message of Christ. But in the sense in which I have been using the term above, the Church arises within the world and as a differentiation of the world: that portion of the world who believe. Without the Church the world is different; without the Church history is different; the Church remains the difference Jesus Christ makes in human history, in the world. Through the Church he remains an historical agent.

It is not, then, as if there is a first moment in which the Church comes to be and then a second moment when it takes a stance in and with regard to the world. The very coming-to-be of the Church is already an engagement in history, a decision in the drama that makes the world what it is. To appropriate the Gospel in faith is to take a stand before the great questions that define any historical moment; it is to identify in the God and Father of the Lord Jesus Christ the origin, center, and goal of human life; it is to recognize the power of sin in oneself and in the world; it is to acknowledge the possibility of forgiveness and reconciliation; it is to have hope that no evil, not even death, not even sin, is stronger or more certain than the power of God; it is to commit oneself to a love that reflects the love of God that has turned one's life around; it is to enter into a community where all this is believed, treasured, celebrated, and made the generative center of common commitments. None of this is simply an individual's experience of transformation; as personal as it is, it is an event that transforms one's interpretation and evaluation of the world, a disclosure of new possibilities for the realization not simply of oneself, but of the world. It is a redefined world that one discovers in the decision of faith.

To what does the Church refer in this understanding? Who are the Church? The Church refers here to the *congregatio fide-*

lium; it is the whole company of believers who are the Church. The word "Church" refers to the totality of people who have been brought into apostolic communion with those who first heard and saw the word of life. The Church does not mean first or even chiefly the clergy or the hierarchy; it means the assembly of believers, within which there are, of course, differentiations based on sacraments and charisms. But it is crucial to keep in the foreground of one's mind the comprehensive, inclusive meaning of the word "Church" to refer to the whole portion of humanity that has appropriated the Gospel of Christ.

Much ecclesiology presupposes a narrower referent of the word "Church," particularly by using it to refer to the clergy, to the canonical structures and institutions, or to the sacramental activities in which its distinctive reality is celebrated in thanksgiving. But an ecclesiology should not be based upon a systematic neglect of the fact that ninety-nine percent of the members of the Church are not ordained leaders of the community of faith and that they live most of their Christian lives outside of formal liturgical services in what is called "the world." It is there that their Chrisitan lives either do make a difference or do not; it is there and through these Christians that Christ continues to be powerful in human history or does not; it is through them that the world is different because of Christ or is not.

Let me use an actual example to illustrate the point. Some years ago, in a parish in the Bronx, a white teenager was murdered by a black teenager, the second such tragedy within a few months. Feelings of anger were widespread, and calls for revenge were being heard. The funeral would take place in the Catholic Church, and a priest had to preach at it.

What was at stake in the liturgy this priest had to lead? There was, of course, the central and Church-defining conviction that even the evil of this brutal and early death did not escape the healing and life-giving power of God, that the light of the resurrection could dissipate the darkness even of this death. Included within that faith-comfort was also a call to reconciliation that would be symbolized when blacks and whites came to receive the one bread and the one cup. But as an inner and inseparable dimension of that Christian worship there was also the call to make that faith and that communion the defining principle of what the members of that assembly would say and do when they left the church. It might be fairly easy to be the Church when assembled for worship; would they be the Church when they left the church? What would the next day's newspapers report about the Bronx? That a black child had been murdered in revenge? That race-riots had broken out? That the spiral of violence had taken another twisting turn? Or that some steps were being taken to reduce racial tensions? That people were talking about forgiveness and reconciliation and looking for harmony? That at least a little ray of hope could now be seen?

The Bronx in this story is the world: a world of sin and death, of grief and anger, a world facing choices about what it will become. In the middle of this world, part of this world, there is a community of Christian believers, trying to believe, hope, and love in the face of evil and before the temptation to return evil for evil. But the question of whether they can realize their distinctive Christian identity and integrity is inseparably also the question of what the world of which they are a part will become. If the community remains faithful to what the Gospel promises and requires, the world will be one thing; if they do not remain faithful, the world will be quite different. And the difference is made, not solely by the preacher, but chiefly by the whole assembly. And whether it is an authentic Church is determined, not solely by what takes place in the church, but also and perhaps chiefly by what takes place outside it.

The dramatic concreteness of this example of the Church-in-the-world is illustrative of many things. It shows the inner link between what is most constitutive of the Church and what is most redemptive of the world. It exemplifies Vatican II's statement that the eucharistic liturgy is at once the summit of the Christian life and the source of its energy. It shows the importance of Christian leadership even as it demonstrates that the redemption of human history is the task of the whole body of believers. And it manifests how the redemptive role of the one Church is only undertaken within local communities of faith, each of which finds itself in particular circumstances, particular "worlds," within which it faces day after day the question of whether it will display the faith, hope, and love that alone can make the Gospel of Christ an effective redemptive light and power.

Theologians in the Church

I wish now to propose some reflections on the role of theologians within the Church so conceived. I will assume a very simple definition of Christian theology as critical and systematic reflection on the event of Christ, understanding by the last phrase all those realities that prepared for, constituted, and follow from the event of Jesus of Nazareth confessed as Lord and Savior.

The first thing to note is that the theologian's task is a differentiation within a common enterprise undertaken in many ways and by many other people. There was a Church before there were theologians in any strict sense, and, in many circumstances, a Church can accomplish its purposes in the world without the presence of theologians.

Secondly, however, theology arises out of certain exigencies intrinsic to the common Christian enterprise. There is, first, the spontaneous desire to understand as fully as possible what one believes, what one has been given, what one finds oneself loving. Because faith is neither sight nor rationally compelled judgment, it does not quiet our mind's restlessness but urges it on to inquiry and thought.[3] Because faith discloses a new world of great depth and breadth and a new self within it, there is no lack of things about which to ask questions. There is also the need, stated already in the New Testament, "to give an explanation [*apologia*] to anyone who asks you for a reason [*logos*] for

3. For a description of Aquinas's effort to combine Aristotelian epistemology and Augustinian religious psychology, see M. -D. Chenu, "La psychologie de la foi dans la théologie du XIIe siècle: Genèse de la doctrine de saint Thomas, Somme théologique, IIa IIae, q. 2, a. 1," in *La parole de Dieu*, I. *La foi dans l'intelligence* (Paris: du Cerf, 1964), 77–104.

the hope that is within you" (1 Pet. 3:15). With the Christian Church a new praxis is introduced, an existential orientation derived from hope, that poses questions to others, and Christians have an obligation to answer them "with gentleness and respect." Finally, there is the need to defend the Gospel both from misunderstandings of it within the Church and from attacks from without. A move towards critical and reflective thought, then, is native to Christian faith and produces the differentiated task that would eventually be called Christian theology.

Thirdly, theology, as I am here discussing it, is in the service of the Church's redemptive presence and role in the world. It arises from within a community convinced that Jesus Christ is the Savior of the world, and the event and message on which it reflects is meant to have an effect upon the course of human history. Theology is thus one of the ways in which the Church seeks to be the sign and instrument by which Christ continues to be historically effective.

This is a point which perhaps especially needs stressing today when, on the one hand, there is a tendency to slacken the ties of theology to the Church, either because of fear of or resentment towards Church authorities or because of a desire to be accommodating to broader criteria of intellectual discipline, and when, on the other hand, some people defend a notion of theology that relates it nearly exclusively to the domestic service of the Church. It can thus appear that the theologian has to choose between primary communities and their respective criteria of loyalty. But if the Church is the bearer of a word that is intended for the redemption of human history, this is an impossible choice.

David Tracy has usefully distinguished three audiences to which a theologian may address himself: society and culture, the academy, and the Church itself. Primary reference to each of these audiences yields also a distinction between practical, fundamental, and systematic theology.[4] It is clear from his book

---

4. David Tracy, *The Analogical Imagination: Christian Theology and the Culture of Pluralism* (New York: Crossroad, 1981), esp. 3–98.

that Tracy's distinctions are not meant to be taken as separations, something confirmed by simple reflection on, first, the Church itself and, second, the situation of the theologian. The Church is indeed the bearer of the distinctive Christian message from generation to generation, but it is this only by embodying it in the lives of communities engaged in history, society, and culture. In every past age one never encounters the Church except as the Church-in-the-world; and one never confronts an articulation of the faith that has not been expressed in specific cultural terms and as a response to historical challenges and opportunities. Similarly, in the present moment the Church comes to be only in the several local communities living in their several worlds and facing the decision whether or not to differentiate themselves in a faith and praxis derived from and carrying forward the event of Christ. The Church has never been "world-less," and even the most sectarian effort to "go out from among them" is a decision within a world and with respect to that world, a decision that makes that world something different. A theology that is principally concerned to serve the Church with systematic reflection on its message must also be an engagement with society and culture.

Furthermore, critical intellectual exigencies are dimensions of a culture and their institutionalization today in the academy represents a particular historical praxis. In a culture in which these exigencies have developed, a Church has no choice but to engage them, something it does even when it is repudiating them, as Tertullian claimed to do when he counterposed Jerusalem and Athens. The broad Catholic tradition has, however, refused that antithesis and chosen to follow rather the examples of Justin Martyr, Clement of Alexandria, and Origen. It is true that with the collapse of the cultural institutions of antiquity, theology was located principally in monasteries, but it should be remembered that these houses were the chief centers of education and learning in the early Middle Ages; and when later economic, social, and cultural developments led to the establishment of the medieval universities, theology quite appropriately moved there also and became "Scholastic," that is, academic. It should also be noted, as Chenu repeatedly stressed, that this move in both the social location and in the methods of theology represented the Church's incarnational and redemptive response to the social and cultural transformations known as the renaissance of the twelfth century.[5]

For theologians today to address the concerns of the academy, then, does not represent a new or alien enterprise, nor need it mean a preference for that audience over the other two audiences, the Church and society. A modern university represents one practical way in which modern societies have chosen to articulate the social distribution of knowledge. But universities do not only transmit a society's cultural heritage to new generations, they subject it to critical reflection, and through a variety of disciplines in the various sciences they also sponsor research that affects the possibilities of transforming the conditions, from the physical to the cultural, in which their society shall live. Universities, in other words, are part of the constitutive praxis of societies. In the circumstances of modern societies, were the Church not engaged in the academy it could not effectively serve its redemptive purpose in history. A theologian's engagement with the academy, then, does not remove him or her from either the Church or society. To the contrary, it represents one of the ways in which the Church tries to embody in contemporary society the redemptive light and power of the Gospel.

Theologians belong to all three of the worlds represented by Tracy's three audiences. As believers, they belong to the Church; as dedicated to critical and systematic reflection, they accept certain rational exigencies that define a science or discipline and today are institutionalized in the academy; as persons, they are not only responsible for what they make of themselves but also participants in the great collective enterprise that their society and culture creates. To withdraw from the Church is to cease to be a Christian theologian; to repudiate standards of critical reflection is to cease to be a theologian; to think one can abstain from the collective engagement is an illusion only conceivable on indefensible notions of self, world, and history.

5. See M.-D. Chenu, *Une école de théologie: le Saulchoir* (Paris: du Cerf, 1985).

The temptation to separate the three worlds or publics of the theologian is strongest where certain modern assumptions about the place and role of religion are accepted. The differentiation of various relatively autonomous social spheres was often accompanied by the assumption that religion has nothing to do with them, but is simply a matter of personal decision or taste, something for those differentiated institutions called "churches" to deal with, but without public valence. Paradoxically, even while repudiating this privatization of religion, the Catholic Church played into the hands of this idea by its own characteristically modern institutionalization and by the pastoral strategy of constructing a countersociety, a small alternative "Catholic world." A premium was placed on institutional unity and loyalty, and theology was conceived largely in terms of its service to this ecclesial world. The result has been that it now requires an argument to overcome two assumptions: first, that religion has no public significance, and, second, that a Catholic theological interpretation of the Gospel is possible without reference to the larger world of collective human history. Distinctions have become separations.

The problem is complicated by certain abstractions which often haunt these discussions, as, for example, in distinctions between "faith" and "reason," "theology" and "philosophy," "theory" and "praxis," "Church" and "world," "magisterium" and "theology," and so on. These various terms can be defined and their use defended as referring to dimensions of the various problematics, but in their abstraction they all run the danger of causing one to forget where the real tensions they describe are encountered: not in the realm of abstractions but in the minds and hearts, in the commitments and communities, of specific people.

Consider, for example, the tensions represented by such distinctions as those between "faith" and "reason" or between "theology" and "philosophy." It is not rare to find the differences described by distinguishing what faith or theology "thinks" or "does" from what reason or philosophy "thinks" or "does." The intention here is to describe certain typical orientations, loyalties, criteria, or methods that characterize what theologians or philosophers do. But it is individual people who "do" these things, not abstractions. Thus the tension between faith and reason does not arise at some second moment, sometime after the decision of faith; it is what is at stake in the very question of the authenticity of faith itself. Whether "faith" and "reason" are compatible is settled already in the act of faith itself as an existential commitment that is not made at the price of surrender of one's intelligence and reason and could not be defended if it demanded such a surrender. To believe is to embrace a new loyalty that specifies and completes the underlying and constitutive loyalty to intelligence and reason that defines human responsibility.

Two difficulties often arise when the relation between "the Church" and "the world" is discussed. The first arises when the Church is defined solely in terms of its divine principles, for example, when it is said to be the community that derives from the word of Christ and the grace of the Holy Spirit, with little attention given to the concrete realization of the Church in actual communities of faith. Similarly, "the world" may be defined simply as that portion of humanity that has not accepted the Gospel of Christ. But while this notion of "world" can be found in the New Testament, the Scriptures also ground a notion of "world" as that great collective enterprise in which both the believing and unbelieving portions of humanity are engaged.

The point is that "the Church" does not actually encounter "the world" except in actual communities, and the genesis of the Church in and out of them is an event within the world's history. There is no Church except in the world, and there is no world except the one in which the Gospel and the Spirit have generated a distinctively Christian engagement with the challenges of individual and collective history. For the Church to come to be, for individuals to commit themselves to it, is then already a decision of human freedom that makes the world different. One has not left the world by entering the Church, then; one has made the world itself to be different from what it would be if one had not made that decision. One literally *cannot* choose between Church and world; to be in the

Church is not to leave the world, but to be in the world, to be the world in a particular way.

In principle, or, to use the older phrase, *per se*, there are no possible conflicts between the various terms distinguished. But that phrase "in principle" itself points to another problem that also can be obscured by abstractions. Conflicts do not arise on the level of abstract definitions, where it is easy enough to come up with notions of faith, the Church, or theology that are not in principle in conflict with easily derived notions of reason, the world, or philosophy. Conflicts are always concrete. They derive from the fact that the abstract notions do not think or do anything by themselves. Concretely there are only people who are more or less faithful to the demands represented in the abstract notions. Catholic theologians have always been aware of this on the one side of the equation, as, for example, when they maintained that there could be no conflict between faith and "right" reason, that adjective being added because often what is considered reason is not "right." They tended, however, to underplay the possibility that faith might not be "right," that believers might not be faithful. (Rationalists, of course, often returned the compliment, comparing their own abstract normative notion of reason to unreasonable statements or actions of believers.) Similarly, it is easy to counterpose an ideal notion of the Church to the concrete imperfections of the world, neglecting the fact that the Church very seldom, if ever, is perfectly realized in the concrete communities of faith in which alone it exists.

There is a similar temptation in the internal discussion of relations between ecclesiastical authority (the "magisterium") and theologians. Once again, it is possible to derive abstract notions and ideals of the two groups and to make the statement that they are not in principle in conflict with one another, but perform complementary roles in the Church. In many treatments of the matter, however, the discussion remains abstract, as when people speak about "magisterium" and "theology" and describe what they do or are supposed to do. In fact, of course, the magisterial role is only carried out by concrete people, popes and bishops, and theology is a task undertaken only by specific men and women.

To point the issue, reflect on some comments by Newman:

Consider the Bible tells us to be meek, humble, single-hearted and teachable. Now, it is plain that humility and teachableness are qualities of mind necessary for arriving at the truth in any subject, and in religious matters as well as others. By obeying Scripture, then, in practicing humility and teachableness, it is evident that we are at least *in the way* to arrive at the knowledge of God. On the other hand, impatient, proud, self-confident, obstinate men are generally wrong in the opinions they form of persons and things. Prejudice and self-conceit blind the eyes and mislead the judgment, whatever be the subject inquired into. . . . The same thing happens also in religious inquiries. When I see a person hasty and violent, harsh and high-minded, careless of what others feel, and disdainful of what they think—when I see such a one proceeding to inquire into religious subjects, I am sure beforehand that he cannot go right—he will not be led into all the truth—it is contrary to the nature of things and the experience of the world, that he should find what he is seeking. I should say the same were he seeking to find out what to believe or to do in any other matter not religious, but especially in any such important and solemn inquiry; for the *fear* of the Lord (humbleness, teachableness, reverence towards Him) is the very *beginning* of wisdom, as Solomon tells us; it leads us to think over things modestly and honestly, to examine patiently, to bear doubt and uncertainty, to wait perseveringly for an increase of light, to be slow to speak, and to be deliberate in deciding.[6]

The paragraph calls for conversion as an inner requirement for religious inquiry, and it would not be difficult to spell Newman's words out as the intellectual, moral, and religious conversions Bernard Lonergan has put at the heart of theological method. Ecclesiastical literature, of course, abounds in appeals that such virtues mark the inquiry of theologians, and Church law provides for occasions in which authorities may and ought to intervene where their absence has led theologians astray. On the other hand, ecclesiastical history has ample evidence of what happens when such virtues are lacking among those who occupy Church offices. Unfortunately, Church law is less care-

---

6. John Henry Cardinal Newman, "Inward Witness to the Truth of the Gospel," in *Parochial and Plain Sermons*, vol. 7 (London: Longmans, Green and Co., 1891), 113–14.

ful to protect the rest of the Church from the consequences of
a lack of modesty, honesty, patience, and deliberation in those
in authority.

The result is a structural imbalance: one side of the problem
is addressed in its full concreteness, while the other tends to be
seen in abstraction from the problems generated by the fact
that the magisterial task is in fact only undertaken also by limited and sinful people—the invocation of the Holy Spirit's assistance often presented, to the neglect of considerable historical evidence to the contrary, as if it somehow, almost miracu-
lously, would render this fact innocent. Theologians are often
reminded of the necessity of conversion and of ecclesial communion and subordination; reminders of similar obligations on
the part of popes and bishops are much rarer. An abstract ideal
of the magisterium, in other words, is paired with a very concrete description of theology. Real progress will only be made
when ideal description is compared with ideal description and
concrete reality with concrete reality.

It is important to note the *ecclesial* dimensions of the problem and not to reduce it to a mere matter of the rights of individual theologians. It is the integrity of the Church and its ability to meet its redemptive role in history that are at stake. Theology is indispensable to the inner life and to the mission of
the Church in our age, and that means that it is also indispensable for those who have the authority to maintain the
faith-integrity of the People of God and to direct its accomplishment of its work as the sacrament of the world's salvation.
There is little evidence that papal election or episcopal conse-
cration substitutes for a lack of theological skills or of intellectual conversion, and when popes and bishops do not themselves have the talent or the time to undertake the critical and
reflective tasks that define theology, they have to rely on the
work of theologians. Official magisterial authority and the dis-
ciplined authority of theologians, then, are reciprocally dependent, and it is a mistake to counterpose them.

The difficulties and tensions that have arisen between magisterium and theologians are not simply a matter of the Church's
internal discipline and integrity. For the last two centuries,

almost all of the crises that have pitted Church authority against various theologians have involved, in one way or another, the Church's engagement with the movements of thought and practice that have shaped modern culture and society: the turn to the subject in modern philosophies, historical consciousness in the form of critical method; economic and political theories; the adequacy of old or new Christendoms; ecumenical relations and cooperation. At times, of course, it was the impact of these challenges for the integrity of the Church's faith that was the most visible concern; but that very concern arose precisely in the historical process by which the distinctively modern world was shaping itself. What was at stake was not only what the Church ought to be in itself but also what the Church ought to be doing in the world and how it was to do it.

This observation places the question of tensions between theologians and representatives of the magisterium into a larger context. It is not simply a matter of the rights of individual theologians within the Church, but a matter of the ability of the Church to meet its historic and redemptive challenge. Abuses of authority did not only violate individual rights, they often also hindered or delayed the Church's redemptive response to new and changing historical circumstances. To cite only one example: when John Courtney Murray argued for the necessity of interreligious cooperation and then, in order to clear the ground of debris that prevented it, urged a reconsideration of Church-State relations, he was opposed by American and Roman critics whose zealous defense of the Church's unique status and rights was accompanied and, it seems, at times inspired by nostalgia for an idealized past, specifically modern departures from which could only be seen as a series of apostasies. The ability of Catholics to cooperate with others in the task of social reconstruction after World War II and in the direction of history since was seriously compromised and delayed. The Second Vatican Council did not merely vindicate Murray over and against his critics; it made its own the strategy for the Church's engagement with the challenges of modern history that he had begun to outline twenty years earlier. It can be argued that it was not only Murray who suffered from the measures taken against him, but the Church itself and the world to which it is supposed to bring an effectively redemptive message and grace.

Murray's case illustrates once again the inner link between the Church's inner life and discipline and its mission in the world. The Church's nature and mission are not separable; the Church's nature only exists, is only realized, in its mission in the world. What the Church becomes in virtue of its most divine and distinctive principles is an event within and in relationship to the world. And this means that this relationship with the world is an inner dimension and implication both of the hermeneutical event by which the Church is reborn in faith each day and of the internal relations that characterize its members. A community is only the Church in a redemptive relationship with a world.

Perhaps it needs restatement that this is not to say that it is the world that defines the Church. Within the world of human history the Church is a differentiation that is defined by normative reference to Jesus Christ. Where this distinctive normative reference is lacking or is compromised, it is something other than the Church that emerges within history, and the world lacks the redemptive word and grace of Christ. It is the worst of mistakes to think that concern for the integrity of faith, for the liberating power of hope, and for the comprehensiveness of love is somehow a retreat from the world. What the world needs for the redemption of its historical project is a Church that is faithful to its own originating center, proclaimed, interpreted, and appropriated as the word of life for all circumstances and challenges.

∼

I am grateful to have had the opportunity to offer these observations in a volume of tribute to Carl J. Peter. They are offered not only in respect and gratitude to him but also as one effort to carry forward a conviction he often stated clearly and loudly. He often invoked a phrase that Pope Paul VI used at the end of the Second Vatican Council when he urged intellectuals and scholars: "Have confidence in faith, that great friend of intelligence!" This great friendship always inspired Carl Peter's life, his teaching, and his writings, and it was his honest commitment to that friendship, stormy and tense as it might sometimes become, that makes one gladly recall his memory and sadly mourn his loss.

4

~

The Collegiality Debate

PATRICK GRANFIELD

Carl Peter and I were colleagues and friends for twenty-seven years. He was dedicated to the study of theology in all its aspects, even though his special fields of interest were Christian anthropology, eschatology, and medieval theology. He taught those subjects and wrote extensively on them. Not an ecclesiologist in the formal sense, he was, nevertheless, well aware of the developments in the theology of the Church through his wide reading, conversation with other theologians, and participation in various Church projects.

His ecumenical work, with its strong ecclesiological dimension, encompassed membership in the Commission of Faith and Order of the National Conference of Churches for two years; in the Roman Catholic-Presbyterian/Reformed Churches Bilateral Consultation for six years; and in the Roman Catholic-Lutheran Bilateral Consultation for nineteen years. During his tenure in the last of these dialogues, he actively participated in discussions on such major ecclesiological themes as papacy, episcopacy, teaching authority, and infallibility.

Furthermore, Carl Peter was engaged in the practical working of episcopal collegiality at the national and international levels. He served as a *peritus* at the meetings of the Synod of Bishops in 1971, 1983, and 1985. At the invitation of Pope John Paul II he served two five-year terms on the important International Theological Commission in Rome. For six years he was advisor to the Committee on Doctrine of the National Conference of Catholic Bishops in the United States. In addition, many bishops often consulted him for theological advice. Ecclesiological issues were the subject of some of his consultations here and in Rome.

I am honored to dedicate this essay on collegiality to Carl Peter in appreciation of his many contributions to theology and of his years of loyal service to the Church that he loved.

～

My intention in this article is to describe some of the main features of the continuing debate on collegiality in the Roman Catholic Church. Because this topic is so broad, I shall limit my remarks to episcopal collegiality: the sacramental communion of bishops as they function collaboratively in the Church with the Bishop of Rome, the head of the College of Bishops. In so doing, I in no way intend to minimize the importance of other forms of collegial cooperation in the Church that take place in diocesan synods, presbyteral councils, pastoral councils, and religious congregations. I shall not be able to treat adequately several other important topics related to collegiality: the theology of the local Church; the *sensus fidelium*; the selection of bishops; and ecumenism.[1]

This essay will have five parts: first, the reaction to the present practice of collegiality in the Church; second, the doctrinal foundation of collegiality; third, the Synod of Bishops; fourth, episcopal conferences; and fifth, some concluding remarks on the continuing challenge of collegiality.

I. The Present Context

The formulation of collegiality at Vatican II did not have an easy passage, but it is now seen as a watershed in the history of ecclesiology. It ushered in a new era of the Church; it encour-

1. I have dealt with some of these topics in *The Papacy in Transition* (Garden City, N.Y.: Doubleday, 1980) and *The Limits of the Papacy* (New York: Crossroad, 1987).

aged cooperation and collaboration; it considered authority as service and not domination; and it promoted local rather than centralized decision-making. Karl Rahner's assessment at the end of the Council was typical: "Here is one of the central themes of the whole Council: the College of Bishops."[2] It seemed that collegiality would transform the Church by introducing a vision of ecclesial authority that would modify a monachical view that had characterized ecclesiology for a century or more. Twenty years after the Council, Cardinal Joseph Ratzinger could say that "episcopal collegiality . . . forms part of the major pillars of the ecclesiology of the Second Vatican Council."[3]

Other, less optimistic voices have also been heard in recent years. They question the success of collegiality and see the return of a monarchical approach to authority. Knut Walf, of the Catholic University of Nijmegen, said that the 1983 Code of Canon Law does not reflect the spirit of collegiality found in Vatican II. He argued that the Code overemphasizes papal authority, diminishes the role of bishops, and has a decided preference for Roman centralism.[4] Edward Schillebeeckx's book on the Church is noteworthy because of the absence of any treatment of collegiality, even in the chapter on democratic rule in the Church. Pessimistically he stated that, in the years after Vatican II, "the breath of the Council was cut off, and its spirit, the Holy Spirit, was extinguished."[5] He noted that the Council encouraged participation in Church life, for example, in national councils, episcopal conferences, and diocesan councils. "But when these institutions bore their varied fruit in practice, they were undermined from above and tamed."[6]

2. Karl Rahner in *Commentary on the Documents of Vatican II*, ed. Herbert Vorgrimler (New York: Herder and Herder, 1967), 1:195.

3. Joseph Ratzinger, "The Ecclesiology of Vatican II," *Origins* 15, no. 22 (1985): 373.

4. Knut Walf, "Kollegialität der Bischöfe ohne römischen Zentralismus?" *Diakonia: Internationale Zeitschrift für die Praxis der Kirche* 17 (1986): 167–73. He makes a similar point in "Dead-End or New Beginnings?" in *Ius sequitur vitam. Law Follows Life. Studies in Canon Law Presented to P. J. M. Huizing*, ed. J. H. Provost and K. Walf (Leuven: Leuven University Press, 1991), 230–41.

5. Edward Schillebeeckx, *Church. The Human Story of God* (New York: Crossroad, 1990), xiv.

6. Ibid., 209.

Several groups of theologians have also lamented the failure of collegiality. The Cologne Declaration, signed by 163 European theologians, objected to excessive hierarchical control which they saw as undermining the local churches: "One of the critical achievements of Vatican II—the opening of the Catholic Church to collegiality between Pope and bishops—is being stifled by recent Roman efforts of centralization."[7] In the United States a statement from some unnamed members of the Catholic Theological Society of America repeated many of the concerns of the Cologne Declaration. They singled out the tendency toward centralization in the Church today, the interference of Rome in some episcopal appointments, and the diminished role of episcopal conferences. Collegiality was also mentioned: "We believe that these and similar actions are not compatible with the teaching of Vatican II on episcopal collegiality and the local churches."[8]

Before dismissing collegiality as a noble but failed experiment, it should be noted that interest in collegiality—in theory and in practice—is still very much in evidence. There is an abundance of theological literature in many languages on the ecclesiology of communion, local Church, papacy, episcopacy, Synod of Bishops, and episcopal conferences.[9] On the pastoral or grass-roots level, there is likewise much interest both in the understanding of presbyteral councils, pastoral councils, and consultation, and in the actual working out of collegial decision-making in dioceses, parishes, and religious orders. Lay participation in Church life and governance continues to increase.

7. "The Cologne Declaration," *Origins* 18, no. 38 (1989): 633. Similar sentiments were also found in a statement signed by sixty-three Italian theologians and intellectuals that appeared in 1989: "Lettera ai cristiani," *Il Regno-Attualità*, 15 May 1989, pp. 244–45.

8. "Statement of Catholic Theological Society of America Members," *Origins* 20, no. 29 (1990): 464.

9. In addition to the works cited in this article, see James Provost and Knut Walf, eds., *Collegiality Put to the Test*, *Concilium* 4 (London: SCM; Philadelphia: Trinity Press International, 1990); in it, see especially Donato Valentini, "An Overview of Theologians' Positions: A Review of Major Writings and the State of the Question Today," 31–42.

II. The Doctrinal Foundation

The term "collegiality" is not found in the documents of Vatican II, even though Yves Congar mentioned "collegiality" in the 1950s in his writing on the theology of the laity. The Council preferred the adjective *"collegialis"* and referred to the assembly of bishops as a *"corpus," "ordo," "coetus,"* or *"collegium."*[10] *Collegium,* however, is not to be understood in the juridical sense of the nineteenth century when it meant a group of equals *(societas aequalium)*. The Fathers of Vatican I rejected its application to the College of Bishops. The *Nota explicativa praevia* (#1) of Vatican II stated that there is no equality between the head and the members of the College of Bishops.

A. The Ecclesiology of Communion

The doctrine of collegiality rests on the ancient idea of the Church as a *communio*—a people united and participating in God's saving grace in Christ and celebrating his presence most visibly through the Eucharist. In the words of Augustine, the Eucharist is the sacrament "through which in the present age the Church is made."[11] The universal Church is a *communio ecclesiarum*—not the confederation or sum of the particular churches but a network of local worshiping communities joined together by a common faith, baptism, and the Spirit of the living Christ.

The concept of *communio (koinōnia)*, according to John Paul II, "lies at the heart of the Church's self-understanding."[12] *Communio* has both a vertical and horizontal dimension. The vertical aspect of communion refers to participation and sharing through grace in the life of the Father through Christ in the

10. See Xaverius Ochoa, *Index verborum cum documentis Concilii Vaticani Secundi* (Rome: Commentarium pro Religiosis, 1967), and Philippe Delhaye, *Concordance de Vatican II* (Louvain: CETEDOC, 1974).

11. Augustine, *Contra Faustum* 12, 20 (*PL* 46:265).

12. John Paul II, "Address to the Bishops of the United States (September 16, 1987)," *Origins* 17, no. 16 (1987): 257.

Holy Spirit. Communion is a gift, the fruit of the Paschal Mystery that establishes a new relationship between God and ourselves. The horizontal aspect of communion is the relationship among believers that is possible because of our relationship to God.

Vatican II and subsequent magisterial teachings have emphasized the importance of the ecclesiology of communion.[13] The Synod of 1985 also linked communion to collegiality: "The ecclesiology of communion provides the sacramental foundation of collegiality. Therefore, the theology of collegiality is much more extensive than its mere juridical aspect."[14] Vatican II insisted on the unity and cooperation between the papal and episcopal offices. Although both the papacy and episcopate exist by divine right and have different functions, together they form one communion. The College of Bishops needs the Pope, and the Pope needs the college of which he is the head; one cannot exist without the other.

Others have also stressed the connection between collegiality and communion. Paul VI, for example, noted that collegiality is a "*quaedam communio*,"[15] and that collegiality is nothing else than ecclesial communion among bishops.[16] Walter Kasper stated in similar words that "*communio* ecclesiology is furthermore the basis for the collegiality among the various bishops, and this collegiality is nothing more than the *communio* of the Church in its manifestation at the level of the shepherds."[17]

---

13. Vatican II used the term "*communio*" over one hundred times with a variety of meanings. For some of the more significant usages, see *Lumen Gentium* 4, 8, 13–15, 18, 21, 24–25; *Dei Verbum* 10; *Gaudium et Spes* 32; and *Unitatis Redintegratio* 2–4, 14–15, 17–19, 22. Also see the Congregation for the Doctrine of the Faith, "Some Aspects of the Church Understood as Communion," *Origins* 22, no. 7 (1992): 108–12.

14. *Extraordinary Synod of Bishops, Rome, 1985: A Message to the People of God and the Final Report* (Washington: NCCB, 1986), 19.

15. Paul VI, "Allocution of October 11, 1969," *Acta Apostolicae Sedis* (hereafter *AAS*) 61 (1969): 717.

16. Paul VI, "Address at General Audience (November 12, 1969)," *L'Osservatore Romano*, 13 November 1969, 1.

17. Walter Kasper, "Apostolic Succession in Episcopacy in an Ecumenical Context" (Bicentennial Lecture at St. Mary's Seminary and University, Baltimore, Maryland, October 3, 1991), 15.

Episcopal ordination is another critical aspect of collegiality among bishops. Collegiality is rooted in ordination, which provides a sacramental, ontological foundation. Ordination is essential for collegiality not simply as a juridical requirement, but because it gives a deeply spiritual and interior quality to episcopal activity. In the words of Vatican II: "One is constituted a member of the episcopal body by virtue of sacramental ordination and by hierarchical communion with the head and members of the body" (*Lumen Gentium* 22). Through the sacrament of ordination the bishop enters into a special relationship of coresponsibility for the universal Church. A bishop, through ordination and membership in the College of Bishops, is obliged to exercise solicitude for the entire Church, even though this is not through an act of jurisdiction (*Lumen Gentium* 23).

In conclusion, episcopal collegiality is part of the very nature of the Church as a communion of believers. Sharing in the life of God through grace, a bishop by his ordination becomes the sign of unity in his particular Church. And, as a member of the College of Bishops, he is also obliged to safeguard the unity of faith in the entire Church. The bishop, therefore, is in communion with God, the people he serves, the other members of the college, and the entire People of God.

B. *The Distinction between Effective and Affective Collegiality*

It is commonplace today to find a distinction between two kinds of collegiality: effective and affective. The Synod of 1969 used this distinction, and in the 1970s many theologians adopted it. John Paul II frequently refers to this distinction.[18] Although the terms "effective" and "affective collegiality" are not present as such in Vatican II, they may be substantially present in some of the conciliar texts. *Lumen Gentium* 22 refers

18. Here are a few examples: John Paul II, "Address to German Bishops (November 17, 1980)," *Origins* 10, no. 25 (1980): 387; "Allocution of June 15, 1984," *AAS* 77 (1985): 54; and "Address to Bishops of the United States (September 16, 1987)," *Origins* 17, no. 16 (1987): 258.

to "a true collegial act" ("*versus actus collegialis*"), which seems equivalent to effective collegiality. *Lumen Gentium* 23 refers to the "collegial spirit" ("*collegialis affectus*"), which seems to be what is meant by affective collegiality. In this sense, effective collegiality would mean the most complete and full expression of collegiality, such as is found in an ecumenical council or in the united action of the dispersed bishops with papal approval or acceptance. Affective collegiality would refer to partial expressions of collegiality—the mutual cooperation and fraternal interaction among groups of bishops on the national, regional, or international level. Some examples of affective collegiality would be the Synod of Bishops and episcopal conferences.[19]

In 1985 the International Theology Commission (ITC) issued a document that described two kinds of collegiality. It did not use the terms "effective" or "affective," but described that distinction:

Episcopal collegiality, which succeeds to the collegiality of the Apostles, is *universal*. In relation to the whole of the Church, it belongs to the *totality* of the episcopal body in hierarchical communion with the Roman Pontiff. These conditions are fully verified in a united action of the bishops throughout the world according to what is set down in *Christus Dominus* 4 (see *Lumen gentium* 22). To some degree they can also be verified in the Synod of Bishops, a true but partial expression of universal collegiality, because "representing the whole Catholic episcopate, it at the same time indicates that all bishops participate in hierarchical communion in the concern for the whole Church" (*CD* 5; see *LG* 23). On the other hand, institutions such as episcopal conferences (and their continental groups) belong to the organization and to the concrete or historical form of the Church (*iure ecclesiastico*). If words such as "college," "collegiality," "collegial" are applied to them, they are being used in an analogous and theologically improper sense.[20]

19. For further analysis of this distinction see Joseph A. Komonchak, "The Roman Working Paper on Episcopal Conferences," in *Episcopal Conferences. Historical, Canonical, and Theological Studies*, ed. Thomas J. Reese (Washington: Georgetown University Press, 1989), 177–204, esp. 188–95.

20. Commissio Theologica Internationalis, *Themata selecta de ecclesiologia* (Vatican City: Libreria Editrice Vaticana, 1985), 34. Translation from Komonchak, 192.

Also in 1985 the Synod of Bishops briefly discussed collegiality. It omitted the last sentence of the ITC report, but it spoke of effective collegiality and the collegial spirit and referred to strict and partial realizations of collegiality. It stated that "the collegial spirit is broader than effective collegiality understood in an exclusively juridical way" and that "the collegial spirit is the soul of the collaboration between bishops."[21] The partial realizations of collegiality—the Synod of Bishops, the episcopal conferences, the Roman Curia, the *ad limina* visits, the pastoral journeys of the Pope—"cannot be directly deduced from the theological principle of collegiality, but they are regulated by ecclesial law."[22] The Synod also recommended that a study be made of the theological status and authority of episcopal conferences.

The first draft of this study on episcopal conferences appeared in 1988 and is often referred to as the "*Instrumentum Laboris*."[23] It employed the distinction between effective and affective collegiality. It also repeated the ITC assertion that only in an analogical and theologically improper sense can the concept of collegiality be applied to affective collegiality.

Theological reaction to the distinction between effective and affective collegiality contained in the documents reviewed above has been mixed. Angel Antón, for example, says that the ITC "is not correct" when it limited the use of the terms "collegiality" and "collegial" only to full actions of the entire episcopal college.[24] He also said that he considered "erroneous" the assertion of the 1985 Synod that partial realizations of collegiality (affective collegiality) cannot be deduced from the theological principle of collegiality.[25] Remigius Sobanski thought that the distinction between effective and affective collegiality may

21. *Extraordinary Synod*, 19.

22. Ibid.

23. The English translation of this document can be found in "Draft Statement on Episcopal Conferences," *Origins* 17, no. 43 (1988): 731–37. No other drafts of this document have appeared so far.

24. Angel Antón, "The Theological 'Status' of Episcopal Conferences," *The Jurist* 48 (1988): 205.

25. Ibid., 207.

"deny affective collegiality legal consequences."[26] Joseph Komonchak claimed the distinction should be abandoned. If a distinction is necessary, he suggested, then it should be made between the full or supreme exercise of collegiality in or outside an ecumenical council and the partial realizations of collegiality, as in episcopal conferences. Partial manifestations of collegiality, however, should not be viewed as theologically improper or inferior.[27]

Some theologians see value in the affective dimension of collegiality. Avery Dulles finds the distinction between effective and affective collegiality "quite legitimate provided that 'affective collegiality' is not sterile and ineffective; it has practical effects."[28] The collegial spirit or disposition should never be absent, since it is at the heart of all forms of collegiality. The collegial attitude of collaboration and cooperation among bishops is essential in the process of transmitting the Word of God and strengthening the unity of the *communio ecclesiarum*.

III. The Synod of Bishops

The Synod of Bishops is an obvious expression of episcopal collegiality. Paul VI established the Synod of Bishops on September 15, 1965, by the *motu proprio, Apostolica Sollicitudo*, in which he explained the nature and authority of the Synod and gave norms for its operation.[29] The Pope felt that the Synod

26. Remigius Sobanski, "Implications for Church Law of the Use of the Term 'Collegiality' in the Theological Context of Official Church Statements," in *Collegiality Put to the Test*, 45. This same point was made earlier by Giuseppe Alberigo, "Istituzioni per la communione tra l'episcopato universale e il vescovo di Roma," *Cristianesimo nella storia* 2 (1981): 249.

27. See Komonchak, 194.

28. Avery Dulles, "Doctrinal Authority of Episcopal Conferences," in *Episcopal Conferences*, 217. In similar manner, Angel Antón has said that affective collegiality "is not to be reduced to a mere sentiment, but, expressing the same ontological sacramental reality as effective collegiality, it preceded it in the historical development of the synodal element in the Church and is ordered to it"; Antón, "Theological 'Status'," 205.

29. *AAS* 57 (1965): 775–80. For a thorough analysis of the thought of Paul VI on the Synod of Bishops during his pontificate, see Giovanni Caprile, ed., *Paolo*

would establish a regular forum for the bishops to share their common solicitude for the whole Church and to exercise their collegiality. In particular he enuntiated a threefold purpose for the Synod: to foster a close relationship between the Pope and the bishops throughout the world; to provide accurate information concerning problems facing the Church and the course of action it should take; and to facilitate agreement in the Church on essential doctrine and procedural matters.

Through 1992, thirteen synods have been held: eight ordinary, two extraordinary, and three special. All the synods have been held in Rome and, with the exception of the special synods, they each had about two hundred participants.

The eight ordinary synods dealt with the following topics: dangers to the faith, revision of the Code of Canon Law, seminaries, mixed marriages, and liturgy (1969); ministerial priesthood and justice in the world (1971); evangelization (1974); catechetics (1977); the role of the family (1980); penance and reconciliation (1983); the laity (1987); and priestly formation (1990).

The first extraordinary synod took place in 1967 and discussed the relationship between episcopacy and primacy; the second extraordinary synod was held in 1985 to celebrate the twentieth anniversary of the ending of Vatican II. Pope John Paul II has convoked three special synods. Two took place in 1980: one dealing with the Church in the Netherlands and another concerned with Ukrainian Catholics. There was also a special synod for Europe held November 28–December 14, 1991. A special synod for the Church in Africa is scheduled to meet in Rome in 1994.

Aside from the canonically established meetings of the Synod of Bishops, there have also been several Vatican consultations with bishops: in June 1981, the bishops of Central America; in October 1984, the bishops of Peru; in January 1983, representatives from the United States bishops' conference and European bishops' conferences discussed the second draft of the American

---

VI. Il sinodo dei vescovi. Interventi e documentazione (Brescia: Istituto Paolo VI; Rome: Edizioni Studium, 1992).

bishops' pastoral letter on nuclear war and peace; in March 1986, twenty-one Brazilian bishops; in March 1989, thirty-five bishops of the United States discussed evangelization and the role of the bishop as teacher; in March 1991, seven Eastern patriarchs and eight presidents of episcopal conferences discussed the consequences of the war in the Persian Gulf; and in May 1992, six bishops of the United States discussed the proposed pastoral letter on women. All of these informal meetings were convened by the Pope and took place in Rome. They provided an opportunity for the Pope and his advisers in the Curia to meet with representatives of various episcopal conferences and to share common concerns. Such meetings have helped link the local churches more closely with the universal Church.

Two particular issues concerning the Synod of Bishops are still being discussed: the precise nature of the collegiality exercised by the Synod of Bishops and the use of a deliberative vote by participants at the synods.

The first issue raises the question: can the Synod of Bishops perform a "true collegial act" (*"verus actus collegialis"*) mentioned in *Lumen Gentium* 22 and Canon 337 of the Code of Canon Law? There are two schools of thought on this matter. Some theologians hold that the Synod can in certain circumstances perform a true collegial act.[30] They contend that the synod can act in a strictly collegial manner and thus be an example of effective collegiality, if the Pope accepts its counsels or if it is granted a deliberative vote and the Pope ratifies its decisions. Their major argument is that the *motu proprio* establishing the Synod of Bishops describes its members as "representative of the entire Catholic episcopacy." Thus the synod can be an example of a nonconciliar, strictly collegial action of the bishops united with the Pope. Supporters of this view refer to the statement from the International Theological Commission in 1985 that a strictly collegial action was possible by the Synod of Bishops.[31]

30. Angel Antón, "La collegialità nel Sinodo dei vescovi," in *Il Sinodo dei vescovi*, ed. Josef Tomko (Vatican City: Libreria Editrice Vaticana, 1985), 55–120; and Edward Schillebeeckx, "The Synod of Bishops: One Form of Strict but Non-Conciliar Collegiality," *IDO-C* Dossier 67–9 (March 12, 1967).

31. Commissio Theologica Internationalis, *Themata selecta de ecclesiologia*, 34.

Other theologians take a different view and hold that the
Synod's actions are not capable of being strict collegial acts.[32]
Their arguments make sense. They insist that the only subject
of a strict collegial act is the entire body of bishops and not a
part of it, pointing to *Lumen Gentium* 22 and the Code of
Canon Law (Canon 337, 2). They also note that the 1985
Synod of Bishops—which has greater ecclesial authority than
the International Theological Commission—says that the collegiality of the Synod of Bishops is to be distinguished from
strictly collegial action. The Synod of Bishops, it says, is only a
partial realization of collegiality and a sign of the collegial
spirit. The synod should not be seen as a mini-ecumenical
council where a few bishops can commit the entire episcopate
to their decisions.

The second issue has to do with the giving of a deliberative
vote to the participants in the Synod of Bishops. The Pope can
confer such a right (Canon 343), but he has not done so. It has
been argued that the granting of a deliberative vote would
strengthen the collegial aspect of the synod and increase its
credibility in the Church. Both in the 1969 and 1985 Synods
the request for a deliberative vote was rejected.

As a relatively new entity in the Church, the Synod of Bishops is still seeking ways to become a more effective institution.
Although the synods have experienced some organizational difficulties and have received some criticism, the Church is still
better off having synods than not having them. The Synod of
Bishops is a unique form of collegiality and will continue to
play an important role in the life of the Church.

IV. The Episcopal Conference

Episcopal conferences are another important manifestation
of collegiality. From the earliest days of the Church, bishops

32. Henri de Lubac, *The Motherhood of the Church Followed by Particular Churches
in the Universal Church* (San Francisco: Ignatius, 1982); and Jérôme Hamer, "La responsabilité collégiale de chaque évêque," *Nouvelle revue théologique* 105 (1983):
641–54.

met to share their faith and to address common concerns. Episcopal meetings, synodal assemblies, and particular councils have a long history in both the East and the West. The Second Vatican Council gave episcopal conferences formal status in its *Decree on the Bishops' Pastoral Office in the Church* (*Christus Dominus*). Paul VI, in his 1966 *motu proprio, Ecclesiae Sanctae,* mandated that each nation or territory establish a permanent conference of bishops, if one did not already exist. The 1983 Code of Canon Law treated episcopal conferences at some length (Canons 447–59).[33]

Today there are some one hundred episcopal conferences throughout the world. The conferences are either national (e.g., United States, Brazil) or regional (e.g., Scandinavia, the Caribbean). There are also some larger episcopal organizations: the Council of European Episcopal Conferences (CCEE); the Latin American Episcopal Council (CELAM); the Symposium of Episcopal Conferences of Africa and Madagascar (SECAM); the Federation of Asian Bishops' Conferences (FABC); and the Council of Pacific Episcopal Conferences (CPEC). The last decade has seen an increase in communication between episcopal conferences; they do not operate in isolation.[34]

Since Vatican II, assessments of episcopal conferences have not been lacking. For the sake of brevity and clarity, they can be divided into positive and negative evaluations. Positively, Paul VI considered the conferences valuable because they could address problems and provide assistance which bishops would be unable to do individually.[35] The official *Relatio* of the 1969 Synod of Bishops made a similar observation. It stated that the episcopal conference has "a doctrinal and pastoral authority among Christian people which is not accorded any individual bishop, whatever his authority or opinion" (*Enchiridion Vatica-*

33. For a thorough analysis of the canonical aspects of episcopal conferences, see Thomas J. Green, "The Normative Role of Episcopal Conferences in the 1983 Code," *Episcopal Conferences*, 137–75.

34. On this point see Ivo Fürer, "Episcopal Conferences in Their Mutual Relations," *The Jurist* 48 (1988): 153–74; and Jesús Hortal, "Relationships among Episcopates," *The Jurist* 48 (1988): 175–80.

35. Paul VI, "Address to the Italian Episcopal Conference (April 14, 1964)," *Insegnamenti di Paolo VI* 2 (1965): 245.

num 3:1712). Diocesan bishops have also stressed the value of the conferences as an important part of their pastoral service and their ministry of teaching.[36]

The episcopal conference, an intermediate organization between the diocesan bishop and the Holy See, has proved most effective in responding to urgent problems that require a timely response. Thus John Paul II described episcopal conferences as instruments in accord "with the needs of our time, effective in ensuring the necessary unity of action by the bishops."[37] Episcopal conferences are expressions of the collegial spirit of solicitude that the bishops have for other churches. The conferences ultimately benefit the People of God. The observation of the 1985 Synod of Bishops on episcopal conferences summed it up accurately: "No one can doubt their pastoral utility, indeed their necessity, in the present situation."[38]

Negatively, some authors question the increased role of episcopal conferences in the Church.[39] These authors, however, are not against episcopal conferences *per se*, but they do raise questions about an excessive dependence on episcopal conferences and some possible abuses. The following criticisms are frequently heard. (1) The episcopal conference, with its prestige, publicity, and sheer output of documentation, may diminish or overwhelm the teaching authority of the diocesan bishop and the Pope. (2) The episcopal conference can easily become an unwieldy bureaucracy with its staff, departments, consultants, meetings, projects, publications, and an ever-increasing budget.

36. For example, see the comments of Bishop James Malone, president of the National Conference of Catholic Bishops, "Evaluating Vatican Council II," *Origins* 15, no. 7 (1985): 101; and of Archbishop James Hickey, "The Bishop as Teacher," *Origins* 12, no. 9 (1982): 142.

37. John Paul II, "Address to Chaldaean Bishops (October 6, 1980)," *Insegnamenti di Giovanni Paolo II* 2/2 (1981): 799.

38. *Extraordinary Synod*, 19.

39. The following remarks are drawn from several sources: de Lubac, *The Motherhood of the Church*; Hamer, "La responsabilité collégiale"; Cardinal Joseph Ratzinger with Vittorio Messori, *The Ratzinger Report: An Exclusive Interview on the State of the Church* (San Francisco: Ignatius, 1985); Hans Urs von Balthasar with Vittorio Messori, *Un Papa nutrito di preghiera per questa Chiesa offesa e ferita* (Milan: Avvenire, 1985); and "Draft Statement on Episcopal Conferences." Also see Joseph A. Komonchak, "Introduction: Episcopal Conferences under Criticism," in *Episcopal Conferences*, 1–22.

(3) The episcopal conference often deals with controversial issues which are not unanimously accepted by the bishops and which have serious political ramifications. (4) The extensive consultative process used by some conferences (including the U.S. bishops) is complicated, expensive, and may raise false expectations. (5) The conference may be susceptible to undue influence by special interest groups. (6) The episcopal conference, under the guise of subsidiarity, may be replacing Roman centralization with episcopal conference centralization. (7) The episcopal conference may become nationalistic, when it is so focused on issues confronting its own local Church that it neglects its relationship to the universal Church.

If the amount of the literature is any indication, the issues mentioned above are not as significant as two major questions about episcopal conferences that are currently being discussed by theologians and canonists: the theological character of episcopal conferences and their teaching authority. Let us examine each of these.

A. The Theological Status

Here again we have two clearly defined positions—one which denies the theological character of episcopal conferences and the other which affirms it. Even during Vatican II the issue of the theological foundation of episcopal conferences was debated.[40] Although the Council did not definitively settle this question, it did say that the collegial spirit (*collegialis affectus*) is present in groups of bishops (*Lumen Gentium* 23) and that "there will emerge a holy union of energies in the service of the common good of the churches" (*Christus Dominus* 37).

The first school of thought argues that there is no theological basis for episcopal conferences, because they are only of ec-

---

40. Bishop Luigi Carli, both at Vatican II and at the 1969 Synod of Bishops, said that the papacy and the episcopacy have authority by divine law and that episcopal conferences are based only in ecclesiastical law. For his interventions see *Acta synodalia concilii Vaticani Secundi* (Vatican City: Typis Polyglottis Vaticanis, 1960–61), II/5, 72–75, and Giovanni Caprile, *Il sinodo dei vescovi* (Rome: La Civiltà Cattolica, 1970), 77.

clesiastical law. The position of Cardinal Joseph Ratzinger is forthright: "We must not forget that the episcopal conferences have no theological basis, they do not belong to the indispensable structure of the Church as willed by Christ; they have only a practical, concrete function."[41] Jérôme Hamer considers the actions of episcopal conferences as "collective" rather than "collegial."[42] This school of thought finds support in some magisterial teachings. Thus, the International Theological Commission, as we have already seen, said that episcopal conferences belong "to the concrete or historical form of the Church (*iure ecclesiastico*)" and cannot be called collegial in a proper theological sense.[43] The 1985 Synod of Bishops taught that episcopal conferences are partial realizations of collegiality "which cannot be directly deduced from the theological principle of collegiality, but they are regulated by ecclesial law."[44]

The second school of thought contends that episcopal conferences have a theological basis, even though they are of ecclesiastical law. I agree with this position. Episcopal conferences are more than simply useful institutions; they have a profound theological underpinning. Remigius Sobanski puts it well: "Bishops' conferences, as also other groups of churches and their synods and councils, are without doubt institutions of ecclesiastical law which developed over time. But this development proceeds by divine providence (LG 23), and for that reason from their historical fruits it can be said that they rest ultimately on divine law."[45] Episcopal conferences, as well as parishes, dioceses, and the Roman Curia, are not of divine law, but, according to Avery Dulles, "they have real authority based on the divinely established order of the Church."[46]

41. Ratzinger, *The Ratzinger Report*, 59.
42. Hamer, "La responsabilité collégiale."
43. Commissio Theologica Internationalis, *Themata selecta de ecclesiologia*, 34.
44. *Extraordinary Synod*, 19.
45. Remigius Sobanski, "The Theology and Juridic Status of Episcopal Conferences at the Second Vatican Council," *The Jurist* 48 (1988): 104. Also see the thorough article by Hermann J. Pottmeyer, "Der theologische Status der Bischofskonferenz—Positionen, Klärungen und Prinzipien," in *Die Bischofskonferenz: theologischer und juridischer Status*, ed. H. Müller and H. J. Pottmeyer (Düsseldorf: Patmos, 1989), 44–87.
46. Avery Dulles, "Bishops' Conference Documents: What Doctrinal Authority?" *Origins* 14, no. 32 (1985): 530. Walter Kasper says of episcopal confer-

B. The Teaching Authority

It is clear that episcopal conferences do teach. Conferences throughout the world regularly issue pastoral letters, statements, clarifications, and admonitions as part of their teaching ministry. The question, therefore, is not whether or not conferences teach, but whether they have formal authority to do so. There is no unanimous opinion among theologians and canonists on this question. However, since all appeal to the same conciliar and canonical texts to defend their view, it will be helpful first to give the pertinent texts and then to explain the differing interpretations. There are three primary texts.

(1) *Christus Dominus* 38,1. "An episcopal conference is a kind of council in which the bishops of a given nation or territory jointly [*coniunctim*] exercise their pastoral office by way of promoting that greater good which the Church offers to human beings, especially through forms and programs of the apostolate which are suitably adapted to the circumstances of the times." This text, with a few changes, is also found in Canon 447.

(2) *Christus Dominus* 38,4. "Decisions of the episcopal conference, provided they have been made lawfully and by the choice of at least two-thirds of the prelates who have a deliberative vote in the conference and have been reviewed [*recognitae*] by the Apostolic See, are to have juridicially binding force only in those cases which are prescribed by the common law of the Church or determined by special mandate from the Apostolic See issued either on its own initiative [*motu proprio*] or in response to a petition of the conference itself." Canon 455, 2 also deals with *recognitio*.

(3) Canon 753. "Although they do not enjoy infallible teaching authority, the bishops in communion with the head and members of the college, whether as individuals or gathered in conferences of bishops or in particular councils, are authoritative teachers and instructors of the faith [*authentici sunt fidei*

---

ences: "They are of ecclesiastical law, but with a foundation in the divine law." See "Der theologische Status der Bischofskonferenzen," *Theologische Quartalschrift* 167 (1987): 3. Yves Congar presents the same idea in "Collège, primauté . . . Conférences épiscopales: quelques notes," *Esprit et vie* 96 (1986): 385–90.

doctores et magistri] for the faithful entrusted to their care, who are bound to adhere to this authoritative teaching [*authentico magisterio*] of their bishops with religious submission of mind [*religioso animi obsequio*]."

The first theological position holds that episcopal conferences have no teaching authority. Cardinal Ratzinger has stated this view on several occasions. At a Roman consultation in 1985, he is reported as saying: "A bishops' conference as such does not have a *mandatum docendi*. This belongs only to the individual bishops or to the College of Bishops with the Pope."[47] In *The Ratzinger Report* the Cardinal stated: "No episcopal conference, as such, has a teaching mission; its documents have no weight of their own save that of the consent given to them by the individual bishops."[48] A developed explanation of this view is given by James P. Green and his mentor at the Gregorian University, Gianfranco Ghirlanda.[49] These authors make a distinction between the *munus docendi* (the teaching office) and the *postestas magisterii authentici* (the power of authoritative teaching). They also focus on the meaning of *coniunctim* in *Christus Dominus* 38,1, and Canon 447. For them, *coniunctim* in these texts means that in an episcopal conference the bishops exercise their authoritative power of teaching as individuals, but they do so jointly (*coniunctim*) with the other bishops. The conference as such, then, has no power to teach authoritatively unless it has a special mandate from the Apostolic See. The bishops in the conference teach as individuals, although they do so with others.[50]

The second position affirms that episcopal conferences do have teaching authority. This interpretation is held by many

47. Reported by Archbishop Jan Schotte, "A Vatican Synthesis," *Origins* 12, no. 43 (1983): 692.

48. Ratzinger, *The Ratzinger Report*, 60. He has also said that "bishops' conferences do not have any teaching authority and cannot make teaching binding"; Joseph Ratzinger, *Church, Ecumenism and Politics: New Essays in Ecclesiology* (New York: Crossroad, 1988), 58.

49. James P. Green, *Conferences of Bishops and the Exercise of the "Munus Docendi" of the Church* (Rome: P. Graziani, 1987). Gianfranco Ghirlanda, the director of Green's dissertation, has also written on this question: "De episcoporum conferentia deque exercitio potestatis magisterii," *Periodica* 76 (1987): 573–603; 637–49.

50. Avery Dulles disagrees with this interpretation, because it goes against the clear meaning of Canon 753 which gives teaching authority to episcopal confer-

theologians and canonists, including Avery Dulles, Ladislas Orsy, Hermann J. Pottmeyer, Francisco A. Urrutia, and Julio Manzanares.[51]

It is impossible to summarize here the views of all these authors, but certain important points should be noted. (1) The use of *coniunctim* in *Christus Dominus* 38,1 should not be overemphasized. Admittedly, *coniunctim* is not the same as *collegialiter*, but one should not differentiate between them too sharply. It appears that the Council selected *coniunctim* in order to avoid entering into a discussion of the collegial nature of episcopal conferences and to leave room for further development. (2) The pastoral tasks of bishops mentioned in *Christus Dominus* 38,1 and Canon 447 includes the magisterial function. Relative to these texts, Cardinal Bernadin Gantin, prefect of the Congregation for Bishops, made an interesting observation in his progress report on the document on episcopal conferences: "From an examination of the replies, the importance that the bishops exercise '*coniunctim*' '*quaedam munera pastoralia*' in the conference is highlighted (Canon 447). Within this, the *munus docendi* cannot be left out. In reality, it is unthinkable to have a pastor who does not teach."[52] (3) The obvious and clear interpretation of Canon 753 is that episcopal conferences have the power to teach. This canon states that bishops both individually and gathered in conferences of bishops or in particular councils are authentic teachers of the faith. (4) There is a connection between particular councils and episcopal conferences.

---

ences. Furthermore, the Green-Ghirlanda view goes against the practice of the conferences whereby statements are issued in the name of the entire conference (Canon 454, 2) and not individual bishops. Avery Dulles, "Doctrinal Authority of Episcopal Conferences," in *Episcopal Conferences*, 217–18. In the same volume Ladislas Orsy presents and critiques Ghirlanda's position; see "Reflections on the Teaching Authority of the Episcopal Conferences," 248–51. Orsy also affirms the teaching authority of episcopal conferences.

51. See the articles of Dulles and Orsy referred to in previous note. Hermann J. Pottmeyer gives a tightly reasoned argument in his article "Das Lehramt der Bischofskonferenz," in *Die Bischofskonferenz*, 116–33. Francisco X. Urrutia takes issue with the views of Ghirlanda in "De exercitio muneris docendi a conferentiis episcoporum," *Periodica* 66 (1987): 605–36. Julio Manzanares gives further canonical arguments in "The Teaching Authority of Episcopal Conferences," *The Jurist* 48 (1988): 234–63.

52. Cardinal Bernadin Gantin, "An Update on the Bishops' Conferences Study," *Origins* 20, no. 22 (1990): 356.

Historical evidence shows that particular councils—assemblies of bishops—have exercised a teaching office and have played a major role in the development of doctrine. (5) The very nature of episcopal ordination and the *munus docendi* of the episcopal office means that bishops—singly and together—have the responsibility of proclaiming, witnessing, and encouraging. This teaching function is undertaken by the bishop in his diocese and also with other bishops in the episcopal conference. (6) The authoritative teaching office of the bishops in conference is distinct from the papal and universal episcopal magisterium. The episcopal conference can never exercise an infallible magisterium.

V. Concluding Remarks

After examining the principal elements of episcopal collegiality and the different interpretations of them, it is appropriate to make a few concluding remarks about the nature of collegiality.

First, *collegiality is unique.* Collegiality is not an ecclesial replica of a secular form of government. A balanced understanding of collegiality must take into account two factors. On the one hand, we should avoid, as the Synod of 1985 reminds us, "a unilateral presentation of the Church as a purely institutional structure, devoid of her mystery."[53] In a similar vein, Henri de Lubac has spoken about the danger of conforming the doctrine of collegiality "to ready-made models taken from the history of human societies or from situations or ideas of our times."[54] The temptation is to apply ideas of representative democracy, for example, to collegial governance and to overlook the unique ecclesial character of collegiality. Collegiality shares in the mysterious character of the Church itself, and to neglect its sacramental and spiritual dimension is to end up with a flawed version of collegiality. On the other hand, the Church is both

53. *Extraordinary Synod*, 11.
54. De Lubac, *The Motherhood of the Church*, 235.

divine and human, invisible and visible, pneumatic and charismatic. These elements form, as *Lumen Gentium* 8 teaches us, "one interlocked reality." We have to be careful, therefore, not to supernaturalize the human elements in the Church to the point where, as Gérard Philips has observed, we end up "emptying the mystery by destroying its earthly reality."[55] A proper understanding of collegiality depends on acknowledging both the spiritual and the human dimensions.

Second, *collegiality is complex*. What makes the analysis of collegiality difficult is its multifaceted character. Collegiality is primarily a theological concept. It rests on the idea of communion—the interaction and collaboration of the individual local churches with their bishops in union with the head of the College of Bishops. In addition, collegiality has historical, pastoral, canonical, and ecumenical aspects that relate to theory, structure, and practice. It is difficult to grasp all of these various elements of collegiality and to apply them both to the life of faith, hope, and charity shared by all Christians and to the specific episcopal *munera* of teaching, sanctifying, and ruling. Yet it is only through an appreciation of the broader context that the full scope of collegiality can be seen.

Third, *collegiality is in process*. Vatican II, the Synods of Bishops, and the Code of Canon Law do not give a complete and unambiguous understanding of collegiality in the Church. We have seen how theologians and canonists interpret differently the same magisterial teaching. Certain difficulties that were mentioned by Cardinal Godfried Danneels in a report at the 1985 Synod are still with us. He said: "There remain problems to be resolved: for example, the relationship between the universal Church and the particular churches, the promotion of collegiality, the theological status of the episcopal conferences, . . . a desire to improve relations with the Roman Curia."[56] Moreover, the institutional expressions of collegiality are historically conditioned and can be improved.[57] The concept of collegiality will

55. Gérard Philips, *L'Eglise et son mystère* (Paris: Desclée, 1967), 1:118.

56. Cardinal Godfried Danneels, "Cardinal Danneels: An Overview," *Origins* 15, no. 26 (1985): 428.

57. Paul VI made this observation in regard to the Synod of Bishops in the

develop, and different manifestations of it will appear. Not all disputes will be settled once and for all by the magisterium; time is needed for truth to develop.[58] The ultimate success of collegiality, of course, will depend on our openness to the direction of the Holy Spirit. In this process contributions will come from the universal Church and the particular churches, from bishops and clergy, from laity and religious, from scholars and parishioners. In that way collegiality can be a critical element in "the Church's task of bringing all human beings to full union with Christ" (*Lumen Gentium* 1).

---

motu proprio, Apostolica Sollicitudo, AAS 57 (1965): 776. He said that the synod is a human institution and "will admit of improvement in its form in the course of time." Also see Paul VI, "Allocution of October 11, 1969," *AAS* 61 (1969): 717, and John Paul II, "Allocution of October 29, 1983," *AAS* 76 (1984): 287.

58. Cardinal Gantin, in speaking of the preparation of the final document on episcopal conferences, gave a sound principle concerning the development of doctrine: "It is not the aim of the new document to settle the open theological issues, but rather to allow time for them to mature"; "An Update," 356.

5

~

"Differences about infallibility . . . too significant to be brushed aside as inconsequential"

JOHN T. FORD

The place was Leipzig, the year was 1519, the month was July, the occasion was a debate between John Eck and Martin Luther—some twenty months after the latter's ninety-five theses had been posted at Wittenberg.[1] Like a medieval tournament, this theological *disputatio* attracted a large crowd:

The debate had been scheduled to be held in the aula of the university; but so great was the concourse of abbots, counts, Knights of the Golden Fleece, learned and unlearned, that Duke George placed at their disposal the auditorium of the castle. Chairs and benches were decorated with tapestries, those of the Wittenbergers with the emblem of St. Martin and Eck's with the insigne of the dragon killer, St. George.[2]

After settling matters of procedure and protocol, the debate began with a lengthy argument about human depravity before focusing on papal and conciliar teaching authority. "Eck asserted that the primacy of the Roman see and the Roman bishop as the successor of Peter went back to the very earliest days of the Church."[3] Luther attacked the credibility of the de-

1. For a revisionist view of the way the theses were "posted," see Erwin Iserloh, *The Theses Were Not Posted: Luther between Reform and Reformation* (Boston: Beacon, 1968).
2. Roland H. Bainton, *Here I Stand: A Life of Martin Luther* (New York: Mentor Books, 1961), 86.
3. Ibid., 88.

cretals that Eck had used to support his assertions. When Eck subsequently appealed to the authority of Church councils, Luther replied:

> I assert that a council has sometimes erred and may sometimes err. Nor has a council authority to establish new articles of faith. A council cannot make divine right out of that which by nature is not divine right. Councils have contradicted each other, for the recent Lateran Council has reversed the claim of the councils of Constance and Basel that a council is above a pope. A simple layman armed with Scripture is to be believed above a pope or a council without it. As for the pope's decretal on indulgences I say that neither the Church nor the pope can establish articles of faith. These must come from Scripture. For the sake of Scripture we should reject pope and councils.[4]

Pronounced in the heat of debate, Luther's assertion proved to be more prophetic than he could have anticipated. Included in this statement were many of the polarities that have characterized centuries of Protestant-Catholic polemics: revealed truth versus human error, Scripture versus tradition, divine right versus historical institution, dogmatic definition versus doctrinal revision, personal freedom versus ecclesiastical authority, and so on. Not surprisingly, this same constellation of issues has formed a major item on the agenda of the official Lutheran-Roman Catholic Dialogue in the United States.[5]

Given their commitment to historical confessions, it is also not surprising that the Lutheran-Catholic Dialogue has revisited Reformation controversies, with Lutherans looking back to such magisterial documents as the *Augsburg Confession*, and Roman Catholics reexamining pivotal teachings such as those of the Council of Trent. Yet, however necessary and beneficial such historical reappraisal may be for two confessional traditions, ecumenical dialogue is not only a matter of re-evaluating, and

---

4. Ibid., 90.

5. See *Papal Primacy and the Universal Church: Lutherans and Catholics in Dialogue V*, ed. Paul C. Empie and T. Austin Murphy (Minneapolis: Augsburg, 1974); *Peter in the New Testament: A Collaborative Assessment by Protestant and Roman Catholic Scholars*, ed. Raymond E. Brown, Karl P. Donfried, and John Reumann (Minneapolis: Augsburg; New York: Paulist, 1973); *Teaching Authority & Infallibility in the Church: Lutheran and Catholics in Dialogue VI*, ed. Paul C. Empie, T. Austin Murphy, and Joseph A. Burgess (Minneapolis: Augsburg, 1978).

hopefully resolving, the divisive controversies of the past; dialogue must also address the current *status quaestionis*. At least on the Roman Catholic side, the question of the Church's teaching authority has been both clarified and complicated not only by post-Tridentine theological developments, but particularly by the pronouncements of the First and Second Vatican Councils. In other words, bilateral dialogues need to treat not only the issues that prompted the original separation, but also the differences that have subsequently arisen during the course of their separate histories.

Such a task might seem hopeless were it not for a commitment to achieve visible unity among Christians. In simplest terms, where many of the disputations of the Reformation seem polemical efforts almost designed to exacerbate differences, contemporary ecumenical dialogue has been motivated by the irenic desire of discovering a basic convergence in belief amid a diversity of doctrinal expressions.[6]

In addition, such efforts have benefited immensely from such "signs of the times" as the establishing of the World Council of Churches and the participation of Protestant and Orthodox observers at Vatican II. In fact, the Lutheran-Roman Catholic Dialogue had the decided advantage of beginning before Vatican II concluded.[7] The *aggiornamento* initiated by Pope John XXIII and continued under Pope Paul VI was still a breath of fresh air, fostering theological *resourcement* and encouraging ecumenical endeavors. Yet Lutheran-Roman Catholic conversations were scarcely underway when the teaching of the First Vatican Council (1869–70) on the "infallible magisterium of the Roman Pontiff" became a topic of heated debate among Roman Catholic theologians.[8]

6. For an overview of the redirection of ecumenical dialogue from "comparative dogmatics" to "ecumenical convergence," see John T. Ford, "Ecumenical Studies," in *A Century of Church History: The Legacy of Philip Schaff*, ed. Henry W. Bowden (Carbondale: Southern Illinois University Press, 1988), 245–93.

7. Paul C. Empie, *Lutherans and Catholics in Dialogue: Personal Notes for a Study*, ed. Raymond Tiemeyer (Philadelphia: Fortress, 1981), viii: "On July 6, 1965, representatives of Roman Catholic and Lutheran churches met to open dialogues between the churches."

8. On July 18, 1870, Vatican I promulgated its "First Dogmatic Constitution on the Church of Christ," commonly cited by its first words, *Pastor Aeternus*; its

On the centennial of the First Vatican Council, Hans Küng, who was one of the most influential theologians at the time of Vatican II, published *Infallible? An Inquiry*.[9] Disenchanted with the slow pace of postconciliar renewal, Küng felt that "pope, Curia, and many bishops, in spite of the unavoidable changes which have taken place, continue to carry on in a largely pre-conciliar way" (p. 12). As a case in point, Küng pointed to *Humanae Vitae*, the most recent of a long list of "errors of the ecclesiastical teaching office in every century" (p. 32). Küng then marshalled a series of arguments—biblical, historical, and philosophical—that indicated that a serious re-examination of "infallibility" was urgently needed. Unlike the relatively minimal response to other works on infallibility which appeared at roughly the same time, Küng's *Infallible?* became the focus of considerable debate.[10] Most Roman Catholic theologians agreed with Küng that a reconsideration of infallibility was needed, though few agreed with Küng's way of discussing the question.[11]

Moreover, there was no way that this debate could remain intramural. The teaching of Vatican I on the primacy and infallibility of the Roman pontiff has long been a bone of contention for Protestant polemicists. With or without Küng, infallibility would necessarily have been placed on the ecumenical agenda. Secondly, while this doctrine had become more intelligible (which is not to say acceptable) to Protestant theologians as a result of the discussion of episcopal collegiality at Vatican II, nonetheless it could be claimed that "papal infallibility" was "*the* ecumenical problem of the Christian Churches."[12]

---

fourth chapter treated the "infallible magisterium of the Roman Pontiff"; the text is given by H. Denzinger and A. Schönmetzer, *Enchiridion Symbolorum*, nn. 3050–75 (hereafter cited as DS).

9. Hans Küng, *Infallible? An Inquiry* (Garden City, N.Y.: Doubleday, 1971); see John T. Ford, "Küng on Infallibility: A Review Article," *The Thomist* 35 (1971): 501–12.

10. Among the numerous reviews of Küng's works, see those of Gregory Baum, George Lindbeck, Richard McBrien, and Harry J. McSorley in *The Infallibility Debate*, ed. J. Kirvan (New York: Paulist, 1971).

11. For a review of this discussion, see John T. Ford, "Infallibility: A Review of Recent Studies," *Theological Studies* 40 (1979): 273–305.

12. See Leonard Swidler, "*The* Ecumenical Problem Today: Papal Infallibility," *Journal of Ecumenical Studies* 8 (1971): 751–67.

Carl Peter on Papal Primacy and Infallibility

Carl Peter became a member of the Lutheran-Roman Catholic Dialogue in 1972, thus at a time, not only when the "infallibility debate" was in full swing, but also when this dialogue was discussing the topic of papal primacy and teaching authority. Though not primarily an ecclesiologist, he did publish several essays that reflected both his participation in and contribution to the ecumenical discussion on papal primacy and infallibility.

In one of these studies, originally presented at a meeting of the Lutheran-Roman Catholic Dialogue in September 1974, Peter discussed the "ecumenical possibilities" of the infallibility debate.[13] Candidly acknowledging that "[n]ot a few Roman Catholics react in an embarrassed fashion when there is mention of papal infallibility," he summarized this debate's ecumenical implications:

a) the resolution of this theological debate among Roman Catholics about the meaning and grounds for the dogma of papal infallibility is not within sight;
b) this lack of consensus among Roman Catholics poses problems for ecumenical efforts aimed at bringing the two traditions represented in this bilateral consultation closer together;
c) progress may nevertheless be made toward greater unity if theologians in the traditions of Trent and Augsburg can arrive at a consensus . . . regarding their belief in the final and unsurpassable character of God's revelation in Jesus Christ.[14]

Turning to the heated controversy about infallibility that had arisen between Hans Küng and Karl Rahner, Peter pointed out that for the former, " . . . even a solemn papal or conciliar definition could (though not necessarily 'must') in principle be not merely 'historically' restricted, limited, inadequate, dangerous, one-sided, mingled with error and therefore open to correction, but—measured by the Gospel itself—downright erroneous."[15]

13. Carl J. Peter, "A Rahner-Küng Debate and Ecumenical Possibilities," in *Teaching Authority*, 159–68.
14. Ibid., 159–60.
15. Ibid., 160, citing Küng's "A *Working Agreement* to Disagree," *America* 129, no. 1 (7 July 1973): 10.

Küng's position posed an important question, not only for Roman Catholics, but for their partners in ecumenical dialogue:

Can solemn papal or conciliar definitions be mistaken or erroneous when measured against the gospel? Küng answered this question affirmatively while Rahner said he had to reply negatively, not merely as a Roman Catholic but as a Christian and theologian conscious of the Church's nature.[16]

Given the prominence of these theological adversaries, as well as the importance of the topic, Peter felt that there was good reason for the Vatican to intervene in the debate: "When an issue cannot be resolved on theological grounds to the satisfaction of the participants, when the dispute is not an idle skirmish or when Christian values are at stake in the view of all involved, one has no right to demand silence from the church's teaching office."[17] Consequently, Peter felt that Pope Paul VI in issuing *Mysterium Ecclesiae* (1973) had done ecumenism a service: "Ecumenical progress may well be fostered by such a candid statement of Catholic convictions."[18] Peter highlighted three areas where *Mysterium Ecclesiae* provided such candor:

1. " . . . the Church and its magisterium can indeed teach the Word of God infallibly."
2. " . . . theologians remain subordinate to the living *magisterium* of the Church."
3. "Bishops and the pope have a unique role in the Church; in teaching they have been promised divine protection from error in certain circumstances."[19]

Nonetheless, although he defended the Vatican's right to speak to the controversy, Peter was less than satisfied with the theological argumentation presented in *Mysterium Ecclesiae:* "If the Congregation for the Doctrine of the Faith felt it should reassert the teaching of Vatican Councils I and II, it might well have tried harder to be convincing."[20] For a satisfactory explanation of infallibility, Peter felt that one needed to look else-

16. "Rahner-Küng Debate," 161–62.
17. Ibid., 164.   18. Ibid., 164–65.
19. Ibid., 162–64.   20. Ibid., 165.

where: "Transcendental method appears, at least in my opinion, to be the most promising philosophical theory to warrant the conviction that time-conditioned language can express infallible truth."[21] Such a discussion would be the concern of another article (see below); for the immediate purposes of the Lutheran-Roman Catholic Dialogue, he insisted on both the provisionality and the significance of doctrinal statements:

Both traditions represented in this dialogue look to the eschaton for the final validation and perfection of faith. From this perspective all confessional formulae are provisional, even the infallible definitions of Roman Catholics. But it is also true that both traditions regard doctrinal differences as obstacles that must not be ignored in efforts to achieve closer union between Christian churches that have been seriously divided for centuries. However provisional the formulations of dogma may be in relation to eternity, differences about infallibility between Lutherans and Roman Catholics are too significant to be brushed aside as inconsequential—this in the name of the unity that already exists between the two confessions.[22]

Peter found corroboration for his conviction that "differences about infallibility" are "too significant to be brushed aside as inconsequential" in the claim of a Lutheran participant, George Lindbeck, that "probably every religion, and certainly Christianity, is committed to affirming the infallibility of at least some of its central affirmations."[23]

There is no doubt that this is the case in Roman Catholicism. The First Vatican Council, for example, taught that "by divine and catholic faith, all those teachings must be believed, which are contained in the written or traditioned word of God and are proposed by the Church to be believed as divinely revealed, either by solemn decision or by the ordinary and universal magisterium."[24] Subsequently, Vatican I condemned anyone who

21. Ibid.
22. Ibid., 168.
23. Ibid., 168, citing George Lindbeck, *The Infallibility Debate*, 108.
24. Vatican I, *Dei Filius* (the dogmatic constitution on the Catholic faith), ch. 3 (*DS* 3011): "Porro fide divina et catholica ea omnia credenda sunt, quae in verbo Dei scripto vel tradito continentur et ab Ecclesia sive solemni iudicio sive ordinario et universali magisterio tanquam divinitus revelata credenda proponuntur." However, it should be noted that Vatican I did not speak of "infallible proposi-

dared to assert that "Blessed Peter did not have, by the institution of Christ Himself or by divine right, perpetual successors in the primacy over the universal church."[25] Other important factors (such as scriptural verification) aside, in what sense can it be said that any ecclesial institution (such as the primacy) exists "by divine right"?

In an article that appeared the year before his presentation at the Lutheran-Roman Catholic Dialogue, Peter explored the "Dimensions of *Jus Divinum* in Roman Catholic Theology."[26] At the outset, he acknowledged the neuralgic nature of the topic: "Talk of institutions existing 'by divine right' sets people on edge these days. It sounds so Byzantine and seems to smack of arrogance."[27]

Nevertheless, as Peter emphasized, *jus divinum* is part of the Roman Catholic tradition and has been used to characterize those "offices and rites" that are "a result of divine institution and mandate."[28] Given the fact that the church's ecclesial offices and sacramental rites incorporate human and historical factors, how can one possibly distinguish the divine from the human in actuality? Such a distinction would be like attempting to divide matter from form: " . . . no theological scalpel can be applied to separate the dimension of nature from that of form in the concrete. Nor can a laser ray be brought to bear to accomplish this purpose."[29]

---

tions" (as Küng has claimed), but of "irreformable definitions" (*DS* 3074); the former is usually understood in a philosophical sense; the latter, however, seems best understood in a juridical sense; cf. John T. Ford, "Infallibility: Who Won the Debate?" *Proceedings of the Catholic Theological Society of America* 31 (1976): 184–85.

25. *Pastor Aeternus*, ch. 2; the canon in its entirety stated (*DS* 3058): "Si quis ergo dixerit, non esse ex ipsius Christi Domini institutione seu iure divino, ut beatus PETRUS in primatu super universam Ecclesiam habeat perpetuos successores; aut Romanum Pontificem non esse beati PETRI in eodem primatu successorem: anathema sit."

26. Carl J. Peter, "Dimensions of *Jus Divinum* in Roman Catholic Theology," *Theological Studies* 34 (1973): 227–50.

27. Ibid., 227; Peter pointed out that "[t]here is no comprehensive study of what Roman Catholics mean when in theologizing today they refer to *jus divinum* and lay claim to it for some of their rites and institutions" (236).

28. Ibid., 227.

29. Ibid., 231.

To explain how the Church has come to consider certain offices and rites to be divinely instituted, even when the New Testament evidence for direct institution by Christ is inconclusive, Peter looked to Rahner, who felt that "subsequent developments, despite their tardy appearance, may be so decisive as to make it impossible to turn the clock back to the way things were earlier."[30] While one might argue that other options might legitimately have been made, these decisions are now irreversible:

Such decisions in the primitive Church may well give rise to a *jus divinum* for subsequent ages. Indeed, he [Rahner] sees no reason why a priori and certainly it is impossible to have a *jus divinum* arise in such a fashion in the postapostolic age, with the "irreversibility" that this would imply.[31]

Irreversibility is another issue that separated Rahner and Küng; for the latter, "episcopate, presbyterate, and diaconate represent a legitimate structuring of the ordained ministry. But the division of functions to which they correspond was not divinely decreed or established."[32] In addition, where Rahner allowed for a postapostolic *jus divinum*, Küng appealed to "the truth of the gospel" as his "only critical norm."[33] "Thus, for Hans Küng some developments of church order are legitimate, but not for that fact obligatory once and for all."[34]

If, at first glance, Küng's thesis of reversibility is appealingly simple and apparently evangelical, on closer inspection it seems basically fundamentalistic, even semirationalistic:

But are the creedal formulae accepted only because of their *evident* connection with the New Testament message? If so, then logical consistency would be the final motive for accepting subsequent dogmatic development. One would not be assenting to the Word of God acknowledged as operative in that development.[35]

30. Ibid., 232.   31. Ibid., 233.
32. Ibid., 234.

33. Ibid. Peter also relied on Raymond Brown: " . . . there can be subsequent normative interpretation of God's action that is not found in Scripture" (235).

34. Ibid., 235.

35. Ibid., 248; as Peter observed, "Computers could probably do a better job of verifying the compatibility of later forms of faith with earlier expressions than any consultation with believing Christians or their leaders" (248).

To restrict *jus divinum* to a one-to-one correspondence between explicit texts of the New Testament and later conciliar teaching is comparable to looking for scriptural evidence that Joseph of Nazareth built the first confessional as a warrant for the Tridentine teaching on the sacrament of penance.[36]

After examining the discussions at the Council of Trent, Peter concluded that the participants were not always able to agree whether a specific question was a matter of *jus divinum* or not, and if so, how. Secondly, "Roman Catholic bishops and theologians at Trent interpreted God's written Word with direct reference to their day."[37] Accordingly, "The difficulty theologians experience today in their efforts to isolate elements of divine right in sacraments and church order from contingent, changeable factors is not new."[38]

In contrast to those who assume that "the validation of later expressions of faith is to be sought primarily in deductive or inductive processes of reasoning linking those expressions with biblical premises or the explicit testimony of tradition,"[39] Peter called for a process combining both historical investigation of and theological reflection on the Christian tradition in the context of the contemporary Church:

Should it be surprising if one group of Christians maintains that the ministry of Peter, however unrepeatable, is nevertheless continued in the exercise of an office through history for men of subsequent ages? The historical demonstrability of such a claim would a priori be expected to be neither totally absent nor apodictic. Far from arguing solely in favor of a purely charismatic ministry, such considerations can tell positively in favor of a succession in the exercise of the Petrine functions in the Church. To put it somewhat differently, if the New Testament presents a chief apostle, a principal spokesman and confessor of the faith, would not a presumption that his function continued in others be at least entertainable as a position Christians might take as believers? I would answer in the affirmative.[40]

---

36. After reviewing the debate at the Council of Trent regarding whether it is *jus divinum* that confession prior to communion is necessary in the case of a communicant in mortal sin, Peter remarked that "Joseph of Nazareth had indeed not built the first confessional, and this was well known" (ibid., 241).

37. Ibid., 243.   38. Ibid., 244.
39. Ibid., 249.   40. Ibid., 247.

Three years later, in a paper delivered at the annual convention of the Catholic Theological Society of America, Peter sketched some of the ecumenical dimensions of papal primacy.[41] Focusing on "the papacy's potential for Christian service to the different local churches throughout the world," Peter noted that the papacy "in our day . . . has already changed notably, perhaps more by way of the personal style of the one exercising its chief role than through statutory reorganization of its functions."[42]

While granting that the way in which John XXIII and Paul VI had exercised their papal role was personal, "[t]here is no good reason to think it cannot or may not be modified more yet while retaining its identity and a continuity with its past in much more than time, space, and name."[43] Peter saw this renewal of the papacy not only as a "peculiarly" intramural task, but also as a necessarily ecumenical endeavor:

In the collective task of renewing the papacy, the insights of all men and women of good will must be welcomed but especially those of fellow Christians. In this case the would-be helper, the papacy, surely needs help from those to be helped. Unless this is admitted the whole venture could be easily dismissed as another instance of Roman Catholic arrogance—triumphalism by another name in another day. But the renewal in question is—all this notwithstanding—a peculiarly Roman Catholic task. Members of that church must be honest enough to recognize and criticize the historical and historic failings of the papacy.[44]

Sympathetic to the necessity of preventing "frightful abuse" in the exercise of papal authority, while not wishing "to eliminate any significant power from the papal office," Peter posed seven questions for beginning discussion of the papacy and contemporary ecumenical developments:[45]

a. Citing Raymond Brown's view of a Petrine trajectory in the New Testament, Peter asked "what it would mean for the suc-

41. Carl J. Peter, "Papal Primacy: Ecumenical Developments," *Proceedings of the Catholic Theological Society of America* 31 (1976): 137–41.

42. Ibid., 137.   43. Ibid.
44. Ibid., 138.   45. Ibid., 138, 139.

cessor of Peter to feed the sheep of Jesus in the last quarter of the last century of the second millennium?"[46]

b. Acknowledging the critique of George Lindbeck, his Lutheran Dialogue-partner, Peter questioned: "How concretely can a Lutheran understanding make a contribution to Roman Catholic efforts to renew the papacy?"[47]

c. Referring to Wolfhart Pannenberg's comment that the Bishop of Rome, as representative of all Christians, needs to speak in such a way as to "gain in credibility outside the Roman Catholic Church," Peter asked: "What would the consequences be if such a *modus agendi* were to be adopted by a bishop of Rome?"[48]

d. Referring to the reflections of Avery Dulles that "it would be conceivable for example that the bishop of another city might hold the primacy, or that the papacy might rotate among several sees," Peter asked: "If so, how could Catholic Christians decide whether pursuing such a line of thought would be ecumenically helpful rather than idle speculation?"[49]

e. Reflecting on the bilateral consensus already achieved in *Papal Primacy and the Universal Church*, Peter inquired: ". . . what limitations are indeed compatible with the nature of the Petrine function exercised by the pope?"[50]

f. In light of the discussion whether Protestant churches, while retaining their own identity, might enter into communion with the bishop of Rome, Peter wondered: "What would the consequences be for the Roman Catholics in their relation to the bishop of Rome if other Christians were officially related to that See very differently?"[51]

g. Finally, with apparent reference to the then current discussions about *Humanae Vitae* and the "infallibility debate," Peter asked: "Does the need for an ultimate court of appeal in faith and morals vary directly, inversely, or not at all with the developments in theology as a discipline?"[52]

46. Ibid., 139.
47. Ibid., 139–40.
48. Ibid., 140.
49. Ibid.
50. Ibid., 141.
51. Ibid.
52. Ibid.

Lutheran-Roman Catholic Convergence

Some answers to these questions were given two years later with the publication of a "common statement" on "Teaching Authority and Infallibility in the Church."[53] Since this document was a cooperative endeavor, it seems inappropriate to ascribe particular passages to any single participant; suffice it to say that Carl Peter's major concerns, as indicated in his previous publications, were reflected in this document.

What is surprising about this common statement is the quantity and quality of theological convergence that the representatives of these two confessional traditions managed to achieve on a topic that for centuries has "occasioned the most violent antagonisms" (I.1). The statement began by recognizing that "papal infallibility" is not a dogma that can be accepted or rejected in isolation from other aspects of a Christian's confession: "Papal infallibility is related to several wider questions: the authority of the gospel, the indefectibility of the Church, the infallibility of its belief and teaching, and the assurance or certainty which Christian believers have always associated with their faith" (I.1).

Simultaneously, the statement acknowledged that in the decades following Vatican I, Roman Catholic treatments of the topic had sometimes produced what Bishop B. C. Butler once called "creeping infallibility":[54]

Despite the careful delimitation of papal infallibility by Vatican I, this dogma was frequently understood more broadly in the period between the two Vatican Councils. Often for the popular mind, and also in theological manuals, it was thought to imply that all papal utterances are somehow enhanced by infallibility. (I.2)

53. In *Teaching Authority*, 9–68. This statement has also been published in *Building Unity: Ecumenical Dialogues with Roman Catholic Participation in the United States*, ed. Joseph A. Burgess and Jeffrey Gros, F.S.C, Ecumenical Documents 4 (New York: Paulist, 1989), 160–216. The statement is divided into (I) "Common Statement," (II) "Roman Catholic Reflections," and (III) "Lutheran Reflections"; citations refer to these divisions and the numbered paragraphs within the respective division.

54. B. C. Butler, "The Limits of Infallibility," *The Tablet* 225 (1971): 372–75.

One productive result of the infallibility debate in the 1970s has been the increased awareness of the need for a careful and conscientious "pruning" of unwarranted exaggerations about papal primacy and infallibility, not only to provide greater doctrinal accuracy as far as Roman Catholics are concerned, but also to allow Protestants to consider the possibility that this doctrine has legitimacy: "Yet Lutherans need not exclude the possibility that papal primacy and teaching authority might be acceptable developments, at least in certain respects" (I.3). Such a possibility, quite unlikely in earlier debates about whether proof for papal primacy and teaching authority could be found in Scripture,[55] was the result of "examining infallibility afresh," first by setting the topic "in the broader horizon of doctrinal authority in the early Church" and secondly, by investigating the topic "in light of linguistic and cultural contexts" that allowed the question to be considered "in ways which are different from earlier discussion" (I.4).

From such a rereading of Scripture, the participants in the dialogue recognized that while "[i]nfallibility is not a New Testament term," nonetheless, "the New Testament is concerned with many of the issues that arise in later theological discussions of the authority and infallibility of Scripture, Church, councils, and popes" (I.16). A concomitant rereading of ancient and medieval church history led to the recognition that "[w]ith the growing practice of appealing to Rome, papal decisions came to be regarded in matters of faith as the last word, from which there could be no further appeal" (I.20). Over the centuries, "infallibility" eventually came "to be associated with the papal *magisterium*" (I.21); in the process, "infallibility" acquired "a new, highly technical meaning" (I.22).

Unfortunately, an appreciation of this technical theological terminology was often lacking in subsequent doctrinal discussions and catechetical presentations. Frequently, the central issue was overlooked: "Whatever one may think about the ap-

---

55. "For while Lutherans see papal primacy as emerging over a long period of time, rather than something taught in the Scriptures, this function could, under proper conditions be acknowledged as a legitimate development, maintaining unity, mediating disputes, and defending the Church's spiritual freedom" (I.3).

propriateness of the term 'infallible,' it points to the unavoidable issue of the faithful transmission of the gospel and its authoritative interpretation, guided by the Spirit" (I.23). The way
that Lutherans and Catholics have envisioned this guidance,
however, has received quite different emphases.

Roman Catholics, on the one hand, maintain that "the transmission of the gospel is the responsibility of the whole people of
God" (I.30); simultaneously they hold that "[t]he highest authority in the transmission of doctrine has been exercised in
definitions of faith made by councils or by the bishop of Rome
speaking *ex cathedra*" (I.32). Nonetheless, such pronouncements
are not arbitrary: "When the bishop of Rome is the agent of the
definition, he acts subject to conditions imposed by the Word of
God and the faith of the Church, with the careful investigation
and study that the seriousness of the action and the conditions
of the time require and permit" (I.33).

In Lutheran churches, on the other hand, "the traditional
organs for continuing this process of interpretation were largely
lost . . . at the time of the Reformation" (I.39). At present,

Lutheran churches are organized in many different forms, episcopal,
presbyterian, and congregational, depending upon the historical
circumstances of their development. Doctrinal interpretation and discipline are accordingly exercised in a great variety of ways. (I.39)

Although such "arrangements have helped to protect" Lutheran communities "from disintegration on the one hand and
from excessive centralization and the sacralization of ecclesiastical power on the other," still they have not been the "most
adequate for Lutherans in the 20th century to confess together
their faith as a world-wide communion" (I.39).

While the dialogue acknowledged such "notable differences
in emphasis and in structure between Lutherans and Catholics,"[56] it also found "considerable common ground" (I.40).
Basic to this convergence is the recognition of the necessity for
"teaching authority" in the Church: " . . . there are Ministries

56. For example, "Lutherans have a tendency to treat Scripture as if it were
identical with the gospel or the Word of God, while Catholics have shown a similar tendency with regard to tradition and church structures" (I.43).

and structures charged with the teaching of Christian doctrine and with supervision and coordination of the ministry of the whole people of God, and . . . their task includes the mandate for bishops or other leaders to 'judge doctrine and condemn doctrine that is contrary to the Gospel'" (I.41). Accordingly, the participants in the dialogue recognized that " . . . there may appropriately be a Ministry in the universal Church charged with primary responsibility for the unity of the people of God in their mission to the world" (I.41).

If the participants were able to concur about the need for the Church to teach authoritatively, they also acknowledged difficulties inherent in exercising that teaching function. Among these is the fact that " . . . no doctrinal definition can adequately address every historical or cultural situation" (I.41). Moreover, while the Church's teaching strives to present the Word of God, "one cannot simply repeat Scripture and tradition in order to be faithful to the gospel, but one must be open to new ways of structuring its transmission in the Church" (I.43).

In such a restructuring, which necessarily includes "a reinterpretation of infallibility" (I.50; cf. II.1), two premises seem particularly important: first, " . . . infallibility does not stand at the center of the Christian faith. Whatever infallibility is ascribed to Scripture, the Church, or the pope, it is wholly dependent on the power of God's Word in the gospel" (I.51). Secondly, from a Roman Catholic perspective, "the doctrine of infallibility aims at safeguarding a basic Christian insight: that the Church, in view of its mission to preach the gospel faithfully to all nations, may be trusted to be guided by the Holy Spirit in proclaiming the original revelation and in reformulating it in new ways and languages whenever such reformulation is necessary" (II.7).

Had these two premises been used in the past as litmus tests for judging interpretations of infallibility, two common exaggerations might have been avoided. For example, infallibility has often been misunderstood as meaning that "the office or officeholder is being somehow divinized and deprived of the capacity for error that is a mark of the human condition" (II.13); however, to say baldly that "the pope in infallible" grossly oversimplifies authentic Roman Catholic teaching:

Vatican Council I did not state without qualification that the pope is infallible. Rather, it taught that when performing certain very narrowly specified acts, he is gifted with the same infallibility which Christ bestowed on his Church (DS 3074). In his explanation of the meaning of the definition, given to the Fathers two days before they voted on the draft, Bishop Vincenz Gasser clearly pointed out that absolute infallibility is proper to God alone and that the infallibility of the pope is limited and conditioned. (II.14)

Another oversimplification comes from considering papal pronouncements that issue from an exercise of infallibility as "infallible propositions." In describing such definitions as *irreformabiles* (but not as "infallible"), "Vatican I was here reacting against the kind of juridical language found in the fourth Gallican article of 1682, in which it was claimed that papal decrees are not irreformable until the assent of the church (*ecclesiae consensus*) supervenes (DS 2284)" (II.17). Thus, "the irreformability of definitions does not rule out further research, interpretation through the hermeneutical process, various applications to the life of worship and piety, and new formulations . . . " (I.33). Irreformability means that such definitions are final in the sense that they are not subject to further canonical ratification (for example, by appeal from the pope to a council); simultaneously, irreformability entails "the trust that, thanks to the *sensus fidelium*, assent to a definition of faith will not be lacking" (I.33).

After the prorogation of the First Vatican Council, John Henry Newman wrote to an Anglican friend who was dismayed by the definition: "Let us be patient, let us have faith, and a new Pope and a re-assembled Council may trim the boat."[57] In fact, nearly a century would pass before the question of infallibility would be reconsidered by another general council. Whether or not one cares to describe the process as "trimming the boat," Vatican II certainly clarified several aspects of its predecessor's teaching about infallibility:

57. Newman to Alfred Plummer, 3 April 1871, *The Letters and Diaries of John Henry Newman*, ed. Charles Stephen Dessain and Thomas Gornall, S.J. (Oxford: Clarendon Press, 1973), 25: 310. Since Vatican I had been prorogued *sine die*, Newman felt that the Council might reassemble; in fact, it never reconvened.

1) . . . the infallibility of the pastors (pope and bishops) must be related to the *sensus fidelium* or the "sense of faith" possessed by the entire people of God. . . .

2) . . . when he defines a matter of faith and morals, the pope should be expected to consult his fellow bishops and proceed in a collegial manner. . . .

3) . . . while no antecedent or subsequent juridical approval by the Church is necessary for the exercise of infallibility, the assent of the Church can never be wanting to an authentic definition "on account of the activity of that same Holy Spirit, whereby the whole flock of Christ is preserved and progresses in unity of faith" (*LG* 25). . . .

4) . . . in the context of a pilgrim church . . . such definitions will inevitably suffer from a certain obscurity.

5) . . . Even while true in the technical sense, a dogmatic statement may be ambiguous, untimely, overbearing, offensive, or otherwise deficient.

6) . . . Will infallibility be able to serve the purpose for which it is intended without far more consultation with Christian communities not in full union with Rome?

7) . . . "in Catholic teaching there exists an order or 'hierarchy' of truths, since they vary in their relationship to the foundation of the Christian faith" (*UR* 11).[58] (II.19)

Even though the Second Vatican Council made these important clarifications, "The state of the doctrine of papal infallibility at the end of Vatican II is not to be taken as the last word on the subject" (II.20).

Nor did the Lutheran-Roman Catholic statement on "Teaching Authority and Infallibility in the Church" claim to be the final word on this topic; it did, however, contribute several important insights to the discussion of infallibility.[59] First, it carefully delineated the relationship between the conciliar teaching and its biblical background; in particular, it pointed out that while Vatican I cited the Petrine texts in Matthew (16:18) and Luke (22:32) in support of its definition,

58. *UR* refers to Vatican II's *Unitatis Redintegratio*, the "Decree on Ecumenism," 21 November 1964.

59. In a comparative study of the Lutheran-Roman Catholic and Anglican-Roman Catholic statements concerned with infallibility, Margaret O'Gara has pointed out an increasing historical sensitivity and theological refinement in treating the topic; see "Infallibility in the Ecumenical Crucible," *One in Christ* 20 (1984): 325–45.

Vatican I did not define the sense of these verses. While we [the Roman Catholic participants] recognize that these Petrine texts have played an important role in the development of the doctrine of papal infallibility, we do not claim that these texts, taken exegetically, directly assert that doctrine. (II.26)[60]

Secondly, the statement was critical, on the one hand, of "ardent papalists, many of whom in the period after Vatican I went far beyond the letter of the Council in claiming infallibility for papal teaching that did not strictly meet the conditions for an *ex cathedra* pronouncement as set forth by Vatican I" (II.27). On the other hand, the statement criticized those who have "alleged that historical research can actually disprove the infallibility of the pope":

No one doubts that popes can err in their teaching as private doctors. In none of the preceding cases can it be shown that the errors, or alleged errors, would have met the requirements specified by Vatican I for an *ex cathedra* pronouncement, and hence these historical difficulties prove nothing against the truth of the teaching of that Council on infallibility. (II.29)[61]

Thirdly, the statement raised questions about the highly problematic area of noninfallible and doubtfully infallible papal teaching: "First, how does one distinguish which papal statements are, or are not to be considered infallible? Second, what obligatory force attaches to noninfallible teaching?" (II.30). In response to these questions, it should be noted that the list of papal pronouncements made under infallibility is remarkably short;[62] indeed, there are "only two papal pronouncements which are generally acknowledged by Catholics as having engaged papal infallibility: the dogma of the Immacu-

60. This position apparently reflects the conclusions in *Peter in the New Testament* (cited in n. 5).

61. This position apparently replied to the position advocated by Hans Küng in *Infallible?* (cited in n. 9).

62. In the past, infallibility has also been claimed for canonizations (II.32), moral teachings (II.35), and condemnations of doctrinal errors (II.33), such as the teachings attributed to Luther and condemned by the Bull *Exsurge Domine* (1520); however, "the Catholic members of this dialogue are convinced that there are no solid grounds for regarding it [*Exsurge Domine*] as an exercise of papal infallibility" (II.34).

late Conception (1854) and that of the Assumption of the Blessed Virgin (1950)" (II.31).[63] In contrast, the list of noninfallible teachings is not only overwhelmingly extensive but highly diverse in content. Due to this diversity, "[t]here exists a vast literature dealing with the highly complex question of the authority of noninfallible papal teaching and the conditions under which this or that form of silent or vocal dissent may be permitted or required" (II.39). In effect, if there is disagreement among Roman Catholics about the binding force of noninfallible teachings, it seems practically impossible to require agreement in these areas as a prerequisite for reunion.

Fourthly, even in the relatively restricted area of "infallible teaching"—which is concerned about "realities and values that are important for the Christian's response to God's word of revelation in Christ, even though they [some dogmas] do not stand at the very center of Christian faith and teaching" (II.43)—the statement recognized that "the community of those who accept these dogmas is not coextensive with the full number of individuals and groups that are rightly called Christian" (II.44). Implicitly, this observation suggests a provocative possibility: would it be possible for other Christians to enter into some form of union with the Roman Catholic Church without an explicit acceptance of Roman Catholic dogmas?[64]

Such a question, of course, goes beyond the immediate concerns of the Lutheran-Roman Catholic statement on "Teaching

63. One might even omit the Immaculate Conception from this list, insofar as it can be considered a joint papal-episcopal exercise of infallibility *prior* to the definition of papal infallibility by *Pastor Aeternus* in 1870; cf. James Hennesey, "A Prelude to Vatican I: American Bishops and the Definition of the Immaculate Conception," *Theological Studies* 25 (1964): 409–19.

64. For example, see the proposal of Heinrich Fries and Karl Rahner, *Unity of the Churches: An Actual Possibility*, trans. Ruth C. L. Gritsch and Eric W. Gritsch (Philadelphia: Fortress Press; New York: Paulist Press, 1983), 7: Thesis I: "The fundamental truths of Christianity, as they are expressed in Holy Scripture, in the Apostles' Creed, and in that of Nicaea and Constantinople are binding on all partner churches of the one Church to be." Thesis II: "Beyond that [expression of fundamental truths] a realistic principle of faith should apply: Nothing may be rejected decisively and confessionally in one partner church which is binding dogma in another partner church. Furthermore, beyond Thesis I no explicit and positive confession in one partner church is imposed as dogma obligatory for another partner church."

Authority and Infallibility." However, in addition to providing a succinct compendium on this topic, the statement highlighted at least four areas for future consideration: (1) the biblical basis and the historical development of infallibility, (2) the need for a clear and accurate presentation of the Roman Catholic teaching on infallibility, (3) a systematic theological explanation of infallibility, and (4) an ecumenical consensus about infallibility.[65]

These four concerns have received considerable attention in the past decade and a half, even though it is generally not possible to divide the literature into such neat categories, since most publications have addressed more than one concern. If there is a common thread running through recent historical, doctrinal, and theological treatments of infallibility, it is an ecumenical concern: with few exceptions, authors have specifically considered the implications of infallibility for the whole Christian community. And if "infallibility" has not received the headlines that it did during the height of the "infallibility debate," it still has continued to receive a steady amount of scholarly attention, some of which will be sampled in the following sections.[66]

Biblical Basis and Historical Development

One ecumenical strategy for resolving divisive issues, such as papal primacy and infallibility, is to reexamine their biblical and patristic bases in hope of achieving consensus. Such was the approach taken by William R. Farmer and Roch Kereszty in their study, *Peter and Paul in the Church of Rome.*[67] In their reappraisal of the "New Testament foundations," the authors discovered a shared apostolic leadership:

65. See the helpful surveys of George H. Tavard, "Infallibility: A Survey and a Proposal," *One in Christ* 22 (1986): 24–43; and Peter Chirico, "Papal Infallibility Since Vatican I," *Chicago Studies* 22 (1983): 163–79.

66. For a comprehensive list of publications on infallibility, see the annual numbers of the *Archivum Historiae Pontificiae*.

67. William R. Farmer and Roch Kereszty, *Peter and Paul in the Church of Rome: The Ecumenical Potential of a Forgotten Perspective* (New York: Paulist Press, 1990).

The New Testament evidence indicates that there was a real partnership among the apostles, particularly between Peter and Paul. This partnership may well have allowed for an authority of Peter which expresses itself in guarding and strengthening the *koinōnia* of faith of all the apostles and in his being chief shepherd, while at the same time it allowed for an authority of Paul which expresses itself in charismatic foresight and theological depth. (51)

In the patristic period, however, "two lines of interpretation emerged." On the one hand, "Irenaeus based the *potentior principalitas* of Rome on its joint foundation by the two apostles Peter and Paul and on their martyrdom as a constitutive part of that foundation" (81). On the other hand, as indicated by Tertullian (during his Montanist phase), "the African church is convinced that the Lord first gave the power of the keys to Peter and through Peter to all the churches in communion with the church of Peter" (81).

Reflecting on their biblical and patristic findings, Kereszty, a Roman Catholic, advanced two theses:

I. The church of Rome has been jointly founded by Peter and Paul. Consequently, the bishop of Rome acts by the authority of both Peter and Paul.
II. According to the New Testament and the early patristic view, the martyrdom of the two chief apostles is constitutive of their apostolic mission, and their martyrdom in the city of Rome is constitutive of the leadership role of the church of Rome. (82)

In his response, Farmer acknowledged that "there is no intrinsic Protestant objection to emphasizing the importance of the Petrine heritage in the holy catholic church" (117), but wondered about "the consequences for church history had the apostles Peter and Paul been martyred in Antioch on the Orontes, meeting place of east and west" (105). In more general terms, a reading of the same biblical and patristic sources does not necessarily lead to the same conclusion: where Kereszty read the texts as the beginning of a Petrine-Pauline primacy, to Farmer "it appears that the case for according a special place for the church of Rome in the divine economy of the holy catholic church rests chiefly, if not entirely, upon 'a theological assertion with some historical foundation' . . . " (106).

In sum, while their *ressourcement* led to some convergence about the essential need for episcopal collegiality in the governance of the Church, Farmer "finds no foundation in the New Testament for even the beginnings of a 'Petrine primacy' over Paul" (122). Kereszty, however, "is convinced that Peter's importance and leadership role ultimately rests on his special call by Christ" (123). Finally, while the authors called for further research on the topic, one wonders whether research alone can resolve what is apparently a basic divergence in ecclesiological hermeneutics: can the Petrine-Pauline (administrative-chariasmatic) tension ever be completely resolved within the same denomination, let alone between different denominations?

In any case, Farmer and Kereszty's book provides a useful compendium of biblical and patristic data about the roles that Peter and Paul exercised in the early Church as well as a useful agenda for future ecumenical discussions on the papacy.

While the biblical and patristic periods furnish only tantalizing anticipations of the modern doctrine of infallibility, " . . . with the discussion of the 13th and 14th centuries it [infallibility] had taken on a new, highly technical meaning."[68] In fact, this late medieval discussion took place in the context of a complicated canonical and theological debate about the nature of the poverty practiced by members of the Franciscan order. The seeds of this conflict were unwittingly sown by Pope Nicholas III (1277–80) in *Exiit qui seminat* (1279), which taught that "Franciscans not only were not allowed to own property or to claim any right to use things, but that they had only the 'simple use of fact.'"[69] Far from settling the issue, "*Exiit* aroused controversy from the day it was promulgated and Nicholas immediately banned all discussion of the decree."[70]

68. "Teaching Authority and Infallibility," I.22.
69. James Heft, *John XXII and Papal Teaching Authority* (Lewiston, Maine: Edwin Mellen Press, 1986), 21.
70. Ibid.

The controversy continued to simmer nonetheless. Peter John Olivi, who had been involved in drafting *Exiit*, claimed that the Spiritual Franciscans' doctrine of absolute poverty was the teaching of the Gospel and thus beyond the power of any pope to change. John XXII (1316–34) thought otherwise. In *Quia quorundam mentes* (1324), he rejected the Spiritual Franciscans' "claim that what the Roman Pontiffs define once through the key of knowledge in faith and morals remains so unchangeable that it is not permitted to a successor either to call it into doubt or to confirm the contrary. . . ."[71]

For a pope to reject the infallibility ascribed to his predecessor is apparently anomalous; Brian Tierney has interpreted this incident in a provocative way:

> There is no convincing evidence that papal infallibility formed any part of the theological or canonical tradition of the church before the thirteenth century; the doctrine was invented in the first place by a few dissident Franciscans because it suited their convenience to invent it; eventually, but only after much initial reluctance, it was accepted by the papacy because it suited the convenience of the popes to accept it.[72]

These conclusions, which appeared shortly after Küng's *Infallible?* seemed to corroborate Küng's argumentation against infallibility.[73]

Denial, however, is easier than proof. Given the technical nature of medieval papal decrees, it is not surprising that Tierney's conclusions have had comparatively few challengers. One of the most comprehensive is James Heft's *John XXII and Papal Teaching Authority*, whose detailed analysis of *Quia quorundam mentes* challenged several of Tierney's premises. One pivotal issue was Tierney's argument that "either the pope is an infallible teacher who can promulgate irreformable doctrines, or he is a sovereign ruler who can revoke all decrees of his predecessors. A pope cannot be sovereign and infallible at the

---

71. *Quia quorundam mentes*, translated by Heft, ibid., 41–42; Latin original, 234.

72. Brian Tierney, *Origins of Papal Infallibility, 1150–1350: A Study on the Concepts of Infallibility, Sovereignty and Tradition in the Middle Ages*, Studies in the History of Christian Thought 6 (Leiden: E. J. Brill, 1972), 281.

73. Cf. Heft, *John XXII*, xxiii.

same time."[74] Heft noted that such an antithesis "is really quite artificial"; instead of seeing the situation as a case of "either/or," it should be seen as one of "both/and": "both sovereignty (in matters which can change) and infallibility (in matters which cannot change)."[75]

Such a response raises another important issue, the object of faith and the scope of infallibility. While "[t]he Franciscans were convinced that there was an article of faith involved in the poverty debate or at least something which was immutable," John XXII did not see the issue as involving what today would be called *dogma*, but "always thought that he could revoke any *disciplinary* or doctrinal (in the mutable sense) decree. . . ."[76] At issue, then, were two different conceptualizations of faith, doctrine, and infallibility, an extensive one on the part of Olivi and his supporters, a more restricted one on the part of the pope.

In addition to its contribution to the study of medieval theology and canon law, Heft's work is important for highlighting how much need there is for nuance in carefully distinguishing (1) infallibility and sovereignty, (2) dogma and doctrine, and (3) discipline and teaching authority. The failure to make such careful distinctions has repeatedly clouded subsequent discussions of infallibility, including those at the Council that first defined the doctrine.

Vatican I

As John Tracy Ellis has observed, "It is doubtful that any event in the history of the modern Church ever gave rise to a greater flow of misinformation than the [First] Vatican Council."[77] This misinformation started to circulate prior to the Council through a highly publicized controversy between "ultramontanes," who advocated a spontaneous definition of "papal in-

74. Ibid., 170–71. 75. Ibid., 173–74.
76. Ibid., 182, 192.
77. John Tracy Ellis, "The Church Faces the Modern World: The First Vatican Council," in *The General Council: Special Studies in Doctrinal and Historical Background,* ed. William J. McDonald (Washington, D.C.: The Catholic University of America Press, 1962), 135.

fallibility," and "cisalpines," who were troubled by the prospects of an aggrandizement of papal authority. Misinformation crescendoed during the Council with heated debates between the "Majority" who favored a definition and the "Minority" who opposed it; and misinformation continued in a more subdued manner after the Council: "maximalists" interpreted the conciliar teaching on infallibility as extending to practically every type of papal pronouncement and "minimalists" restricted the use of infallibility to matters of dogma.[78]

In a sense, the "infallibility debate" that began in 1970 represents the reappearance of historical problems and theological questions that were not resolved a century earlier. Several recent studies provide better information about the Council and offer some answers to the theological questions left unresolved.

One of the most fascinating studies is Margaret O'Gara's *Triumph in Defeat*, which focused on the twenty-two French bishops who were part of the Minority during the Council and decided to absent themselves on July 18, 1870, when the final ballot was taken and the dogma promulgated.[79] The French Minority was not a united party but "a group of groups" that included both liberals and Gallicans who were rallied by a common adversary: ultramontanism. Surprisingly, while the Minority bishops felt obliged to oppose the definition of infallibility, still they were personally devoted to the pope. In fact, their opposition was quite specific: they acknowledged the infallibility of the Church, but opposed "any definition of separate, personal, or absolute papal infallibility" (77).

The debate at the council was wide ranging; it not only involved scriptural, historical, theological, and canonical arguments, but was amply seasoned with ecclesiastical politics. Sort-

78. The classic history in English is still Cuthbert Butler's *The Vatican Council, 1869-1870, Based on Bishop Ullathorne's Letters*, originally published in 1930 and reissued in an edition edited by Christopher Butler (Westminster, Md.: Newman Press, 1962); also, see J. Derek Holmes, *The Triumph of the Holy See: A Short History of the Papacy in the Nineteenth Century* (London: Burns & Oates; Shepherdstown, W.V.: Patmos Press, 1978).

79. Margaret O'Gara, *Triumph in Defeat: Infallibility, Vatican I, and the French Minority Bishops* (Washington, D.C.: The Catholic University of America Press, 1988); cf. John Ford et al., "Review Symposium," *Horizons* 16, no. 2 (1989): 353–72.

ing through this mixture of arguments has always been complicated, if not confusing, and O'Gara has devised three useful
categories for understanding the motives underlying the
Minority's opposition: timeliness, definability, and truth.

First, the Minority considered the definition "untimely":
they saw it as a threat to the internal unity of the Church. In
addition, some considered it a needless ecumenical obstacle,
while others feared that it would prompt a hostile response
from civil governments. In contrast to those who have dis-
counted such objections as merely "inopportune," O'Gara has
insisted that the Minority saw the proposed definition not
simply as a case of "bad timing," but as creating a long-term
problem for the Church.

Secondly, many of the Minority were troubled about the "definability" of infallibility. In part, their fears stemmed from the
exaggerated interpretations of infallibility that were not only
circulated by ultramontane journalists before the Council, but
were advocated by some Majority bishops during the Council.
Nor were the Minority's fears calmed by a text that lacked "the
certitude and clarity that must characterize a definition of
faith" (135). In fact, even after a prolonged process of drafting
and emending, the final text of *Pastor Aeternus* still did not
offer a definition of "infallibility" as such, but only described
the conditions under which the pope may exercise "that infallibility with which the Divine Redeemer deigned to endow His
Church."[80]

Thirdly, in regard to the "truth" of papal infallibility, the Minority wanted a definition that excluded the ultramontane
claim that infallibility was the pope's exclusive prerogative. At
the Council, the French Minority was prepared to acknowledge
that "the pope could speak infallibly when he spoke in accord
with the bishops, with Scripture and tradition, with the whole
Church" (171); however, when the French Minority bishops' efforts to emend the text to this effect were rejected, they decided not to attend the final session.

80. DS 3073: " . . . ea infallibilitate . . . qua divinus Redemptor Ecclesiam
suam . . . instructam esse voluit. . . ."

O'Gara's categories are particularly helpful in answering a question that has long puzzled historians: how could the French Minority so strenuously oppose the definition of papal infallibility during the Council, yet afterwards honestly accept the definition? Some have suggested a lack of good faith, others have hinted that the French bishops capitulated to Roman pressure. O'Gara has proposed that the basic motive for their opposition eventually provided a suitable rationale for their acceptance: at the heart of the Minority's opposition was the belief that infallibility was primarily a gift to the Church; once the Minority bishops became convinced that *Pastor Aeternus* respected the ecclesial character of infallibility, they were able to accept it. Moreover, even those who had once questioned the "truth" of the proposed teaching could maintain that their opposition had prevented the promulgation of an ultramontane-style definition that would have given the pope *carte blanche* in doctrinal matters; as Bishop Maret claimed: "The minority has triumphed in its defeat" (xvii).

O'Gara's very readable study, an admirable combination of careful historical research and perceptive theological analysis, not only has furnished a fuller portrait of the French Minority than had previously been available, but also has corrected some of the misinformation about the motives of the Minority at Vatican I.

Another important source of information on the Council is Gustave Thils's recent study of the "primacy and infallibility of the Roman Pontiff at Vatican I."[81] In contrast to the tendency of many interpreters who concern themselves only with the fourth chapter of *Pastor Aeternus*—and sometimes only with that chapter's paragraph that contains the Council's "definition" of infallibility—Thils has treated infallibility in the context of the conciliar teaching about the "institution of the apostolic primacy in Peter," the "perpetuity of Peter's primacy in the

---

81. Gustave Thils, *Primauté et infaillibilité du Pontife Romain à Vatican I et autres études d'ecclésiologie*, Bibliotheca Ephemeridum Theologicarum Lovaniensium 89 (Leuven: University Press, 1989).

Roman Pontiffs," and the prerogatives of that primacy, among which is the papal exercise of the Church's infallibility.[82]

Thils has investigated the discussion of papal primacy, which began in the preconciliar theological commission and continued during the Council before being enunciated in *Pastor Aeternus*. From this investigation, it is evident that the Council fathers were concerned about such long-dead adversaries as Gallicans, Febronians, and Richerists. Thus, *Pastor Aeternus* in general and particular terms like "full supreme universal power" and "immediate and ordinary jurisdiction"—terms that caused so much controversy at Vatican I and have continued to be misinterpreted—need to be read in the light of controversies of the seventeenth and eighteenth centuries, rather than those of the twentieth.

Thils's treatment of the discussions on infallibility also indicated that the infallibility of the Church was not really in question at Vatican I; likewise, it was generally agreed that the Church's infallibility could be collectively exercised by the bishops, either in council or dispersed throughout the world. The point of contention was whether the pope could exercise the Church's infallibility and, if so, under what conditions and for what teaching. The Minority feared that the pope would act alone and make arbitrary decisions. Such fears have continued to the present, so that it still needs to be emphasized that the pope exercises not his own, but the Church's infallibility and that he acts in and for the Church. In addition, the "object" of infallibility—defined by Vatican I as *doctrina de fide vel moribus ab universa Ecclesia tenenda*—continues to be a matter of debate, as the Lutheran-Roman Catholic Dialogue noted.[83]

Thils's detailed, historically based explanation about both what Vatican I taught concerning papal primacy and infallibility and, equally important, what it did not teach and thus left unsettled, is an important corrective to a lot of misinforma-

82. These topics are treated, respectively, in the first three chapters of *Pastor Aeternus*, whose fourth chapter treats the "infallible magisterium of the Roman Pontiff."
83. DS 3073; "Teaching Authority and Infallibility," II. 30–41.

tion generated in the recent infallibility debate.[84] In other words, if biblical exegetes have come to employ a critical historical reading of scriptural texts, theologians should do no less in interpreting conciliar texts.

Unfortunately, such a critical approach is lacking in the "theological synthesis" of James O'Connor's *The Gift of Infallibility*.[85] Statements such as "It is the gift of infallibility which brings the words of Christ to us pure and unadulterated, which preserves His truth and sews [sic] it unmixed in the world, gives us certitude and thus nourishes our hope" (97) seem more like the enthusiastic ultramontane journalism of Louis Veuillot,[86] rather than the Scholastic theological distinctions of Vincenz Gasser (1809–72), whose conciliar *relatio* O'Connor has translated in this book.

On July 11, 1870, during the concluding week of the debate on infallibility at Vatican I, Gasser, the prince-bishop of Brixen (Bressanone), spoke for four hours on behalf of the Council's doctrinal commission. Since this commission was charged both with drafting *Pastor Aeternus* and recommending emendations to it, Gasser's report is extremely important in interpreting the text. Only excerpts of Gasser's speech have previously appeared in English—a fact that is not completely surprising, since the speech took some four hours to deliver and was replete with terminology difficult to translate. To his credit, O'Connor has furnished a readable text, though one might differ about the translation of a specific phrase or term.[87]

84. In particular, Küng's *Infallible?* would have benefitted from a careful reading of Thils' earlier work, *L'infaillibilité pontificale: source-conditions-limites* (Gembloux: J. Duculot, 1968); much of the material from this book has been incorporated into Thils's *Primauté et infaillibilité*.

85. *The Gift of Infallibility: The Official Relatio on Infallibility of Bishop Vincent Gasser at Vatican Council I*, trans. with commentary and a theological synthesis on infallibility by James T. O'Connor (Boston: St. Paul Editions, 1986). The "synthesis" is given on pp. 93–125.

86. Cf. Marvin L. Brown, Jr., *Louis Veuillot: French Ultramontane Catholic Journalist and Layman, 1813–1883* (Durham, N.C.: Moore Publishing Company, 1977).

87. The translator has also provided explanatory notes, though readers unfamiliar with Vatican I may still be puzzled by the Council's procedures; it would also have been helpful if O'Connor had translated in full Gasser's important speech of July 16, 1870, instead of giving excerpts from it in the notes.

What is the importance of Gasser's speech?[88] Should it be seen as the definitive explanation of the Council's teaching? Doubtlessly, it represented the mind of the doctrinal commission. Also, it was presumably a generally acceptable explanation of *Pastor Aeternus* for the bishops who voted in favor. Yet the fact remains that the bishops were voting to accept *Pastor Aeternus*, not Gasser's *relatio*. If at first sight this distinction seems nitpicking, it must be recalled that after the Council, different interpretations of *Pastor Aeternus* were proposed by the bishops who voted for it. For example, the interpretation of infallibility given by Archbishop Manning of Westminster, a member of the conciliar doctrinal commission, was not the same as that of Bishop Joseph Fessler of Sankt-Pölten (Austria), the Council's Secretary General.[89] In effect, *pace* Gasser, *Pastor Aeternus* was "received" in different ways. After Vatican I some, like Manning, continued to interpret infallibility in an ultramontane sense; others, like Newman, were able to find moderate interpretations with which they and others could live.

Interpretations of Infallibility

After the proclamation on infallibility at Vatican I, many British Roman Catholics, as well as the intelligentsia of the Church of England, were remarkably curious about *What will Dr. Newman do?*—the title of John R. Page's dissertation on the historical development of Newman's views on infallibility.[90] As is well known, Newman accepted the definition, but what Page's impressive study makes clear is that Newman's acceptance of *Pastor Aeternus* was more personally problematic than has usually been acknowledged.

88. Cf. "Teaching Authority and Infallibility," II.14.
89. Cf. Butler, *The Vatican Council*, 455–65; also Robert Ippolito, "Archbishop Manning's Championship of Papal Infallibility, 1867–1872," *The Ampleforth Journal* 77, no. 2 (1972): 31–39.
90. John R. Page, *What will Dr. Newman do? John Henry Newman and the definition of papal infallibility, 1865–75* (Ph.D. diss., Georgetown University, 1990; Ann Arbor, Mich.: University Microfilms, 1990).

Prior to the Council, Newman had been irritated by the extravagant claims of pro-infallibilists like W. G. Ward, editor of *The Dublin Review*, who would have liked an infallible papal pronouncement every morning at breakfast along with his cup of tea and copy of *The Times*. For personal reasons, Newman decided not to reply to Ward, but instead encouraged a fellow member of the Birmingham Oratory, Ignatius Ryder, to write *Idealism in Theology: A Review of Dr. Ward's Scheme of Dogmatic Authority* (1867). Newman did, however, collect material about infallibility and sketch his own views in his private papers;[91] he also shared some of these reflections with a few trusted correspondents.

Rumors were afloat concerning Newman's views, but he managed to keep his thoughts from public scrutiny until one of his letters, a confidential statement of his concerns written to his bishop during the second month of the Council, was inexplicably leaked to the press:

When we are all at rest, and have no doubts, and at least practically, not to say doctrinally, hold the Holy Father to be infallible, suddenly there is thunder in the clear sky, and we are told to prepare for something we know not what[,] to try our faith we know not how. No impending danger is to be averted, but a great difficulty is to be created. Is this the proper work for an Ecumenical Council?[92]

This letter, which summarized Newman's reservations about the proposed definition, scandalized some, but others were relieved that he had voiced his misgivings about its timeliness and definability.[93]

Newman's hope that no definition would be made was soon dashed, but once he saw the text of *Pastor Aeternus*, his worst fears were alleviated: "I saw the new Definition yesterday, and am pleased at its moderation, that is, if the doctrine in question

---

91. These papers have been published in *The Theological Papers of John Henry Newman on Biblical Inspiration and on Infallibility*, ed. J. Derek Holmes (Oxford: Clarendon Press, 1979), 99–169.

92. Newman to Ullathorne, 28 January 1870, *Letters and Diaries* (cited in n. 57), 25:18.

93. "Memorandum on the Definition of Infallibility," 27 June, 1970, *Letters and Diaries*, 25: 151.

is to be defined at all. The terms used are vague and comprehensive; and, personally, I have no difficulty in admitting it."[94] Yet Newman's state of mind seems to have been less sanguine than these words suggest at first sight. Five months after the definition, he again indicated his acceptance of the Council's teaching but expressed his repugnance at its "violence": "As little as possible was passed at the Council—nothing about the Pope which I have not myself always held—but it is impossible to deny that it was done with an imperiousness and overbearing willfulness, which has been a great scandal. . . . "[95]

What Page's study so clearly shows is the complexity of Newman's "reception" of *Pastor Aeternus*. Newman accepted the Council's teaching, but he interpreted it in a moderate, if not minimalist, sense. In castigating the manipulations of Manning and other ultramontane bishops at the Council, he hoped that a reconvened Council might "trim" the definition. After the Council ended, he was angered by those who pressured Catholics to subscribe immediately to the definition. In contrast, he felt that those who were troubled by the definition should be allowed time for reflection, perhaps because he had also needed time to "receive" the definition. Page's account of Newman's reception of *Pastor Aeternus* provides an important theological as well as pastoral lesson: "reception" is not always an instantaneous assent to what a pope or council teaches, but a process of coming to terms with that teaching.

Newman's views on infallibility might well have remained private, shared only with trusted correspondents, had not William Gladstone, the British prime minister, acidulously attacked the teaching of Vatican I in *The Vatican Decrees in Their Bearing on Civil Allegiance* (1874). Newman always needed a "cause" to write, and Gladstone inadvertently furnished one in

94. Newman to Ambrose Phillipp de Lisle, 24 July 1870, *Letters and Diaries*, 25: 164.

95. Newman to Mrs. William Froude, 2 January 1871, *Letters and Diaries* 25:252. August Hasler (*How the Pope Became Infallible: Pius IX and the Politics of Persuasion* [Garden City, N.Y.: Doubleday, 1981], 181) mentioned Newman's description of the Council as "scandalous" but failed to indicate that Newman accepted the definition. Also see John Ford, "Different Models of Infallibility?" *Proceedings of the Catholic Theological Society of America* 35 (1980): 217–33.

which Newman reached his rhetorical zenith: *A Letter to His Grace the Duke of Norfolk* (1875). This *Letter*—in fact, a book—utilized Fessler's *The True and False Infallibility of the Popes* (1875), which had been translated by Ambrose St. John, a fellow Oratorian and Newman's closest friend; thus, strategically as well as theologically, Newman's moderate interpretation of infallibility had "official" support.

Newman's *Letter* was a three-pronged attack. First, to Gladstone's allegation that Roman Catholics could hardly be considered good citizens, Newman respectfully replied that a Catholic must be loyal to the Queen in civil matters and to the Pope in ecclesiastical matters, but above all faithful to conscience. Secondly (and with a great deal of rhetorical flourish), he pointedly reminded Manning, Ward, and other ultramontanes that dogmatic definitions are not self-interpreting but need to be scrutinized by the *schola theologorum*, who must eventually hammer out the precise meaning of every dogma.[96] Thirdly, to Döllinger and the leaders of the *altkatholisch* movement, he sympathetically but firmly emphasized that a Catholic does not believe in a dogma because of the historical proofs that can be advanced in its favor.[97] All three of these points—the responsibility of conscience in responding to church teaching, the role of theologians in interpreting church teaching, and the importance of historical investigation in understanding church teaching—are still very much at issue today.

Page's dissertation not only provides a definitive historical study of the development of Newman's view of infallibility; it also lays to rest the accusation that Newman was inconsistent, even cowardly in accepting the definition, as well as the assumption that Newman had no difficulty in accepting it. In addition, Page's study is helpful in illustrating both the spectrum of different interpretations of infallibility that existed after Vati-

96. By addressing his *Letter* to the Duke of Norfolk, who was the ranking peer of the realm and the leading British Roman Catholic layman, Newman made it difficult for the ultramontanes to counterattack without alienating a prominent benefactor as well as giving credence to Gladstone's charges.

97. Cf. Wolfgang Klausnitzer, *Päpstliche Unfehlbarkeit bei Newman und Döllinger: Ein historisch-systematischer Vergleich*, Innsbrucker theologische Studien 6 (Innsbruck: Tyrolia, 1980).

can I and the pastoral flexibility that Newman espoused in "receiving" the Council's dogmatic teaching.

Another convert for whom the definition created problems has been portrayed by William Portier in *Isaac Hecker and the First Vatican Council*.[98] Even before he became a Catholic in 1844, Hecker (1819–88) had hoped for an ecumenical council that would settle the doctrinal controversies of the past and steer the Church in a new direction. Hecker, the founder of the Paulists as a religious community committed to adapting Roman Catholicism to the American scene, welcomed the announcement of the forthcoming Council. Named as the procurator for Bishop Rosecrans of Columbus, Hecker journeyed to Rome via England and Germany, where he acquired information about the ultramontane campaign for the acclamation of the personal infallibility of the pope. Döllinger, whom Hecker met in Munich, later commented that Hecker "seems profoundly convinced that the triumph of ultramontanism would be fatal to the Church in America" (36).

Hecker arrived in Rome, confident that infallibility would not come before the Council. When it became evident that the Majority wanted a definition, Hecker worked as the theologian of Archbishop Martin Spalding of Baltimore to prepare a compromise proposal.[99] As the extra-conciliar debate over infallibility intensified, compromise became impossible and Hecker, dismayed by the increasing controversy, left Rome at the end of April before the discussion on infallibility began on the floor of the Council. Once the doctrine of papal infallibility was promulgated, Hecker "accepted it in faith even though it had not completely resolved his theological difficulty" (173). Five years later, the same year that Newman published his *Letter to the Duke of Norfolk*, Hecker published "An Exposition of the Church in View of Recent Difficulties and Controversies and the Present Needs of the Age."[100]

98. William L. Portier, *Issac Hecker and the First Vatican Council*, Studies in American Religion 15 (Lewiston, Maine: Edwin Mellen Press, 1985).
99. Cf. Roger Aubert, "Documents concernant le tiers parti au concile du Vatican," in *Abhandlungen über Theologie und Kirche: Festschrift für Karl Adam* (Düsseldorf: Patmos, 1952), 241–59.
100. *Catholic World* 21 (April 1875): 117–38.

Hecker's "Exposition" set the definition of infallibility within a providential interpretation of history:

The Church had already begun to prepare for the greater outpouring of the Holy Spirit which the needs of the age required. Vatican I's definition of papal infallibility would be the first step. It ushered in "a new and fresh phase of life" for the Church (151).

While Hecker's "uniquely American religious commentary" (173) may have been too much a product of its time and its author's own personal problematic to find much appreciation today, Portier's study still has provided an interesting case study of the diverse ways in which the doctrine of infallibility was received immediately after the Council.

Ecumenical Interpretations

Just as there were various interpretations of infallibility after Vatican I, an even broader spectrum of interpretations has appeared since Vatican II.[101] At one extreme are a few treatments that tend to be ultramontane in their interpretation; in an extensive middle ground is a diversity of studies that generally employ the methods of biblical and historical criticism in interpreting doctrinal statements; at the other extreme are some treatments that minimize infallibility practically, if not explicitly, to the point of extinction. Yet there is one characteristic that differentiates most of the studies of infallibility that have been written in the past quarter-century from those published earlier: an ecumenical concern.

This concern is prominent in Luis Bermejo's study of Vatican I and Conciliar Reception in *Towards Christian Reunion*.[102] Taking

101. For reviews of earlier studies, cf. John T. Ford, "Infallibility: A Review of Recent Studies," *Theological Studies* 40 (1979): 273–305, and "Papal Primacy and Infallibility in Ecumenical Perspective," *Religious Studies Review* 8 (1982): 342–47.

102. Luis M. Bermejo, S.J., *Towards Christian Reunion: Vatican I: Obstacles and Opportunities* (Lanham, Md.: University Press of America, 1984). After four chapters on "Vatican I and Conciliar Reception," the next two chapters treat "Rome and Canterbury in Dialogue" and the final chapter considers "Protestant Churches." Bermejo's more recent study, *Infallibility on Trial: Church, Conciliarity and Communion* (Westminster, Md.: Christian Classics, 1992), was received too late to be included in this section.

his cue from Pope Paul VI, who once described his primatial office as "the greatest obstacle in the path of ecumenism," Bermejo has portrayed infallibility as a major roadblock to Christian unity. Few would challenge either party; the question is how to remove or at least to surmount the double barrier of papal primacy and infallibility.

Bermejo began his response by asking whether "conciliar infallibility [is] part and parcel of Revelation . . . " (10–11). To answer this question, he surveyed the biblical, patristic, and medieval evidence, and concluded that "it is exceedingly difficult to determine with any degree of certainty which decrees of the earlier councils are infallible and which are fallible, and, as such, subject to correction—which shows that the distinction is not particularly helpful" (53). Prescinding from the usefulness of the distinction, one gets the impression that Bermejo has attempted to find the teaching of Vatican I explicitly enunciated in earlier centuries; such an endeavor is curious insofar as Vatican I would have had little reason to issue its definition had its teaching been clearly defined by earlier popes and councils.

Unfortunately, Bermejo's historical study of infallibility is not a disinterested investigation, but seems to be slanted toward a rejection of conciliar infallibility.[103] Moreover, there is a systemic flaw in his expectation that "[t]heological deductions, in order to be acceptable, should be subject to and dependent upon, history" (55–56). In effect, Bermejo has seemingly fallen into a position against which the Roman Catholic participants in the Lutheran-Catholic dialogue cautioned, namely, that "historical research can actually disprove the infallibility of the pope."[104] Ironically, Bermejo dismissed the findings of this bilateral dialogue as "a rather disappointing piece of work" (135).

After questioning the "alleged infallibility of councils," Bermejo turned his attention to the *reception* of Vatican I. Again, his use of history is debatable; for example, the Minority bishops certainly raised the question of episcopal freedom and

103. In particular, I must take exception to Bermejo's inference (178, n. 174, in reference to "G. Ford") that I "tacitly" approve of Hasler's treatment of the Minority; in addition to my remarks in *Theological Studies* 40 (1979): 298–301, see those in *The Catholic Historical Review* 65 (1979): 667–69.

104. "Teaching Authority and Infallibility," II. 29.

"moral unanimity" during Vatican I, but was the Minority any less free at Vatican I than their counterparts at earlier ecumenical councils? And didn't the Minority bishops eventually accept the definition, albeit with minimalist, even ambiguous, interpretations (172–76)? At issue in Bermejo's presentation are not the facts, but the conclusions that he has derived; for example, is it fair to conclude from the facts available that "[c]onciliar infallibility can hardly be considered as a case of legitimate doctrinal development" (68)?

Similarly questionable is Bermejo's contention that "an increasingly large number of *Catholic* theologians have of late dared raise explicitly the spectre of a possible error in the dogmatic teachings of Vatican I" (72–73). There is no doubt that Küng's *Infallible?* produced a flood of commentaries on infallibility; however, few Roman Catholic theologians have followed Küng in contending that Vatican I was in error. Instead, practically all Roman Catholic theologians have found that Vatican I needs to be more carefully and exactly interpreted. Consequently, most would agree with Bermejo that "[t]he Vatican 'dogma' of infallibility is not above reconsideration," even though they might not want to consider the dogma as resembling "a mighty medieval cathedral resting on a rather shaky foundation" (88). However, for Bermejo, this "reconsideration" seemingly should lead to a renunciation of Vatican I, not its "re-reception," as Congar and others have proposed.[105]

Nonetheless, Bermejo was correct in focusing attention on the ecumenically significant question: "How far is the universal primacy of jurisdiction of the bishop of Rome a Church structure willed by God and part of the deposit of faith?" (125–26). In regard to jurisdictional primacy by divine right there is no doubt that "modern biblical scholarship may not support in every respect the exegesis of the Petrine texts prevalent in 1870" (101). Moreover, since the terminology involving divine right "has no clear interpretation in Roman Catholic theology" (123), it is not surprising that there are divergent opinions, not

---

105. Cf. Yves Congar, "Le Concile Vatican I en question: recension d'ecclésiologie conciliaire," *Revue des sciences philosophiques et théologiques* 68 (1984): 449–56.

so much about the *factual* development of the papacy, but the weaving of those facts into a theological background, as Carl Peter well noted in his treatment of *jus divinum*.

In similar fashion, one can readily grant that Vatican I has a "relative value," but the same could be said of any council, insofar as its decisions may be emended by a later council. But what should be done with the teachings of Vatican I? Bermejo proposed that "the only realistic solution is a decisive return to the ecclesiological conception of the first millennium" (138). However appealing such a return might be to the scholarly imagination, is it really possible? Secondly, while today it might seem "difficult to detect any historical upheaval that would have necessitated the dogmatisation of papal infallibility" (181), the challenging task for historical theologians is to deal with history as it happened, not as they would like for it to have happened. The fact remains that the Majority at Vatican I felt that the definition of infallibility was necessary.

As the conclusion to his analysis of Vatican I in the light of recent ecumenical findings, Bermejo made four proposals for removing the infallibility-roadblock:

a) Rome could acknowledge, without any loss of self-identity, that Vatican I is not an ecumenical Council proper, to be placed on the same footing as the first seven Councils of the first millennium. (314)

b) . . . no Catholic dogma defined after the separation should be imposed on the reluctant non-Catholic Churches as a condition for reunion. (314)

c) . . . it would be illusory to expect that Rome will ever officially disavow any of the Catholic dogmas defined after the separation. (315)

d) . . . the Pope could officially proclaim his readiness to return to the effectively synodal form of government that prevailed even in the Church of Rome, until the sixteenth century. (315)

Whatever fascination these proposals might have for ecumenical discussion, Bermejo seems correct in considering their official disavowal "illusory."

In contrast to Bermejo's quixotic proposals, Patrick Granfield has analyzed *The Limits of the Papacy*[106] with far more balance

---

106. Patrick Granfield, *The Limits of the Papacy: Authority and Autonomy in the Church* (New York: Crossroad, 1987).

and advanced ecumenical proposals with much greater care. In spite of the fact that "the Orthodox Church has survived over nine hundred years without the papacy and the Protestant churches nearly five hundred years" (171–72), still "more and more Christians . . . are beginning to recognize that a universal ministry of unity is necessary for a united Church" (171). This recognition of the need for visible unity is the result of a growing awareness that Christian divisions are counter to the will of Christ and damage the preaching of the Gospel.

Since "[i]n the minds of many Protestant and Orthodox Christians the papacy is often identified with arbitrary authoritarianism" (178), the pope should take concrete steps to exercise his authority differently than in the past. One way that this might be done would be for the pope voluntarily to share his authority so that in the future, papal decisions would be made in a collegial or synodal manner, as Bermejo has also suggested. Another way would be for the pope to de-emphasize the use of jurisdictional authority and to concentrate more on moral leadership. In addition, the papacy needs to be concerned not only about the substance of the decisions it makes, but also its "style" in making them; as the Methodist-Roman Catholic Conversations observed, "half-a-dozen more John XXIII's or Paul VI's in the next century would do more than anything to dispose of a thousand years of conflict and misunderstanding."[107]

Although there are several parallels between Granfield's treatment of the "Pope and Other Christians" and that of Bermejo, the tenor is quite different. For example, while Granfield has suggested that the pope "could voluntarily agree not to demand complete uniformity from those Churches desirous of reunion with Rome, but to accept their traditions insofar as they did not contradict the faith or destroy the communion of the Churches" (181), he has candidly noted some formidable difficulties in proposals similar to Bermejo's of not requiring as a condition for reunion the acceptance of any Catholic dogma

107. "Denver Report" #106 (1971), in *Growth in Agreement: Reports and Agreed Statements of Ecumenical Conversations on a World Level*, ed. by Harding Meyer and Lukas Vischer, Ecumenical Documents 2 (New York: Paulist Press; Geneva: World Council of Churches, 1984), 333.

defined after separation. Such a reunion would presumably need to tolerate different lists of obligatory doctrines for two churches in communion with each other; the result could be an anomalous situation where a Lutheran, for example, would not be required to accept the dogma of infallibility, but a Catholic would be. Such a reunion would not only be artificial but would have little respect for doctrine.

Whether such anomalies can be avoided through a "re-reception" of Vatican I remains to be seen; in any case, doctrinal divergence might be avoided in the future by involving non-Catholic Christians in the teaching task of the Catholic Church. Since a precedent for such a shared *magisterium* was established by the important contribution made by the non-Catholic observers at Vatican II, the Lutheran-Roman Catholic Dialogue has recommended inviting Lutheran authorities "to participate in the formulation of Catholic doctrine in a consultative capacity. . . . "[108]

The question of "Where Do We Go From Here?" also loomed large in J. Michael Miller's status report, *What Are They Saying about Papal Primacy?*[109] After comparing and contrasting the variety of views held by Lutherans, Anglicans, and Roman Catholics regarding the papacy, Miller concluded that future discussion would be clarified by carefully distinguishing between a structure by *divine institution*—one that has "the direct and immediate intervention of the historical Jesus at the origin of such a structure"—and a structure by *divine design*—one whose "structure derives from the divine will" yet where "the community and contingent historical factors played a formative role in determining its shape . . . "(87). In terms of this distinction, the Petrine function would be considered to be of "divine institution," while the papacy would be considered to be of "divine design."

In such a view, which would presumably be acceptable not only to Roman Catholics but also to many Lutherans and Anglicans, the papacy would be seen to have "appeared in history

108. "Teaching Authority and Infallibility," II. 58b.
109. J. Michael Miller, *What Are They Saying about Papal Primacy?* (New York: Paulist Press, 1983).

when the Christian community needed a personal embodiment of the Petrine function" (89). Such a view also allows for
future modifications:

To acknowledge the papacy as God's design for the Church avoids the
impression of an institution determined once and for all in the past.
Considerable room is left open for development in the way that the
Pope will fulfill the Petrine function in the future. (90)

Thus, Anglicans and Lutherans who acknowledge the continuing existence of a Petrine ministry in the Church might also be
able to acknowledge that the papacy is an historically conditioned manifestation and implementation of this function. One
wonders whether the same distinction might be helpful in discussing infallibility: the Church's gift of infallibility would be a
matter of *divine institution*, but its papal and episcopal exercise
(as taught respectively by Vatican I and Vatican II) might be
considered as a matter of *divine design*.

Theological Treatments

The theological explanation of infallibility continues to be
problematic. The debate at Vatican I was prompted in large part
by the lack of a coherent theology of infallibility. The debate
about infallibility after Vatican II has suffered from the same
deficiency: much of that debate has centered on specifics like
"infallible propositions," while comparatively little effort has
been given to formulating a comprehensive contemporary view
of infallibility.

A notable exception, as well as one of the most useful ecclesiastical treatments of infallibility, is Francis A. Sullivan's *Magisterium: Teaching Authority in the Catholic Church*.[110] Sullivan has
located the question of *magisterium infallibile* within the "indefectibility of the Church":

For a great many Christians besides Roman Catholics, it is a matter of
faith that the Church of Christ has a divine assurance of its remaining

110. Francis A. Sullivan, *Magisterium: Teaching Authority in the Catholic Church*
(New York: Paulist Press, 1983).

not only in existence, but also of its being maintained in fidelity to Christ and his Gospel, until the end of time. (4)

Within this perspective, Sullivan first analyzed the "biblical and historical basis for the Teaching Authority of Bishops" and then systematically explained the Church's teaching on infallibility.

Sullivan's study has managed both to handle a large amount of biblical and historical data with considerable finesse and to use technical terminology with a great deal of clarity. By providing a generally reliable explanation of what the two Vatican Councils actually taught, his book effectively dispels a great deal of the still prevalent misconceptions about the nature and extent of infallibility; indeed, had this book been available before Küng's *Infallible?* the theological world might well have been spared a great deal of needless debate about "infallible propositions."

Yet, without detracting from the usefulness of Sullivan's work, at times his laudable penchant for objectivity sometimes seems overly optimistic; for instance, his treatment of the response due to noninfallible pronouncements seems sugar-coated, at least in the wake of the Vatican's recent actions against a number of theologians.[111] Also, on some technical points, Sullivan's interpretation is at least debatable; such is the case with his explanation of the meaning of "irreformable propositions": "All that this adds is a guarantee, provided by the assistance of the Holy Spirit, that the solemnly defined proposition is true, and will always be true" (81). However, as the Lutheran-Roman Catholic Dialogue has indicated, interpreting "irreformable" in a theological sense, rather than in a juridical sense, both ignores the Gallican background of this term and also provides the potential for philosophical misunderstanding.[112]

Sullivan has provided a generally reliable doctrinal guide to interpreting infallibility; in contrast, Peter Chirico has taken a much more innovative direction in *Infallibility: The Crossroads of Doctrine*, which presented "an extended unifying hypothesis

111. Cf. Granfield's frank discussion of some recent Vatican actions in *The Limits of the Papacy*, 4–31; also see the *Report of the Catholic Theological Society of America, Committee on the Profession of Faith and the Oath of Fidelity* (1990).

112. "Teaching Authority and Infallibility," II. 16–18.

which envisions infallibility as the recurring generic process by
which the Church, because of the nature of the witnessed
saving reality which dogmatic statements express, can come to
certitude in judgment about that reality" (xvi).[113]

The creative aspect of Chirico's work is his attempt to formulate a universal perspective that will "account for many facets
of the old infallibility data" (xvii). Basic to his hypothesis is the
claim that

there are universal transcultural meanings that are, at least potentially,
aspects of the genuine development of all peoples. Some of these universal aspects can be known through reflection on ordinary human experience; others can be known only by reliance upon the apostolic witness. (xvii)

These "universal meanings"—identified as "differentiations of
experience that exist or can exist as moments of the legitimate
and ultimately necessary development of every person of every
age and culture" (xxii)—provide the grounds for Chirico's assertion "that there is a natural infallibility of the human mind
which operates in certain limited cases of universal meanings"
(xix). Parallel to this postulated human infallibility is the
Church's infallibility, "an extension of a universal capacity of
the human mind" (xiii). Just as human infallibility is concerned with "universal meanings," the Church's infallibility is
concerned with the "essential identifying traits of all Christian
groups"—essentials which "alone are the object of the exercise
of infallibility" (xiii).

Chirico's "hypothesis" has many attractive features, not the
least of which is the direct connection that it makes between
the personal and Christian development of all persons and "the
notion highlighted at Vatican II that all revelation is in Christ
and that there is no revelation not reflected in his humanity"
(xv). Equally praiseworthy is his "attempt to look at infallibility
from a new perspective, to ask a new set of questions, to pre-

113. Peter Chirico, S.S., *Infallibility: The Crossroads of Doctrine* (Kansas City:
Sheed Andrews and McMeel, 1976; 2d printing: Wilmington, Del.: Michael Glazier, 1983). References are to the second printing (which has additional material
in the introductory section).

serve the old doctrine not by repeating it but by attempting to fulfill and enrich it with the insights of a Church on the move" (xv).

Like every new vision, however, Chirico's has its oversights and blind spots. First, the apparent keystone to Chirico's "hypothesis" is his postulation of "universal meanings"; but how does one find such "universal meanings" behind historically conditioned expressions? By his own admission, he has "not attempted to justify these transcultural interpretations by historical investigations because such investigations were both practically impossible and at least at this stage of the endeavor, unnecessary" (xvii–xviii). However, without such investigations, readers may well feel unconvinced. In addition, Chirico's case seemingly stands or falls with the existence of "universal meanings" both human and ecclesial. But are "universal meanings" absolutely necessary for an exercise of infallibility? On the human side, Newman was able to make a convincing case for the "indefectibility of certitude" on the basis of the activities of the human mind without postulating "universal meanings."[114] On the ecclesiological side, neither of the Vatican Councils restricted the exercise of infallibility to "universal meanings." Is it necessary or even justifiable to link infallibility to "universal meanings"?

Another problem with Chirico's "hypothesis" is that of methodology. There is no question that an author has every right to propose a "hypothesis" on infallibility independently of any or all doctrinal teaching on the topic. However, at some point, most theologians want to know how such a "hypothesis" relates to doctrinal teaching. Unless the hypothesis and the doctrine do not correlate at all, one needs to show either how the doctrine is explained by the new hypothesis or how the hypothesis serves to transcend the doctrine. Chirico has claimed that his hypothesis does the latter, but on several issues it appears to be a procrustean fitting. For example, Chirico has insisted that Vatican I "rejected the notion that . . . [the

114. John Henry Newman, *An Essay in Aid of a Grammar of Assent* (London: Longmans, Green, 1903), ch. VII, sect. 2.

pope] *had to* consult the Church beforehand" (224) even though the Council's proceedings indicate otherwise (xxxv).

A third and more pervasive problem is the fact that Chirico has "utilized new and varying terminology in the hope that it will challenge the reader to find those elements in his or her experience which underlie the new framework I am attempting to convey" (xxi). Every author, of course, has the liberty to create new terminology; indeed, theology would never develop without such creativity, not only in terminology but also in method. However, if readers are even to follow an author's thought, much less to accept it, consistency is mandatory. Unfortunately, Chirico's varying usage has sometimes created more confusion than comprehension.[115]

Finally, Chirico has indicated that his work was "not intended to be an erudite work; it is more reflective than scholarly" (xxiv); indeed, he has left "others to take up the work of proving or disproving the hypothesis by detailed studies in their various specialties" (xix). Unfortunately, without such supporting studies, even the most promising hypothesis remains unsubstantiated, if not unconvincing.

Whereas Chirico's creative approach is undercut by methodological lacunae, a collaborative effort to apply Lonergan's theological method to *Papal Infallibility* seems to have been overburdened by excessive loyalty to methodological categories.[116] Under the leadership of Terry J. Tekippe, a team undertook a study of papal infallibility with "three interconnected aims: to provide a concrete application of Bernard Lonergan's theological method, to make a significant theological contribution on a topic of Roman Catholic and ecumenical interest, and to experiment with theological teamwork" (xi). In accord

115. Cf. *Infallibility*, xxi. Another opportunity for confusion appeared in his statement that "secondary objects of infallibility . . . manifest universal saving meanings." Then he stated that "these expressions cannot be called infallible truths, any more than Scripture can be called an infallible document. Infallibility should be restricted to the grasp of universal meanings." Later, Chirico claimed that he "explicitly" stated that "the secondary objects of infallibility are not objects of infallibility at all (p. 288)" (xxv, n. 1).

116. *Papal Infallibility: An Application of Lonergan's Theological Method* (Washington, D.C.: University Press of America, 1983).

with Lonergan's list of theological specialties, the team dili-
gently considered papal infallibility in terms of (1) research, (2)
interpretation, (3) history, (4) dialectic, (5) foundations, (6)
doctrine, (7) systematics, and (8) communication.

In the process of working within these specialties, the team
encountered a number of difficulties both practical and theoretical. The most obvious problem is the unevenness of the
individual contributions and the fact that they "rarely mesh
perfectly at the seams" (330). In addition, while one may logically distinguish research, interpretation, and history as three
distinct functional specialties, examining a topic under each of
these headings resulted in considerable duplication, which suggests that these specialties cannot really be exercised independently. But the weakest link was the dialectic: while one might
argue that intellectual, moral, and religious conversions are
necessary for theologizing, the editor's valiant effort to utilize
conversion as a criterion vis-à-vis infallibility ran into insur-
mountable difficulties.

These flaws suggest a more basic problem: is Lonergan's
method really meant to be applied in the way that this team
attempted? If Lonergan's specialties constitute a program for
theologizing, then another team might still do better. However,
if these specialties are really a reflective description of theological inquiry, then a team project was basically a misguided approach from the start.[117] Nonetheless, the project still has value
as a useful compendium of data on infallibility. In addition,
Robert Kress's systematic study suggested a very creative and
potentially helpful approach to infallibility:

As sacraments do not presuppose the absence but the presence of grace
which is, then, brought into socio-historical visibility in the sacrament,
so also infallibly declared dogmas do not presuppose the absence of the
truth, but its presence, which is then given a sacramental socio-
historical visibility in the Church's celebration of its relationship to the
infallibly truth-full and trust-worthy God. (29)

117. Cf. the trenchant critique of V. Gregson in *Method, Journal of Lonergan
Studies* 1(1983): 223–32. Compounding the methodological problem is a suspicion that the topic of infallibility, as a doctrine which cross-cuts other doctrines,
may not lend itself to Lonergan's categories.

In Kress's sacramental approach, "Solemn definitions are the magisterial-liturgical celebrations whereby the truth of God expressed in dogmas is exhibited to the Church so that the whole Church may publicly rejoice in this truth and celebrate it" (35). Unfortunately, Kress's proposal is visionary and only sketched in broad strokes; hopefully, he will eventually fill in the details.

Concluding Reflections

Although the number of publications on infallibility has decreased since the heyday of the debate about Küng's *Infallible?* the seriousness of the contributions has generally improved. Indeed, as Carl Peter perceptively remarked, the discussion about infallibility has itself been "too significant to be brushed aside as inconsequential." From the above survey of some of the literature that has appeared since the publication of *Teaching Authority and Infallibility in the Church*, it seems possible to offer a general assessment of the *status quaestionis* and to make some suggestions for future exploration.

First, in regard to the biblical basis and the historical development of infallibility, solid work continues to be done, though this usually appears to be a matter of adding details to a canvas that is well outlined. While one hopes that such biblical and historical research will continue, there are two larger problems that need further exploration: the first, as Carl Peter observed, is the question of the "divine institution" of papal primacy and infallibility; the second is the nature of doctrinal development, particularly in regard to infallibility.

Second, while clear and accurate presentations in English of the Roman Catholic teaching on infallibility are now available, they need to be utilized in catechesis. Insofar as infallibility is a doctrine concerned with the faithfulness of the Church to the teaching of Christ, a cavalier rejection of infallibility can easily damage the acceptance of the Gospel, just as an ultramontane presentation can destroy ecumenical understanding.

Third, considerable work still needs to be done in elaborating theological explanations of infallibility. Some creative proposals have been made, but such visions need to be correlated systematically with the historical development of this doctrine and the teaching of the Church.

Fourth, considerable and surprising progress has been made in ecumenical discussions about infallibility. On the one hand, Roman Catholics have been much more sensitive in the way that they present infallibility; on the other hand, their dialogue-partners have come to an appreciation of a doctrine that is alien to their ecclesial traditions. While infallibility is definitely an ecumenical roadblock, at least there are cooperative discussions about how to deal with it.

Fifth, a topic that has recently moved into the forefront of discussion is the "reception" of noninfallible pronouncements; while this topic was not directly treated above, it is certainly one that is both ecumenically sensitive and intramurally neuralgic.[118] In response to noninfallible teaching, there is need to balance respect for all teachings of the magisterium with the rights of conscience and due freedom for theological research.

In Memoriam

Carl Peter was keenly interested in all of these developments; in fact, at the time of his death, he was doing research on one aspect of the fifth topic: academic freedom at The Catholic University of America. As is evident from his publications, Peter approached such topics as a "traditional theologian" in the best sense of the term: in investigating any theological topic, such as infallibility, he always consulted the teaching of the magisterium and other Roman Catholic theologians; he also examined the topic in light of its ecumenical significance;

118. See, for example, Philip S. Kaufman, O.S.B., *Why You Can Disagree . . . and Remain a Faithful Catholic* (Bloomington, Ind.: Meyer Stone Books, 1989); on the controversy created by this book, cf. Dawn Gibeau, "Benedictine stays calm amid theological storms," *National Catholic Reporter* 28, no. 32 (19 June 1992), 7.

then, he offered his opinion, with the firmest of convictions, tempered by an awareness of the historically conditioned character of every theological position; he cautioned both his colleagues and his students that progress in theology "will take study, reflection, prayer, and courage. Patience and a sense of humor will also help."[119]

119. Carl Peter, "Papal Primacy" (see n. 41), 138.

6

~

Justification by Faith
and Ecclesial Communion

Pointers from the Lutheran-Catholic Dialogue

ERIC W. GRITSCH

Cardinal Johannes Willebrands envisioned the future of ecumenism in an "ecclesiology of communion in all its dimensions."[1] He explicated his point of view in an exegesis of the
statement in Vatican II that the Church "subsists in [*subsistit in*]
the Catholic Church."[2] After a frank narration of the arduous
route of changing the text from "the Church *is* [*est*] the Catholic Church" to the final reading, the cardinal viewed ecclesiology within the triangle of "*communio,*" "*koinonia,*" and "*sacra-
mentum.*" So viewed, non-Roman Catholic Christians, who have
been properly baptized, "are brought into a certain, though imperfect communion with the Catholic Church." Differences in
doctrine, discipline, and ecclesiastical structure do create "serious obstacles to full ecclesiastical communion." But "all those
justified by faith through baptism" are Christians and should be
properly regarded as brothers and sisters in the Lord by the
members of the Catholic Church.[3] This conclusion represents

1. Johannes Kardinal Willebrands, "Die Communio-Ekklesiologie des zweiten
Vatikanischen Konzils," in *Mandatum Unitatis. Beiträge zur Ökumene*, Konfessions-
kundliche Schriften 16 (Paderborn: Bonifatius Verlag, 1989), 341–56.
2. "*Subsistit in*" is found in *Lumen Gentium* 8. See *The Documents of Vatican II*,
ed. Walter M. Abbott and trans. Joseph Gallagher (New York: Guild, America, and
Association Presses, 1966), 23.
3. *Unitatis Redintegratio* 3. *Documents*, 345.

161

what some ecumenical linguists call a "convergence" short of
"consensus," "agreement," and "full communion."[4]

In 1987, the Lutheran Church in America (now merged with
other Lutheran churches in the Evangelical Lutheran Church in
America) and the Lutheran Institute for Ecumenical Research in
Strasbourg, France, sponsored a convocation on "Fundamental
Consensus and Church Fellowship." Lutheran and Catholic participants discussed the issue of basic consensus/basic differences,
assisted by Episcopalians, Methodists, Reformed, and Orthodox.[5]
A major topic was the "fundamental consensus" on justification
by faith in the U.S. Lutheran-Catholic Dialogue in 1983.[6] This
consensus was stated as a "fundamental affirmation":

> Our entire hope of justification and salvation rests on Christ Jesus and
> on the gospel whereby the good news of God's merciful action in
> Christ is made known; we do not place our ultimate trust in anything
> other than God's promise and saving work in Christ.[7]

But the Dialogue offered two concessions: 1) The christocentric
affirmation is not the full equivalent of the Reformation teaching on justification, and 2) the lack of full agreement raises the
question whether the remaining differences need to be church-
dividing.[8]

At the 1987 convocation, two members of the Dialogue discussed the criteriological implications of the consensus on
justification by faith. The Lutheran participant, Gerhard O.
Forde, contended that the "consensus" will remain a constant
source of "difficulty and suspicion" as long as the Reformation
emphasis on the eschatological component of the consensus is
ignored. As Forde put it: "Justification by faith alone as the article by which the church stands and falls recalls the church to
the realization that its true power is simply the power of the
gospel, the unconditional promise of the new eschatological

4. Joseph A. Burgess, ed., *In Search of Christian Unity. Basic Consensus/Basic Differences* (Minneapolis: Fortress Press, 1991), 4.

5. Pierre Duprey, "Fundamental Consensus and Church Fellowship. A Roman
Catholic Perspective," in *In Search of Christian Unity*, 139.

6. *Justification by Faith. Lutherans and Catholics in Dialogue VII*, ed. H. George
Anderson, T. Austin Murphy, and Joseph A. Burgess (Minneapolis: Augsburg Publishing House, 1985), 74.

7. Ibid., 72.

8. Ibid., 16.

kingdom."[9] The Catholic participant, Carl J. Peter, argued that one could move from consensus to agreement only if the criteriological function of justification by faith is not viewed as *unconditional* and is accompanied by "another critical principle." As Peter put it:

That principle in my judgment is both catholic and ecumenical. It too commends ultimate hope and trust in God alone as it urges: "Seek in faith to recognize God's grace in Jesus Christ and through the Holy Spirit, grace that because of the divine promise has been at work, is working yet, and will work in the future in individuals and institutions despite sin and abuse."[10]

Peter's insistence on *conditions*, over against the Lutheran language of *unconditionality*, is grounded in three postulations which disclose the enduring doctrinal differences between Lutheranism and Roman Catholicism:

a) the trustworthiness of the church according to the divine promise; b) the preservation of at least some degree of freedom and goodness in creation in spite of the fall; and c) the place of grace-wrought acts of charity.[11]

This paper takes another critical look at these enduring differences with special attention to ecclesial communion. First, I shall sketch the significance of justification by faith in the doctrinal tradition. Then I shall assess the 1983 Lutheran consensus on the gospel in the light of that tradition. Finally, I shall distill some implications and imperatives relating to ecclesiology.

The Tradition of "Justification"

Whereas the biblical view of justification by faith has been extensively researched and debated, its postbiblical importance

9. Gerhard O. Forde, "Justification by Faith Alone. The Article by Which the Church Stands or Falls?" in *In Search of Christian Unity*, 75.

10. Carl J. Peter, "A Catholic Response," ibid., 82–83. See also by the same author, "Justification by Faith and the Need of Another Critical Principle," in *Justification by Faith*, 304–15. The terms "Protestant principle" and "catholic substance" have been used by Paul Tillich, *Systematic Theology*, 3 vols. (Chicago: University of Chicago Press, 1956), 1:37; 3:6, 245. Justification is the "Protestant principle," and church tradition is the "catholic substance."

11. Peter, "A Catholic Response," 81.

received only minor attention.[12] The message of justification by faith and of salvation by grace is a basic theme in Scripture.[13] Even when the terms "righteousness" and "justification" are not used, this theme is prominent. At its center is the message of salvation in Christ. Thus Lutherans and Catholics can say together that "Scripture has a christological center which should control the interpretation of those parts of the Bible which focus on matters other than the center itself."[14] Paul's letters disclose more than any other biblical writings the radical difference between divine and human righteousness. But the Pauline tradition survived only until the third century, giving room to what has been called "Christian pharisaism."[15] It represents a compromise between the freedom of faith through grace and the Jewish zeal to fulfill the divine law through human moral efforts. Penitential discipline moved to the center of Christian life; eschatology diminished. Doctrine and piety settled for the enduring notion of cooperation between human nature and divine grace. "There is no longer a trace of Paul's view of baptism, and faith in the righteousness of God runs the risk of being transformed into an ecclesiastical ideology in the service of social accommodation."[16]

St. Augustine revived Pauline thought in the controversy with Pelagius. But he did so under the influence of Neoplatonic mysticism, advocating an understanding of grace as a transcendent, impersonal power which makes humans "adhere to God {adhaerere deo}." Grace is infused in their souls through the administration of sacraments. Augustine viewed this process of

12. For a summary of biblical research see the "Common Statement" in *Justification by Faith*, 58–68. This dialogue also generated the work of John Reumann, *Righteousness in the New Testament* (Philadelphia: Fortress Press; New York: Paulist Press, 1982). The German Lutheran scholar Ernst Käsemann started an enduring debate on the question whether or not justification is the "center of Scripture" or the "canon in the canon." Such and other issues are summarized and discussed in the pioneering work of the Waldensian scholar Vittorio Subilia, *Die Rechtfertigung aus dem Glauben. Gestalt und Wirkung vom Neuen Testament bis heute*, trans. Max Krumbach, (Göttingen: Vandenhoeck & Ruprecht, 1981). I am indebted to Subilia for much of this section of my paper.
13. Subilia, *Rechtfertigung*, 13–20.
14. "Common Statement," 68.
15. Subilia, *Rechtfertigung*, 45.
16. Ibid., 47. This and other translations are mine.

infusion together with a divine decision to elect the ungodly to become members in the kingdom of God. There is, then, an ambiguity in Augustine's understanding of justification: on the one hand, there is the well-known emphasis on the divine initiative, on predestination; on the other hand, there is a view of grace as the power that enables believers to cooperate with God in the process of salvation. This ambiguity prompted critics of Augustine to regard him as an initiator of semipelagianism rather than as a defender of Paul's doctrine of justification.[17]

Augustine's ambiguity in regard to justification generated the two major theological schools of the Middle Ages, Dominican Thomism and Franciscan Scotism. Thomas Aquinas stressed grace as the power that elevates believers to a level where they can be worthy of a relationship with God. Using Aristotle, Thomas tried to communicate the apostolic promise of salvation to people who differentiated between "material" and "formal" reality. Accordingly, "matter" is ineffective and powerless unless it receives "form." Thus Thomas can speak of faith as ineffective matter which, when formed by love, becomes a powerful agent in the process of salvation. One is therefore justified by love rather than by faith. Divine grace transforms sinful human nature in a way that it is able to turn to God with love. Divine *caritas* effects human love for God; in this sense, love is the fulfillment of the law (Rom. 13:10). Believers attain the *habitus*, grounded in love, to please God in their lives. For God will not be in relationship with creatures who cannot honor and please God. Here is Thomas's link between divine grace and human nature, between the love of God and human merit. According to Thomas, faith is justifying because it is grounded in a love given by God who in this way effects the human ability to merit a relationship with God. "Love is the form of faith insofar as the act of faith is completed and formed by love."[18] One can speak of four moments of the process of justification according to Thomas: (1) Divine grace

17. This is the view of some Protestant critics, especially Karl Barth, who regarded Augustine's view of grace as a "poison" that invaded the healthy body of the Christian church. Ibid., 53.

18. Quoted ibid., 58.

initiates the process by infusing love into the human soul, giving it a new *qualitas* or *habitus*. (2) The human will is free, despite sin, to accept or reject this infusion. (3) If the human will accepts it, nature moves from sin to grace and cooperates with God. (4) Cooperation leads to the forgiveness of sin.[19] One can speak of justification only when all four moments are realized.

Critics of Thomas have charged that his doctrine of justification is no longer as christocentric as that of Paul. "Christ is not our justification, but the staircase we can use in order to build our own justification."[20] One can no longer speak with Paul of the justification of the ungodly, but of the justification of the godly who rely on their own efforts to please God. Paul, on the other hand, rejected any justification by law; otherwise Christ would have died in vain (Gal. 2:21).[21]

But Thomism tried to create a proper balance between the sacrifice of Christ and the human response to it. Justification begins with Christ's sacrifice on the cross and continues when believers rely on this sacrifice as the only source of their salvation. Whatever believers do in the process of justification, they never "merit" their salvation but only cooperate with Christ through his church in order to complete their justification.

Franciscan Scotism viewed cooperation in justification in the context of an ascetic rejection of the world, especially through the vow of poverty. While Thomists stressed divine grace in the process of justification, Franciscan Scotists emphasized human cooperation. Its advocates were Alexander of Hales (ca. 1170–1245), John Bonaventure (1221–74), and Duns Scotus (ca. 1270–1308). Scotus taught a "finely woven" (*subtilis*)[22] doctrine of justification: Perceiving God as absolutely free and good,

19. Ibid., 58–59.
20. Ibid., 59.
21. Ibid. Subilia views the demise of the Pauline doctrine of justification and the rise of the medieval focus on cooperation of sin and grace as a return to "the Jewish-Christian tradition." This tradition is virtually synonymous with the Roman Catholic tradition of justification as defined by the Council of Trent which creates "the justifying church" (ibid., 89–99). Subilia remains more skeptical than I and others who see a growing convergence between Luther and Rome on the question of justification. Compare, for example, Subilia (60, n. 21) and the consensus stated in the "Common Statement," 74.
22. Scotus became known as "*doctor subtilis.*"

Scotus contended that God, who is good, wills the salvation of sinners by "ordained power" (*potentia ordinata*), even though God, who is free, need not do so. Humans have the free will to decide for or against the salvation offered in Christ. If they decide to accept what God ordained for them, their acceptance is accounted as "merit" by God. Thus Scotus can talk about merit without talking about works-righteousness; the human acceptance of the divine offer is counted as merit.[23] William of Occam (ca. 1280–1349) radicalized Scotism by rejecting any rational proof for the existence of God, who remains absolute and totally free. Like Scotus, Occam viewed the justification of sinners as the divine acceptance of a freely willed repentance, linked to unconditional faith in what God did in Christ; such faith is traditioned by the Church which must guard against rationalist attempts to explain divine revelation and salvation.

Martin Luther may have learned from Occam and the "nominalist" school to guard against speculative theology.[24] In any event, his rediscovery of the christocentric apostolic tradition, mainly through Paul, led Luther to a rejection of Aristotelian thought structures.[25] Thus Luther made "justification by faith alone" the "article on which the church stands and falls" (*articulus stantis et cadentis ecclesiae*).[26] It was Scripture that taught

23. This has been clearly elaborated by Werner Dettloff, "Duns Scotus," in *Theologische Realenzyklopaedie*, ed. Gerhard Krause and Gerhard Mueller (Berlin and New York: Walter de Gruyter, 1976), 9:227–28. Dettloff sees a great similarity between Scotus and Luther, who linked justification to the absolute freedom of God who cannot be appeased by any human action.

24. Whether or not Luther was an Occamist during his formative years is a much-debated issue. The Catholic historian Joseph Lortz contended that Luther viewed Occamism as works-righteous. But since Occamism was never formally accepted as "Catholic," Luther "overcame in himself a Catholicism that was not Catholic." See Joseph Lortz, *The Reformation in Germany*, 2 vols., trans. Ronald Walls (New York: Herder and Herder, and London: Darton, Longman and Todd, 1968; German ed. 1939–40), 1:176. I disagree and side with Dettloff (above, n. 23). See Eric W. Gritsch, "Joseph Lortz's Luther: Appreciation and Critique," *Archiv für Reformationsgeschichte* 81 (1990): 32–49.

25. This has been clearly demonstrated by Leif Grane, *Modus Loquendi Theologicus. Luthers Kampf um die Erneuerung der Theologie*, Acta Theologica Danica 12 (Leiden: E. J. Brill, 1975), esp. 192–99. See also Eric W. Gritsch, "The Origins of the Lutheran Teaching on Justification," in *Justification by Faith*, 163–67.

26. The phrase is derived from Luther's *Smalcald Articles* (1537) in *The Book of Concord. The Confessions of the Evangelical Lutheran Church*, trans. and ed. Theodore G. Tappert (Philadelphia: Fortress Press, 1959), 292:1–5. Hereafter cited *BC*. The

168   ERIC W. GRITSCH

Luther that penance (*poenitentia*) meant total concentration on Christ crucified rather than an effort to cooperate with Christ in the process of justification. Any theological enterprise, therefore, must become a "theology of the cross." There can be no room in the church for what Luther called a "theology of glory" which focuses on the invisible, hidden God and on how human creatures can use their God-given image to claim some self-righteousness.[27] "This is the reason why our theology is certain: it snatches us away from ourselves, so that we do not depend on our strength, conscience, experience, person, or works, but depend on that which is outside ourselves, that is, on the promise and truth of God, which cannot deceive."[28] Such promise is communicated through word and sacrament as the good news, the gospel, that God became incarnate in Christ to reveal mercy and love to sinners. According to Luther, one must distinguish between the gospel and the "law": the divine demand for unconditional loyalty, manifested in the first commandment of the decalogue ("you shall have no other gods"). The law was violated by the sin to be like God (Gen. 3:5); its proclamation reveals the endurance of this sin (Rom. 3:20).

Luther saw the distinction of law and gospel as the eschatological condition of Christian existence which will be fully enjoyed after the second advent of Christ. In the meantime, often a mean time, one concentrates on the means of grace, word, and sacrament as the instruments of the gospel.[29] For justification is not only a concept but a liturgical experience, a

---

section is entitled "Christ and faith" as the "first and chief article." The phrase appears for the first time in Valentine E. Loescher's antipietist essay *Timotheus Verinus* (Wittenberg, 1718). See Friedrich Loofs, "Der articulus stantis et cadentis ecclesiae," *Theologische Studien und Kritiken* 90 (1917): 323–420. See also Eric W. Gritsch, *Martin—God's Court Jester. Luther in Retrospect*, 2d ed. (Ramsey, N.J.: Sigler Press, 1991), ch. 9: "A Christocentric Theology."

27. Luther, *The Heidelberg Disputation* (1518) in *Werke*, Kritische Gesamtausgabe (Weimar: Böhlau, 1883–), 1:361.32–362.3. Hereafter cited *WA*. American edition: *Luther's Works*, ed. Jaroslav Pelikan and Helmut T. Lehmann, 55 vols. (Philadelphia: Fortress Press; St. Louis: Concordia Publishing House, 1955–86), 31:40. Hereafter cited *LW*.

28. Luther, *Lectures on Galatians* (1535). *WA* 40/1:569.25–28. *LW* 26:387.

29. Luther speaks of several instruments of the gospel: the spoken word, baptism, eucharist, penance, and "mutual conversation and consolation"; *Smalcald Articles*, *BC* 310:iv.

"rhapsody," as Luther once called it.[30] All of Christian life is to be shaped by faith in Christ alone. That is why Luther could speak of justification without even mentioning the term.

I believe that Jesus Christ, true God, begotten of the Father in eternity, and also true man, born of the Virgin Mary, is my Lord, who has redeemed me, a lost and condemned creature, delivered me and freed me from all sins, from death, and from the power of the devil, not with silver and gold but with his holy and precious blood and with his innocent sufferings and death, in order that I may be his, live under him in his kingdom and serve him in everlasting righteousness, innocence, and blessedness, even as he is risen from the dead and lives and reigns in all eternity.[31]

Luther rethought the dogma of the Trinity in soteriological terms, especially in the light of Pauline and Johannine christology.[32] He did not identify justification with the *sola scriptura* principle, as some Lutherans contend. Rather, Luther affirmed Scripture as the history of salvation, centered in God's incarnation in Christ.

The Lutheran Confessions, anchored in *The Augsburg Confession* of 1530, affirmed the ancient dogma of the Trinity as the source of justification. Philip Melanchthon, who drafted the *Confession* and its defense (*Apology*), stressed the soteriological function of the ancient trinitarian creeds and then demonstrated how Christ rules believers through the Holy Spirit in word and sacrament until he returns.[33] Thus the dogmatic section of the *Confession* is a rigorously christological interpre-

30. See the title of Luther's incomplete attempt to write a treatise on justification: *Rhapsodia seu concepta in Librum de loco Iustificationis* (1530), WA 30/2:657.

31. Luther's explanation of the second article of the Apostles' Creed in the *Small Catechism* (1529), BC 345:4.

32. Luther called Paul and John "two high commanders" who are on his side in his fight against Erasmian humanism and its insistence on "free will"; *The Bondage of the Will* (1525), WA 18:757.9–10; LW 33:247.

33. This is the real intention of the Confession when it is read from the viewpoint of Melanchthon's *Apology* of the Confession. See Robert W. Jenson, "On Recognizing the Augsburg Confession," in *The Role of the Augsburg Confession. Catholic and Lutheran Views*, ed. Joseph A. Burgess (Philadelphia: Fortress Press), 153. How justification is the hermeneutical norm in the Lutheran Confessions has been shown by Eric W. Gritsch and Robert W. Jenson, *Lutheranism. The Theological Movement and Its Confessional Writings* (Philadelphia: Fortress Press, 1976).

tation of the work of the Holy Spirit, grounded in the affirmation that believers are justified through grace by faith in Christ alone.[34] Justifying faith is transmitted through the divinely instituted office of the ministry of word and sacraments, the means by which the Holy Spirit "produces faith, where and when it pleases God, in those who hear the gospel."[35] Melanchthon and the signers of the *Confession* thought that they were asserting the core of the ecumenical dogmatic tradition when they focused on justification. Moreover, they reminded their opponents that their teaching was not contrary to the Roman Catholic Church "in so far as the latter's teaching is reflected in the writings of the Fathers."[36] But the Catholic opponents did not agree, and the *Confutatio* of 1530 described the Lutheran doctrine of justification as "diametrically opposed to the evangelical truth, which does not exclude works."[37] The Lutheran Confessions, of course, teach the necessity of good works, albeit as a thanksgiving for the gift of faith active in love to the neighbor.[38] In this sense, good works are the ethics of the interim between the first and second advent of Christ.[39]

Post-Reformation views of justification disclose the influence of various thought structures. Both Lutheran and Catholic views place justification either into an "order of salvation" (*ordo salutis*), as did Lutheran "orthodox" theology in the seventeenth century, or into a process of salvation, as did the Council of Trent in response to the Reformation. Thus Lutherans tried to describe how justification became "applied grace" (*gratia applicatrix*), generating conversion, sanctification, and eventual glo-

34. The articles on the Trinity focus on original sin (1–3) which must be combatted by the Holy Spirit through ministry, sacraments, and the church (4–17). *BC* 27:1–38:5.

35. *The Augsburg Confession, BC* 5:2.

36. End of the first part of the *Confession, BC* 47:1.

37. Herbert Immenkoetter, ed., *Die Confutatio der Confessio Augustana vom 3. August 1530*, Corpus Catholicorum 33 (Münster: Aschendorff, 1979), 90:18–21. The English translation is *The Augsburg Confession: A Collection of Sources with an Historical Introduction*, ed. and trans. J. M. Reu (Chicago: Wartburg Publishing House, 1930; reprinted, St. Louis: Concordia Theological Seminary, 1966), 352.

38. *The Augsburg Confession*, art. 20, *BC* 45:27. On love of neighbor see Gritsch and Jenson, *Lutheranism*, ch. 10.

39. The eschatological background of the Lutheran doctrine of justification has been clearly shown by Subilia, *Rechtfertigung*, 160–66.

rification.[40] Catholic Tridentine theology reaffirmed the Augustinian notion of the primacy of grace without, however, abandoning the notion of human merit as part of divine grace.[41]

Protestant Reformed views of justification, grounded in the theology of John Calvin, were christocentric, but without the strong eschatological emphasis disclosed in Luther. Whereas Luther viewed justified life as existence in the context of the imminent second advent of Christ, Calvin saw Christ centered in holy living. There is then a contemporaneousness of justification and sanctification in Calvin's theological system; the focus is on the God-willed moral witness in an immoral world, based on the conviction that knowledge of God means obedience to God.[42] This theocentric context of justification was later intensified by Karl Barth, who opposed any distinction between faith and good works in order to eliminate any notion of human cooperation in justification. That is why dogmatics and ethics are inseparable.[43]

Eighteenth-century Lutheran Pietism also stressed sanctification as the experience of justification, albeit in a subjectivist fashion that deemphasized sacramental and ecclesial communion. German and Scandinavian pietists saw the evidence of justification in penitential struggle, conversion, and rebirth, issuing in a holy and moral life.[44]

40. Melanchthon already began to systematize Luther's view of justification, but without the Aristotelian categories introduced by seventeenth-century Lutheran theologians. See *Justification by Faith*, 38.

41. Augustine's famous dictum was revived: "God wishes his own gifts to be their merits." Quoted ibid., 35.

42. The Reformed tradition has been well summarized by Subilia, *Rechtfertigung*, ch. 4, 216–18, 230–36.

43. Barth summarized his view of the Reformed doctrine of justification in his typical dialectical way: "Reformed doctrine does not so much stress that humans are justified by *faith* rather than by *works*, but that it is *God* and not *humans* who executes this justification." Quoted ibid., 219.

44. "Orthodox" and "pietist" Lutheran theologians reflect an intra-Lutheran debate about the relationship of justification and sanctification. Luther, at times, spoke of "forensic" justification (from *forum*, the Roman marketplace where judicial and other business was conducted). It meant to him and to other reformers "pronouncing" or "declaring" the sinner righteous on account of Christ before God's tribunal. Orthodox Lutherans liked to emphasize forensic justification while pietists stressed sanctification, "making" the sinner righteous. The Lutheran Confessions tend to move towards forensic justification in order to guard against any notion of self-righteousness. *BC* 541:17.

Nineteenth-century Protestant theology revived the dogmatic interest in justification, with special attention to its biblical and Reformation roots. A renaissance in Luther research at the beginning of the twentieth century intensified this interest in justification. Cardinal Newman paid attention to justification from the Catholic side,[45] and Hans Küng spurred ecumenical discussion with a major work on justification in the thought of Karl Barth.[46] The 1963 Assembly of the Lutheran World Federation tried to make justification once again the cornerstone of Lutheranism. In a lengthy debate before and during the Assembly an attempt was made to modernize justification in the context of questions raised after World War II rather than in the context of the sixteenth century. Influenced by theologians like Paul Tillich, many delegates suggested that the modern quest was no longer for a gracious God, as Luther had asked, but for a gracious neighbor and the meaning of life. Moreover, justification is communicated not just by Scripture alone (*sola scriptura*), or forensically as a divine verdict about human sin, but as life in the church, with rich sacramental enactment and moral witness in an immoral world. Delegates from Africa and Asia argued for a communication of a christocentric faith which may no longer need the term "justification." Yet no consensus was reached at Helsinki, and the discussion on justification continued.[47]

Vatican II paid little attention to justification. It stressed the unique mediation of reconciliation in Christ, and it asserted the primacy of the word of God as the ultimate norm in the

45. He tried to reconcile the two sides. See John Henry Newman, *Lectures on the Doctrine of Justification* (Westminster, Md.: Christian Classics, 1966; 1st ed. 1838), 278, 348. How contemporary Catholic theology has moved closer to Lutheran theology on justification has been shown by Avery Dulles, "Justification in Contemporary Catholic Theology," in *Justification by Faith*, 256–77.

46. Hans Küng, *Justification: The Doctrine of Karl Barth and a Catholic Reflection*, trans. T. Collins et al. (New York: Thomas Nelson, 1964). More useful for the contemporary discussion is Otto H. Pesch, *Hinführung zu Luther* (Mainz: Matthias Grünewald Verlag, 1982), 264–71. Pesch contends that Luther's *solus Christus* is the "article" that unites Catholics and Lutherans (270).

47. On the proposals and their discussion at Helsinki, see "'Justification Today,' Document 75—Assembly and Final Versions," *Lutheran World* 12, no. 1, Supplement (1965): 1–11. A summary of the event is offered in *Justification by Faith*, 45–46.

church which stands in need of a continual reformation.⁴⁸ Karl Rahner, who was most influential at Vatican II, tried to make the Catholic view of justification more palatable to Protestants by contending that justification is "applied christology": justification and its reception, indeed, human cooperation with it, is always a free gift of God through Christ, ruling out Pelagian claims of human merit.⁴⁹ Other Catholic theologians, like Edward Schillebeeckx, have said that the gracious gift of justification cannot be experienced privately, but only in selfless service to others; and the Brazilian Catholic theologian Leonardo Boff prefers the term "liberation" to "justification."⁵⁰

A Neuralgic Consensus

In the wake of Vatican II, an International Lutheran/Catholic Study Commission dealt for five years with the question of "the gospel and the church." When the results of the dialogue were published in 1971, the dialogue team declared that "a far-reaching consensus is developing in the interpretation of justification," but more work needed to be done on the subject and its implications.⁵¹ The Lutheran-Catholic Dialogue in the United States continued this work from 1978 until 1983 when it published "a fundamental affirmation," labeled "a fundamental consensus on the gospel."⁵² At the same time, the Dialogue declared:

Agreement on this christological affirmation does not necessarily involve full agreement between Catholics and Lutherans on justification by faith, but it does raise the question whether the remaining differences on this doctrine need be church-dividing.⁵³

48. On Christ the mediator see *Lumen Gentium* 8 (Abbott and Gallagher, 22). On continual reformation, *Unitatis Redintegratio* 6 (Abbott and Gallagher, 350).
49. *Justification by Faith*, 44.
50. Ibid., 44.
51. The Commission was appointed by the Lutheran World Federation in Geneva and by the Secretariat for Promoting Christian Unity in Rome. Its report, "The Gospel and the Church," was published in *Worship* 46 (1972): 326–51, and in *Lutheran World* 19 (1972): 259–73. See sect. 26.
52. *Justification by Faith*, 74.
53. Ibid., 16.

The "Common Statement" discloses disagreement regarding thought structures:[54] Catholics view justification in a "transformationist" way as a process in which sinners are transformed by grace. This Augustinian view was elaborated at Trent with the understanding that human merits are part of God's transforming work. Lutherans, on the other hand, stress God's justifying word, which promises salvation to those who trust in Christ alone. How the word functions is sketched in a "hermeneutical perspective."[55] A member of the dialogue, George A. Lindbeck, prefers the term "performative" for what the Lutheran Confessions call "forensic." "Words sometimes function as performances or deeds that themselves constitute the actuality of what they speak."[56] Here the emphasis is on the power of the external word as the means by which "the Holy Spirit produces faith, where and when it pleases God, in those who hear the gospel.[57]

There are, then, two different ways of identifying the place of trust: Catholics tend to look at themselves as believers who have experienced the infusion of grace through the ministry of the church; Lutherans insist on trusting the external word alone as the way in which God saves sinners through Christ, the living word. One could say that Lutherans are more concerned about the danger of anxiety or unfaith. Catholics, on the other hand, want to express the human response to divine grace as praise and thanksgiving for the transformation of sinners.[58] Both Lutherans and Catholics agree "that ultimate hope and trust for salvation are to be placed in the God of our Lord Jesus Christ, and not in our own goodness, even when this is God-given, or in our religious experience, even when this is the experience of faith."[59] Both partners in dialogue concede that their consensus is threatened by abuse, be it by an under-

54. Ibid., 49–57.

55. Ibid., 47–48.

56. George A. Lindbeck, "Justification by Faith. An Analysis of the 1983 Report of the U.S. Lutheran-Roman Catholic Dialogue," *Lutheran Partners* 7 (December 1984/January 1985): 10.

57. *BC* 31:3.

58. Lindbeck, 11.

59. *Justification by Faith*, 73.

standing of merit "bordering on legalism" on the Catholic side;[60] or by "neglecting the means of grace" and a "fostering of individualism" by Lutherans.[61] But both Lutherans and Catholics also admit that "the consequences of the different outlooks seem irreconcilable, especially in reference to particular applications of justification by faith as a criterion of all church proclamation and practice."[62]

The "Common Statement" offers some insights into the limits of doctrinal and ecclesial diversity. The Lutherans in the Dialogue go as far as to state that they "do not exclude the possibility that such teachings [as purgatory, the papacy, and the cult of the saints] can be understood and used in ways consistent with justification."[63] Catholics agree that "practices, structures, and theologies of the church" need to be tested by justification as a criterion.[64] Both hope that the remaining differences are not church-dividing.

Official responses by the respective churches suggest that the remaining differences are still church-dividing. The Lutheran response expresses doubt whether Catholics pass the test of justification. "If the consensus on this application [of justification as a criterion] cannot be broadened, then agreement on the doctrine itself will need to be reconsidered."[65] The official Catholic response is quite skeptical about the "consensus," stating that justification as the "criterion of authenticity"[66]

> may well point to a profound ecclesiological difference between Catholics and Lutherans. . . . One must apply the full apostolic heritage in interpreting the gospel. One single doctrine or principle does not suffice. . . . We do consider purgatory, the papacy, and the role of the saints as fostering the life of faith. These three realities also have dogmatic standing in the Catholic Church. Thus adequate agreement on them, in accord with the hierarchy of truths, will be necessary. . . . [67]

60. Ibid., 54.   61. Ibid., 56.
62. Ibid., 57.   63. Ibid., 69.
64. Ibid.

65. "A Response to Justification by Faith," Lutheran Church in America, adopted by the 1986 Convention, 6.

66. *Justification by Faith*, 56.

67. "An Evaluation of the Lutheran-Catholic Statement *Justification by Faith*. The Roman Catholic Bishops of the United States," *Lutheran Quarterly* 5 (1991): 66–67, 70.

It is interesting that a Lutheran theologian shares the same concerns, albeit for different reasons. He contends that the two different thought structures, the transformationist model and the Reformation model, cannot be reconciled. "The difference between these two models of justification is bound to be generative of vastly different styles of ecclesial practice."[68]

This and other dialogues have created linguistic-hermeneutical problems by using words and methods in a confusing manner. How is one to differentiate between such terms as "consensus," "convergence," "affirmation," and "agreement"? Are these terms opposed to such words as "basic difference," "divergence," "dissent," and "disagreement"? What is the difference between a "hierarchy of truths" and specific levels of understanding something as true? George A. Lindbeck has tried to clarify the nature and function of doctrines. He conceptualizes their nature as "cultural-linguistic" and views their function as "regulative."[69] A cultural-linguistic approach assumes the priority of a cultural communication pattern embodied in language, concepts, rituals, and other means of communication. Change or innovation, therefore, do not come about "because of an upwelling of new or different ways of feeling about the self, world, or God," but because an older system of communication can no longer be applied to new contexts. Thus change or reform is generated. The doctrine of justification is a case in point.

Luther did not invent his doctrine of justification by faith because he had a tower experience, but rather the tower experience was made possible by his discovering (or thinking he discovered) the doctrine in the Bible. To be sure, the experience of justification by faith occasioned by his exegesis then generated a variety of fresh expressive symbolisms [like the music of Johann Sebastian Bach]. . . . Yet logically, even if not causally, a religious experience and its expression are secondary and tertiary in a linguistic-cultural model.[70]

68. Carl E. Braaten, "Justification," in *Lutherans and Catholics in Ecumenical Dialogue. A Reappraisal*, ed. Joseph A. Burgess (Minneapolis: Augsburg, 1990), 87; see also 98.
69. George A. Lindbeck, *The Nature of Doctrine. Religion and Theology in a Post-liberal Age* (Philadelphia: Westminster, 1984), 18.
70. Ibid., 39.

Religions, then, are "idioms for dealing with whatever is important—with the ultimate questions of life and death." The same religious experience may generate two different types of reactions, for example, a catatonic trance or strenuous activity. Thus different religions generate different experiences of what is human. "The empirically available data seem to support a cultural-linguistic rather than an experiential-expressive understanding of the relation of religion and experience."[71]

But how does one explain radical differences within the same religion, such as Christianity? Lindbeck's test of such differences, exemplified in the dogma of the Trinity and the "infallible" Marian dogmas (Immaculate Conception [1854] and Assumption [1950]), concludes with the observation that "the Roman, Reformation, and Orthodox positions on infallibility continue to be irreconcilable in the present situation."[72] There are no infallible rules that regulate forever what is eternally true, for there are no infallible theories in ontological disputes, for example, whether Augustinian or Thomistic theological theories explicate the reality of the triune God. "Which theory is theologically best depends on how well it organizes the data of Scripture and tradition with a view to their use in Christian worship and life."[73] That is why the truth of the gospel is "intratextual," that is, it "can only be presented, not proved," by those who "renew the ancient practice of absorbing the universe into the biblical world."[74]

To apply Lindbeck's thesis to the consensus in this dialogue: the "fundamental affirmation" of Christ as the source of "ulti-

71. Ibid., 41.   72. Ibid., 104.
73. Ibid., 106.
74. Ibid., 135. Lindbeck's analysis of the nature of doctrine is quite complex. But when he tests the "cultural-linguistic" theory with reference to "christology, mariology, and infallibility" (ch. 5), his application of the theory as grammar or rule for reading the historical development of dogma becomes both helpful and controversial. This application is helpful insofar as the theory labels some doctrines or dogmas, e.g., the trinitarian creeds, as "permanently authoritative paradigms" because they have been abidingly important in Christian history (95–96). It is controversial insofar as the theory focuses on "intratextuality" as the guardian of faithfulness (113–24). Thus the emphasis is on narrative, i.e., reading Scripture and tradition within the church, as the means of the faithful transmission of the gospel. But who reads the tradition rightly? All the people of God? The magisterium? Once again, one is faced with the difficult issue of authority.

mate trust" in how God saves human sinners could represent a
rule which, like rules of grammar, determines the "cultural-linguistic" context of Lutherans and Catholics; they could have a
common worship and life. But disagreements on what is infallible make this rule neuraligic—creating pain along the curves
of the nerves in the respective church bodies.

Implications and Imperatives

Robert W. Jenson contends that ecumenical theology,
grounded in the work of ecumenical dialogues, is virtually para-
lyzed by "a basic flaw": a lack of thorough christological reflection regarding the relationship between God, time, and the
church.[75] Concentrating on the West, specifically, the relationship between the Protestant and Catholic theological traditions,
Jenson offers a superb critical analysis of the dialogues and
drives home the ecclesiological point that "our Christology
must enable us to say straightforwardly that Christ now has the
church as his body."[76] The "most drastic key to all questions of
the dialogues" is the recognition that "the church *is* the world's
historical continuity"; and the eucharist is the sign of the
church's "dramatic continuity," disclosing "the creation's participation in the difference and unity of the Father and the
Spirit."[77] Thus the church is a community of the interim, looking "forward to God as clearly as it looks back to him," experi-
encing "the temporal unity of its own communal self as the
personal unity of the risen Son."[78]

Such an ecumenical vision of the church ought to compel
churches to strive for full ecclesial communion, for what
Lutherans call "pulpit and altar fellowship" or what a Catholic
theologian calls "the church of churches."[79] Such a church
should no longer seek institutional or doctrinal uniformity, but

75. Robert W. Jenson, *Unbaptized God. The Basic Flaw in Ecumenical Theology*
(Minneapolis: Fortress, 1992), 132–47.
76. Ibid., 127.   77. Ibid., 145–46.
78. Ibid., 147.
79. J. M. R. Tillard, *Church of Churches: The Ecclesiology of Communion* (Collegeville: Liturgical Press, 1992).

embody a unity in diversity: "genuine Church fellowship, including as essential elements the recognition of baptism, the establishing of eucharistic fellowship, the mutual recognition of Church ministries, and a binding common purpose of witness and service."[80]

So far, Lutherans and Catholics have not agreed on the implications of their "consensus" on justification. Whereas Lutherans insist that all traditions and institutions must be judged by the criterion of justification, Catholics indicate that all doctrines have a like critical function.[81] Only one recommendation on the list of the Roman Catholic/Lutheran Joint Commission has been debated and awaits implementation: the removal of the mutual condemnations in the sixteenth century.[82] Everything else has either not yet been received and evaluated by the two communions, or has fallen victim to the winter of discontent that has created a harsh ecumenical climate.

But the stated consensus on justification at least has implications for Lutherans and should help thaw the ecumenical ice generated by theological and nontheological factors. These implications are of a liturgical rather than strictly doctrinal nature. It is the insight from the Lutheran Confessions that the event of justification is an act of worship. Article VII of *The Augsburg Confession* states the criteriological function of justification in the context of the *lex orandi*: the church "is the assembly of all believers among whom the gospel is preached in its purity and the holy sacraments administered according to the gospel."[83] If the truth of the gospel is hope in Christ who alone justifies, then word and sacrament are the only instruments of media-

---

80. *Facing Unity. Models, Forms and Phases of Catholic-Lutheran Church Fellowship* (Geneva: Lutheran World Federation, 1985), 17.

81. This judgment is based on convincing evidence provided by Jenson, 21.

82. Karl Lehmann, ed. *The Condemnations of the Reformation Era: Do They Still Divide?* (Minneapolis: Fortress, 1989). The findings on justification have been criticized in "An Opinion on *The Condemnations of the Reformation Era*. Part I: Justification. The Theological Faculty, Georgia Augusta University, Göttingen," *Lutheran Quarterly* 5 (1991): 1–62. The "opinion" opposes the document because it does not sufficiently focus on the "antithetical" character of the relationship between God and sinners (56).

83. *BC* 32.

tion. Moreover, Lutherans understand the "performance" of word and sacrament to be in faithful continuity with apostolic teaching and ancient church tradition. Consequently, the gospel, that is, justification, creates unity as an ongoing event. "For the true unity of the Church it is enough [*satis est*] to agree concerning the teaching of the gospel and the administration of the sacraments."[84] Given the long and powerful tradition of justification in Christian history, Lutherans have lifted up its originally Pauline aspect of dying and living with Christ (Rom. 5–6), linking the liturgy of baptism with the church's worship as the ongoing event of justification. As one of Carl Peter's students put it: "What Lutherans have only recently discovered in their fundamental tradition is that 'the gospel' is not a dogmatic definition, but is *a liturgical act*."[85] In that act, Christ is truly present and functions as the chief priest in the church militant, leading it to the transformation of the church triumphant. It is also a long-acknowledged fact that dogma follows life. As Yves Congar put it: "The faith of the Church, its unity, was in the *life* of the faithful. . . . The confessing community lives out its faith by celebrating it."[86] Dogma guards doxological life; it does not create such life.

The Lutheran-Catholic Dialogue has generated a consensus that points to some, perhaps limited, forms of ecclesial communion.[87] Why should *liturgical* communion be totally conditioned by agreement in doctrine and structure? Lutherans have begun to move from a traditionally narrow, indeed individualistic, view of justification towards a broader, communion-oriented view.[88] Catholics have begun to view the consensus on justification as an opportunity to raise questions about the re-

84. Ibid.
85. Mark E. Chapman, "The Unity of the Church and the Truth of the Gospel," *One in Christ* 26 (1990): 74.
86. Yves Congar, *Diversity and Communion* (Mystic, Conn.: Twenty-Third Publications, 1985), 13, 100.
87. It should be quite possible to permit intercommunion for couples in a mixed marriage, i.e., Lutheran and Catholic. Marital bonding should encourage eucharistic bonding.
88. See, for example, Oswald Bayer, "Twenty-Five Theses on the Renewal of Lutheranism by Concentrating on Justification," *Lutheran Quarterly* 5 (1991): 73–75. See especially theses 1, 10, 16.

lationship between justification and the ecclesiastical office.[89] The time has come to put the basic differences not only through the mill of theological minds and before the tribunal of officers of oversight, but also before God as a sacrifice of penance. There is a dire need for cruciformity on all levels of ecclesial life. We have to do penance for much of our triumphalist institutionalism in order to appreciate the adiaphorist character of institutionalization. Much of what has become institutionalized needs to die before it can live as a faithful witness to God's justification in Christ. What the apostle Paul said about his body also applies to the body of the church: "always carrying in the body the death of Jesus, so that the life of Jesus may also be manifested in our bodies" (2 Cor. 4:10).

89. Walter Kasper, noted by Jenson, *Unbaptized God*, 44. The issue is ordination; see ch. 4.

7

~

Justification by Faith

A Post-Conciliar Perspective

The troubles of our proud and angry dust
Are from eternity, and shall not fail.

A. E. Housman

STEPHEN J. DUFFY

With the ecumenical thaw that has marked our century, punctuated as it is by sixteen ecumenical dialogues on justification by faith since 1956, the Lutheran doctrine of justification is no longer the bone that sticks in the Catholic throat. Otto Pesch has argued that Luther was practically Thomistic; Harry McSorley, that he was Catholic in his theology of grace; and Hans Küng, that Barth's understanding of justification is Tridentine. Yet outside of ecumenical dialogue, Roman Catholics speak little of justification.[1] All this suggests there may be an

---

1. For example, Aquinas devoted one *quaestio* to justification, *Summa theologiae* I-II, q. 113; M. Schmaus's *Katholische Dogmatik* refers to justification only in passing; K. Rahner's *Schriften* contains but three essays on justification and his *Grundkurs* does not treat of it; R. McBrien's two-volume *Catholicism* refers to justification on only three of its 1200 pages; and the two-volume *Systematic Theology* recently edited by F. Fiorenza and J. Galvin devotes three pages to it. Even among Protestant thinkers outside the Lutheran tradition, justification gets short shrift. See, e.g., G. Wainwright's *Doxology: Praise of God in Worship, Doctrine and Life: A Systematic Theology* (New York: Oxford, 1980), 138–42, 167, 410–12; B. Gerrish, "Justification," in *The Westminster Dictionary of Christian Theology*, ed. A. Richardson and J. Bowden (Philadelphia: Westminster, 1983), 314–15; J. Macquarrie, *Principles of Christian Theology*, 2d ed. (New York: Scribner's, 1977), 342–43; and P. Hodgson and R. King, *Christian Theology* (Philadelphia: Fortress, 1985), 9, 230–31.

elusive subtlety to the doctrine. The topic is massive and here we can only attempt to suggest that it may have found a fresh relevance for many post-conciliar Catholics in view of an important shift in Catholic piety. This is not to deny that for many, especially those more concerned with the justification of God than of humans, the doctrine is hopelessly meaningless. On closer examination, however, even for these the doctrine grounds a much-needed anthropological corrective.

The Matrix of Luther's Problematic

To understand any doctrine one must find its location and function within the total teaching and life of a community.[2] The link between confessional statements or theology, on the one hand, and piety, on the other, is critical. For fifteen centuries Christian teaching and preaching did not focus on a doctrine of justification. Even for Paul it was not the organizing and governing principle of his writings.[3] When it did appear and became a bone of contention in the sixteenth century, it was an attempt to respond to specific developments and problems in the life of Christians. Although there appeared many doctrines of justification, one can more clearly than the others be singled out as the doctrine of justification, namely, Luther's, worked out between 1515 and 1520 and held to his dying day.[4] Luther maintained that as children of Adam we are in all our acts sinners. Striving for righteousness *coram Deo* through our acts, we are doomed to fail. Indeed, such striving itself embodies our sinfulness. God justifies the elect, forgives their sins and their sinfulness solely because of the righteousness of Christ.

2. Cf. J. McCue, "The *Sitz im Leben* of the Doctrine of Justification," *Clergy Review* 67 (1982); 269–74.

3. For a good survey of discussions of justification in recent scriptural studies, see J. Plevnik, "Recent Developments in the Discussion Concerning Justification by Faith," *Toronto Journal of Theology* 2 (1986): 47–62; *What Are They Saying About Paul* (New York: Paulist Press, 1986), ch. 4; above all, J. Reumann, *Righteousness in the New Testament* (Philadelphia: Fortress, 1982).

4. On the galaxy of approaches to the doctrine of justification, see A. McGrath, *Iustitia Dei: A History of the Christian Doctrine of Justification*, vol. 2 (Cambridge: Cambridge University Press, 1986).

Faith is grateful acceptance of God's forgiveness. Solely by God's forgiving grace received in faith are we justified.

Luther can appeal to the tradition, but he has introduced something novel. What is traditional in his teaching appears in a *scholion* of his 1515–1516 *Lectures on Romans*.[5] His doctrine cuts down all human wisdom and accomplishment, no matter how authentic or wonderful they may be, and makes clear the depth of human sinfulness, however unconscious of it humans may be. Luther can cite Augustine, who reminds us that Paul was at war with those who were filled with presumptuous and arrogant pride in their good deeds.[6] In agreement with Augustine's reading of Romans, and in agreement with many, though not all, medieval theologians, Luther teaches the classical doctrine of original sin. All are born marked with the inherent guilt, corruption, and waywardness of Adam. Election, grace, and salvation are sheerly gratuitous. But Luther's reading of Romans moves beyond Augustine and introduces something new, and of import for our own time. Luther was theologizing within a matrix almost nonexistent in Augustine's day and only embryonic in Thomas's time. Augustine had thought it possible with grace to do good works. For Luther, this slighted the complexity of the matter. The grace of forgiveness does change the fabric of one's existence and agency. Yet in each and every phase of life the human being stands in need of continual forgiveness. This line of thought is not clearly found in Paul. Augustine thought that Christians sin often and inevitably, and these sins, if strictly judged, would merit condemnation, even though we might consider them inconsequential. But the thought is marginal in Augustine, who seems not to have waxed anxious about finding a gracious God, and it never clearly feeds into the mainstream of his thinking. Luther was to tap into this line of thought left unpursued in Augustine. Indeed, it was to become the life-source of all his theologizing.

---

5. M. Luther, *D. Martin Luthers Werke: Kritische Gesamtausgabe* (Weimar: H. Böhlan, 1883–) 56:157. 1–5. (hereafter *WA*).
   6. *WA* 56: 157. 6–7.

To better grasp this move by Luther, one must attend to the changes occurring in the everyday life of the Church in the thousand years separating the bishop of Hippo and the Wittenberg lecturer. There was in Augustine's time, except for very serious sins punished by extended banishment from the Eucharistic table, no fully developed penitential rite. Augustine was well aware that Christians sin repeatedly. But those who prayed the Lord's prayer could be sure of forgiveness, if they were themselves forgiving persons. Counting up and confessing one's sins were not conditions of forgiveness; nor were any other particular acts, aside from that of forgiving others, which looms large in Augustine's homilies. These were simpler times, not prone to introspection and anxiety over sin.[7]

Time changes all, however—even the Catholic tradition. By the sixteenth century the situation is vastly different and its characteristics were to perdure into the Roman Catholicism of only a generation ago. A full-blown penitential rite had emerged over the centuries.[8] Now one must specify and tally one's serious sins, repent, at least out of fear of hell, confess to a priest, receive absolution, and carry out the prescribed penance. Self-scrutiny and self-judgment by everyone for everyday sins are the order of the day. A line cleanly separates being in the state of grace from being in a state of sin. This penitential process had achieved maturation by the mid-thirteenth century and with it entered a new legalism, an individualistic conception of sin, and, hard on their heels, anxiety.[9] From the dawning of the fourteenth century the scrupulous conscience

7. "Those listening to Augustine's sermons are never invited to plumb the depth of their consciences to recognize their own sinfulness. . . . The focus is not on what are one's own sins, but on the forgiveness to be given to others. For the ordinary Christian . . . detailed examination of conscience in search of sins would have been purposeless." J. McCue, *"Simul Iustus et Peccator* in Augustine, Aquinas, and Luther: Toward Putting the Debate in Context," *Journal of the American Academy of Religion* 48 (1980): 84.

8. Cf. B. Poschmann, *Penance and Anointing of the Sick* (New York: Herder & Herder, 1964); T. Tentler, *Sin and Confession on the Eve of the Reformation* (Princeton: Princeton University Press, 1977); J. Dallen, *The Reconciling Community* (Collegeville: Liturgical Press, 1986); K. Osborne, *Reconciliation and Justification* (New York: Paulist Press, 1989).

9. Cf. J. McCue, "Luther and the Problem of Popular Preaching," *Sixteenth Century Journal* 16 (1985): 33–43.

becomes a common phenomenon.[10] How can one be sure one had done everything required for forgiveness? Late Scholasticism tinkered with the system to make it more liveable. If an earlier stress on contrition was too demanding and left many enervated and unsure, it could be replaced by attritionism. Difficult ethical imperatives could be softened by casuistic interpretation that nurtured hope of fulfillment, though this opened a door to minimalism, often the bedfellow of legalism; the finer the net, the more the holes. Confessors' manuals could thus leave the impression that sinlessness is indeed possible and should be strived for. Though the effort called for grace, according to the Augustinians, many embraced a neo-semi-Pelagianism.[11] Forgiveness and a right relationship with God now appear mediated by the clear conscience.

By 1515 Luther had come to sense that Augustine's dialectical view of every Christian's life as sinful/sinless, reflected in liturgical prayer, had been nudged into oblivion by the theology and penitential practice of the day. Now it was held that Christians could perform acts of unalloyed good and clearly distinguishable from sin. Indeed, such acts were requisite for salvation. This was the situation Luther addressed in retrieving and moving beyond Augustine. His concern was not so much the source of any good act, grace, or the human will, but more the insight that at the end of the day even the best of Christians has absolutely nothing to fall back on but merciful divine scrutiny. The Pharisee in the parable of the Publican and the Pharisee (Luke 18:9–14) speaks much like a Scholastic Augustinian contemporary of Luther. Loudly he thanks *God* that he is not as certain others. Even if Luther had not yet elaborated his position on justification, the key ingredients were already

10. After the dawning of the fourteenth century, more detailed instructions for dealing with the scrupulous conscience begin to appear in the *Summae confessorum*. The early classics of this genre, appearing in the thirteenth century, do not treat of scrupulosity. This development in the piety of the late Middle Ages indicates that dread and despair were seeping into Catholic consciousness as people wrestled with uncertainty over their salvation due to the impossibility of ever knowing that one was properly repenting and being freed of one's sins.

11. Cf. D. Janz, *Luther and Late Medieval Thomism: A Study in Theological Anthropology* (Waterloo: Wilfrid Laurier University, 1983).

there: forensic or external justification, grace primarily as forgiveness, not empowerment, the *simul, sola fide, sola gratia*.[12]
The *simul peccator et iustus* was to cudgel the self-righteous who
think their lives can bear up under divine scrutiny.

What was novel in Luther's position? Though the penitential,
confessional piety might conduce to smug self-righteousness, it
seems more often to have led to despair and scrupulosity, tor-
tured as people were by uncertainty concerning their fulfillment of the conditions for salvation.[13] Luther himself drank the
dregs of despair. Ignatius Loyola saw such anxiety a temptation
commonly afflicting sincere Christians[14] and it almost pushed
Ignatius himself to suicide after he began to take Christianity
seriously. Two centuries later, Alphonsus de Liguori was to open
his classic, *Theologia Moralis*, with *De Conscientia Scrupulosa*. In
pre-Reformation days a common enough argument for the
divine institution of penance as a sacrament was that no mere
human could levy such a harrowing onus.[15] Nor could the onus
be lifted merely by falling back on the Augustinian teaching on
grace. Luther himself experienced all this. Between 1515 and
1519 or 1520 he came to see that his assertion that *all* human
deeds are contaminated by egoism, while a broadside against
the proud and self-righteous, was at the same time, paradoxically, a solace to those wracked by despair over the impossibility of the requisites of genuine repentance. Full repentance,

12. *WA* 56:272, 17.

13. McCue finds an example of the torture in Matthew of Cracow (late fourteenth–early fifteenth century): "Wicked thoughts that have been sought and accepted with pleasure are all to be explained (in confession) so far as one can; how
many, how long, how often. But no matter how bad one's thoughts, if not pur-
posely sought, if not accepted with pleasure, if not persevered in for a while in
the heart; and if you have not given rise to them by intemperate eating or drink-
ing; if they came suddenly and just as suddenly disappear, if you have been dis-
pleased by them, if as soon as you are aware of them you drove them out or tried
to by busying yourself in meditation or reading, then such thoughts are not to be
confessed, because not only does one not offend by them, but one merits greatly
for one's struggle and victory." Matthew goes on: those who do confess such
thoughts may commit a sin of vainglory, showing the confessor how advanced
they are. See "Luther and the Problem of Popular Preaching," 36.

14. *The Spiritual Exercises of St. Ignatius*, trans. L. Puhl (Chicago: Loyola University Press, 1951), §§ 315, 345–51; Ignacio de Loyola, *St. Ignatius' Own Story*
(Chicago: H. Regnery Press, 1956).

15. T. Tentler, *Sin and Confession*, 69.

plumbing the depths of one's sinfulness, is neither possible nor necessary for salvation. Forgiveness does not depend on a checklist of conditions fulfilled. Examining our lives without self-deceit, we see that we are forever falling short of what God asks, and that this, far from being a mere foible, is symptomatic of our real sinfulness. Yet God's forgiveness does not ride on anything other than God's graciousness. Forgiveness is needed not just for the past, but for the future as well because of our abiding sinfulness. Acceptance of the forgiveness of God because of Christ, which is mediated through God's word of pardon and sacraments, is faith. One can and must trust in God's word of pardon no matter how overwhelmingly negative the dark underside of one's sinfulness.

What is to be said to those beyond the Lutheran pale who stress the need for growth in sanctification, and hence think Luther's position misguiding, if not antinomian? Simply this. Luther was well aware that not all could hear and find meaningful the doctrine of justification by faith.[16] It will strike a resounding chord only in hearts that take the law of God seriously, struggle to meet its demands, and become mired in their own moral impotence. Untimely ripped from the price exacted by the law, *sola fide* is antinomian. Law as well as gospel forms the content of preaching, and the former is antecedent to the latter. More than a doctrine in a theological system, forensic justification by faith through grace is the proclamation of the gospel. Proclamation of justification by faith presupposes Christian life is seriously engaged, that there is growth. Luther knew well that what is the heralding of the gospel for one group might well be an inducement to sin for another, indeed for most, according to the *Third Antinomian Disputation*.[17] What

16. See, e.g., WA 1:571.10–572.15; 574.5–11. Cf. J. McCue, "Luther and the Problem of Popular Preaching."
17. Luther had no illusions about his Christian contemporaries. In remarkably straightforward ways his message often enough was: disobey the law and you will be damned; obey and you will be saved. His message sounded much like what was resounding from Roman Catholic pulpits. His first task was to get people to take the law seriously, to strive to obey it, which will beget its own problems, the solution to which is the good news of justification by faith. See, e.g., WA 30/1:58.10–11; 66.9–11 and 16–18; 68.20–69.2; 75.19–21; 47:763.3–765.7; 1:571.10–572.15; and 574.5–11.

Luther rejects is the naive optimism that thinks a Christian can arrive at a point where he or she is no longer in need of forgiveness and that final judgment is the lavishing of rewards on our achievements. Some, like Calvin, may insist that the work of grace in us does not cease with our justification, but is at work throughout the long process of sanctification as it moves to its end. God alone can bring to fulfillment what God has begun. Luther nuances this by contending that there is a beginning in every new now; justification is ever the condition of the possibility of any movement in sanctification. As Melanchthon said, it may be possible to be a better Christian today than yesterday, but if one considers oneself better, one would be a worse one.[18] Preoccupation with growth easily becomes preoccupation with self. But one is forever in need of divine acceptance and forgiveness. Only when reassured on the basis of justification by grace alone can one ward off despair and sustain the effort to meet the radicality of God's impossible expectations that are new each day.

A Failed Compromise

If Christianity did not self-destruct for a millennium and a half without this doctrine of justification by faith, and if the *Sitz im Leben* of its emergence, the terrified conscience of the confessional piety of late medieval Catholicism, all but vanished a generation ago, can the churches now do without this doctrine?

Generally, Roman Catholic theology did not take kindly to the doctrine of justification by faith until recently, and perhaps in some ways Catholic piety and practice have made this new openness possible. Despite the *lex orandi lex credendi* axiom, the gap between Catholic theology and Catholic piety had over centuries widened.[19] The captivating debate over the notion of

18. *Corpus Reformatorum*, ed. K. G. Bretschneider and H. E. Bindseil (Brunsvigae: C. Schwetschke et Filius, 1834–1860), 26, 9.

19. For example, C. La Cugna, in *God For Us: The Trinity and Christian Life* (San Francisco: Harper-Collins, 1991), shows the widening gap between Trinitarian theology and Catholic piety in the years following the Nicene resolution of the

double justification at the Council of Trent makes all this clearer. A most significant statement in the seventh chapter of Trent's decree on justification concerns the *single* formal cause (*unica formalis causa*) of our justification. It was a deliberate attempt to silence any opinion introducing more than one formal cause of a twofold justification. The contention that there was more than one formal cause was especially associated with Girolamo Seripando, general of the Augustinians.[20] Despite the lack of any explicit reference to it, the possibility that a *iustitia aliena imputata* might be a contributing cause of justification was effectively rejected by the decree. According to Trent, each one receives his or her own justice in the measure meted out by the Spirit, who gives to each as the Spirit wishes and in accord with the cooperative disposition of each. Into the hearts of the justified the love of God is poured, and they are engrafted into Christ.[21] The conviction that the phrase "formal cause of justification" was meant to convey appears with greater frequency than the phrase itself. This was the conviction that justification entails a real, interior transformation in and of the subject. What makes the just to be just, each in his or her own distinctive way, is a created justice distinct from that of God and Christ, an inner renewal or change dependent on union with Christ in his Spirit. This inner righteousness, given to the just as their own and as the formal cause of their justification, they "may bear before the tribunal of our Lord Jesus Christ and have eternal life." Thus eternal life can be merited because of the goodness of good works.[22] Thus, too, a situ-

---

Arian crisis with the end result that the Trinitarian dimension of Christian life was generally without influence in Catholic spirituality. Michael Buckley, in *At the Origins of Modern Atheism* (New Haven: Yale University Press, 1990), argues that in the sixteenth century Lessius tore the question of God from its roots in Catholic theology and in piety and, with ultimately disastrous consequences, handed it over to the philosophers. My own reading of this complex and debated issue is that this uprooting began long before Lessius, in the Nicene area, and is already reflected in Aquinas's sundering of *De Deo Uno* and *De Deo Trino*. Lessius and theologians after him mark the end of a long trajectory.

20. On Seripando, see H. Jedin, *Papal Legate at the Council of Trent: Cardinal Seripando* (St. Louis: Herder, 1947). The translation is not always reliable.

21. H. Denzinger and A. Schönmetzer, *Enchiridion Symbolorum*, 32d ed. (Freiburg im Breisgau: Herder, 1963) 1529 (hereafter DS).

22. DS 1531, 1582, 1548, 1545.

ation seems to be envisioned that is contrary to the one envis-
aged by Luther in his *Against Latomus*. There the renewal of the
just, marvel though it be, is deficient and they stand ever in
need before God's tribunal. Here in chapter seven of the decree
it appears that they do not. All the irritation festering in the
"habitus" language surfaces again with a vengeance.

To understand how the adjective *unica* made its way into the
decree, one has to look more closely at the lively debate over
the notion of a double justice championed by Seripando.[23] The
notion achieved prominence at the Regensburg Colloquy in
spring 1541. This effort at a Catholic-Protestant rapprochement
forged a far-reaching consensus, even on justification, that was
rejected by Rome and Luther. Martin Bucer and the Catholic
theologian Johann Gropper had arrived at a compromise description of justification (Article V), one claiming the authority
of Augustine and intertwining the Protestant idea of imputed
justice and the Catholic idea of inherent justice or infusion of
caritas.[24] We cannot, it was agreed, wholly rely on an inherent
but imperfect righteousness; ultimately, assurance lies only in
the imputed righteousness of Christ's merits and in the promise
of God. Rome found this view ambiguous and unacceptable;
Luther spurned this "gluing together," as he called it. Yet the
Regensburg formula or some variant of it won the support of
such major Catholic theologians as Cajetan, Catharinus, Pflug,
and Pighi, as well as the support of the Venetian diplomat and
lay cardinal, Gasparo Contarini, and the English cardinal, Regi-
nald Pole.[25]

On 8 October 1546, Seripando, addressing the Council a
third time and citing Gropper and Contarini, stated that the
"question is whether we who have been justified and are con-

23. Cf. J. McCue, "Double Justification at the Council of Trent: Piety and Theology in 16th Century Roman Catholicism," in *Piety, Politics, and Ethics*, ed. C.
Lindberg (Kirksville: Sixteenth Century Journal, 1984), 39–56. The notion of
double justice is found embryonically in a 1519 sermon of Luther, "De duplici
iustitia," *WA* 2:145–52.
24. *Concilium Tridentinum*, ed. Societas Goerresiana (Freiburg im Breisgau:
Herder, 1911), 5:487 (hereafter *CT*). See H. Jedin, *A History of the Council of Trent*
(St. Louis: Herder, 1957), 2:168–69; 200–201; 257–58.
25. On Pole, see D. Fenlon, *Heresy and Obedience in Tridentine Italy: Cardinal
Pole and the Counter-Reformation* (Cambridge: Cambridge University Press, 1972).

sequently to be glorified . . . are to be judged before the divine tribunal by one justice alone . . . the justice of our works proceeding from God's grace in us or by a twofold justice, our own, first, and secondly, the justice of Christ fulfilling . . . the imperfection of our own justice."[26] Leaving room for an inherent justice, Seripando suggested that in the end, the chief cause of justification is Christ's justice imputed to us. Inherent justice depends on imputed justice as its cause. What led to the demise of the irenic double-justice proposal after rigorous debate was its opponents' belief that the inherent justice of the justified was being tagged as inadequate over the long haul and in need of supplementation by another subsequent, inherent justice, though Seripando had never claimed that. The question of double justice thus came to be construed as a question of double justification and identical to the question whether justification has a twofold formal cause. A vote on 9 December marked the definitive rejection of *duplex iustitia*.[27] To most it was a viewpoint with no past and they were not of a mind to provide it with a future.

Asserting that one is really, if inchoately, justified in this life, while adding that at death one is in need of appealing to the justice of Christ to cover the imperfection of one's justice, appeared to undermine Catholic realism concerning justification, though the Council never separated the justice of the just from the justice of Christ. Moreover, *iustitia imputata* (a term Seripando rarely used) was a novelty, unknown to the Catholic theological tradition.[28] In view of the real renovation effected by justification, it appeared superfluous. So it was that on 11 December 1546, the decree was amended to read: "The sole [*unica*] formal cause of justification is that justice of God not whereby he himself is just, but whereby he makes us just *coram ipso*."[29] This view captured and has held the field into our own time. Justification is at once acquittal and a making righteous in the full ethical sense; it is both relational and behavioral renewal, all due to a single formal cause.

26. *CT*, 5:486 and 821. See also Jedin, *Papal Legate*, 348ff.
27. *CT*, 5:666–76, 691. Jedin, *A History of the Council of Trent*, 2:286–87.
28. Cf. *CT*, 5:564.38–39; 569.8; 579.5–6.
29. *CT*, 5:700.

Perhaps we can salvage the insight contained in the notion of double justice in this way. Trent rejected a double judgment, one a declaration of righteousness for sinners *in via*, the other, an eschatological judgment at the end of life or history. Rather, the initial transforming declaration already carries within it the seeds of eschatological reality. When God accepts sinners, God accepts them definitively, though they can still turn from God. The one perduring sentence of merciful forgiveness creative of inherent justice and counting it worthy of eternal life is pronounced from start to finish of any Christian's life. If this is so, Trent's position on inherent righteousness as the *unica formalis causa* of justification is compatible with Luther's mini-drama in *Against Latomus.*[30] Inherent righteousness is the effect, not the cause, of the divine declaration that a sinner is now just. Real as it is, the justified cannot boast of their justice or rely upon it *coram Deo* as absolute perfection, achievement, or possession. Trent did reject a twofold justification with a double formal cause; it did not formally condemn Seripando's view on a *duplex iustitia.*[31]

A Tension Between Theology and Piety

Though Seripando could not carry the day, the debate on his proposal lays bare a critical tension in sixteenth-century Catholicism, a tension between piety and theology. Seripando's position bore within it a protest against the way in which Catholic theology in the West had been done for four centuries. Theology had torn loose from its mooring in experience and hence had difficulty giving voice to the actualities of Christian life. The term *duplex iustitia* was of little concern to Seripando, nor whether the Council spoke of a single or of a double justice. In a short work, written in the heat of the 1546 debate, he was able to lay out his position without resorting to the expression "double justification."[32] Two things, however, were cru-

---

30. *WA* 8:43–128.
31. See P. Pas, "La doctrine de la double justice au Concile du Trent," *Ephemerides Theologicae Lovanienses* 30 (1954) 5–53.
32. *CT,* 5:486.32–35; 12:613–36.

cial to him: 1) Christian life involves a transforming gift given because of Christ and it must translate into good works; 2) no matter how "good" our works, we must always and continually rely on God's forgiveness, for even the best acts of the best men and women fall short of what God requires. These are traditional concerns, voiced by Augustine and classical monastic writers and woven into the liturgy.[33] Catholics thought Lutherans had jettisoned the first concern; Lutherans thought Catholics has jettisoned the second.

Seripando was saying that justification is too important to be left to theologians. "The doctrine of justification should be open, clear, easy, so that those for whom Christ died might not be repelled from it by difficulties." Though he thought highly of Thomas, Seripando cited him but once, and aside from citing Cajetan, he invoked no author later than Bernard of Clairvaux. Seripando steered clear of the human wisdom of technical theology. Instead of turning to the great Scholastics for light, one should, he thought, seek guidance on this issue from great sinners who experienced God's justifying grace: David, Paul, Augustine. What experience taught them was that our good works are "*quasi pannus menstruatae*" (Isa. 64:6, Vulg.). Only the justice of Christ is full and true. None of our works is good enough in God's eyes to win salvation. If we ask, "On what basis is the Christian justified before God's tribunal, by works or by the justice of Christ given through God's grace?" the answer has to be that "we are made just not by our own justice [*iustitia propria*] but by the justice of God in Christ communicated to us, for before the divine tribunal truly our justices are *quasi pannus menstruatae*." This use of Isaiah 64:6 to label the works of even the justified traces back to John Cassian and to medieval writers who used it in similar fashion.[34] We need the justice of Christ, said Seripando in his 8 October address, "not in the sense that it informs or assists us," but in the sense that "it is given to us through the sacraments that it

33. J. McCue, "Double Justification," 40.

34. John Cassian, *Conferences of the Fathers*, trans. E. Gibson, in *A Select Library of the Nicene and Post-Nicene Fathers of the Christian Church*, ed. P. Schaff and H. Wall (Grand Rapids: Eerdmans, 1978), 23, 4 and 17; pp. 521, 529–30.

might count in our favor, might make up for our shortcomings. It is like what we do for the dead; these things are said to belong to them because by the power of our charity they count in their favor."[35]

To Seripando this was Augustinian orthodoxy, but more important, it was the only proper stance of a Christian *coram Deo*. Traditional and correct piety was, he thought, endangered. That piety knew its own paradox, for it insisted at once on the necessity of good works and on their insufficiency in meeting divine scrutiny. No matter the breadth and depth of one's good works, one will stand in need of mercy at the judgment. Yet not only then. One's entire life, though energized by grace, must at every step be accompanied by that merciful forgiveness. The issue was not speculative and academic, but practical, Seripando told the Council fathers in his address. Each one must envision himself before the divine judge and consider whether he wishes to be judged exclusively on the basis of his works. One could hear echoes of Luther claiming that experience alone makes theologians, a claim that was to resound again in Schleiermacher. According to the latter, one who had not experienced would not understand.

Seripando's most important Council intervention came on 26 and 27 November. In an impassioned and deeply religious address he asked: "Should those soon to die trust in only one justice, that of works deriving from grace, or in a double justice, of works born of grace and the justice of Christ, his passion, merit, satisfaction?" Trust in a double justice is not to occur only at death and judgment, but throughout the course of life. There may be some (certainly there was one) so perfect that they need not be judged with merciful pardon. But this issue concerns the real, what is, not the possible (*de possibili*), what might be; it concerns the vast majority, not the exception, said Seripando. Theologians should not overlook their experience in the interest of their theories (*et non dimitteretur sensus propter intellectum*). Let each theologian speak of himself, play his own drum and not someone else's.[36] This *ad hominem* attack puts the finger on

35. *CT*, 5:486.29–487.33.
36. *CT*, 5:668.29–33.

the schizoid character of late Scholasticism. Theology and experience had been locked in separate compartments. Seripando theologizes out of lived experience. The quarrel over double justice is rooted in the question of the relationship between experience and theology. Most were blind to this. While maintaining that inherent, transforming justice is a necessary condition for salvation, Seripando also insisted that in the end, it is insufficient and cannot be the basis of our trust. Our basic trust must rest on God's forgiveness because of Christ.

Seripando's argument is two-pronged. First, it is dubious that any of our works is what it should be. God's judgment is not ours. We do not do all the good we should and the good we do is alloyed with sin. In approaching the Eucharist we may doubt whether we receive grace; not that God's mercy is questionable, but our performance is. With reason we flee to divine mercy, which will accept us because of Christ's perfect justice. The two justices are very different. To the question, what are we to rely on as we stand before God, the answer is not, partly on each justice. Though our inherent justice is a *sine qua non*, we ultimately trust in divine mercy. Good works we must do, but ultimately we rely not on them but on God's forgiveness for salvation. Secondly, there is the *lex orandi*. The Church teaches trust in a twofold justice, for while it teaches the righteousness of grace-animated actions, it also teaches the need for the justice of Christ if liberation from sin is to be real. In her prayer the Church begs for freedom from sin and death "not through inherent grace, not through works done in grace, but through the justice of Christ."[37]

Seripando thought it better strategy to counter Lutherans by playing down works while preaching the grace of God. "What can slay them is this: that daily we abound more in good works, yet praise only God's grace and mercy." As for those who put greater stock in works and cited Augustine to the effect that the law can, with grace, be fulfilled, Seripando again appealed to them to consider their experience. Who at death will claim that he or she has fulfilled the law? Who will be able to say with Ezekiel: "I have walked before thee with a perfect

37. *CT*, 5:670.14–16 and 42–46.

heart" (Isa. 38:3, *sic*). Rather, will we not cry with David: "Do not enter into judgment with your servant, Lord" (Ps. 143:2)? We ought to pray as the church does for the dead who it thinks died in grace: "Do not enter into judgment with your servant, Lord, for before you no one will be justified unless given through you forgiveness of all his sins."[38] Seripando is not concerned with providing an elaborate theology of justification. Against what he takes the Reformers to be saying, he affirms the necessity of good works; against Scholastic theologians, the necessity, even for the just, of relying ultimately on God's merciful acceptance. Grace effects a real change in us. Yet we do not love wisely or well. However good our lives and loves appear to us, we must in every moment and at judgment throw ourselves into the arms of divine mercy.

The Augustinian general did not stand alone. Gregory of Padua, an Augustinian and a theological adviser at the Council, argued the same view syllogistically. If one justified by grace does good works by that same grace, fulfills the law, and perseveres, he or she will merit heaven. Here is a summary proposition. But who can supply a minor for this major? Who can say, "But I am such a one!"? Who is so sure of his or her deeds that he or she can say: "All you commanded, Lord, I have done since my youth!" Do not all fall daily? Even a saint would not provide the minor and say, "I am that just one!" Gregory also appealed to the canon of the Mass, where we turn not to our merit but to God's mercy: "To us also, sinners, . . . trusting in the multitude of your mercies, grant . . . fellowship with your holy apostles . . . into whose company we pray you admit us, not weighing our merits but freely granting us forgiveness."[39] There is no ground on which we may worthily stand before God except in Christ, who did for us what we cannot do for ourselves. Nevertheless, it seems that several fathers at Trent offered themselves as the minor Gregory sought. One opponent of Seripando even claimed he would indeed go to the final judgment fully confident in his good works.[40]

38. *CT*, 5:663.2; 673.11–29.
39. *CT*, 5:580.1–15 and 47–50.
40. *CT*, 5:569.29–570.5; 552.30–48; 630.19–40.

Lorenzo Mazocchi and Stephen of Sestino also sided with Seripando. Stephen's address returns to the underlying issue. "Let us not speak of abstractions, nor square the circle with logic. Rather, let us speak of what each of us experiences in himself." And what is that? "There is in the justified . . . however much they live in grace, an ongoing struggle against evil. . . . You know our infirmity . . . do not posit a human being cured in every way, justified in every respect, but rather one infirm . . . and carnal."[41]

In the end, however, the proponents of double justice could not muster support. The opposition, led especially by the Spanish Jesuit Diego Laynez,[42] without formal repudiation of Seripando's position preferred a more familiar Augustinian Scholasticism that undercut the presuppositions of double justice. Two clinching arguments told against double justice: it seemed 1) to negate any serious consideration of merit and 2) to dissolve the realism of inherent justice. Moreover, how could it be squared with purgatory and a many-mansioned heaven? Seripando considered the notion of merit traditional and hence quite legitimate, though he sought another language for it, one that would not lead Christians to think they command their due before God. He cited Bernard of Clairvaux, the medieval writer Luther most admired: as for merit, it suffices to know that merits do not suffice; just as for merit it suffices not to presume on merits, so also to be without merits suffices for judgment.[43] To be bereft of the merits of good deeds suffices for condemnation; on the other hand, good deeds cannot be clung to as claims upon God. Seripando was not alone in his severe approach to merit. Aquinas evidenced a similar austerity.[44]

Far from being just another dead end in the history of theology, the debate over double justice carries no little significance. Through it all, the opposition and wonderment that Seripando met was due to the fact that, like Luther, he was redefining, un-

41. *CT,* 5:609.14–20.
42. On Diego Laynez, cf. C. Maxcey, "Double Justice, Diego Laynez, and the Council of Trent," *Church History* 49 (1979): 269–78.
43. *CT,* 5:373.38–45; 374.15–18.
44. *Summa theologiae* I-II, q.114.

consciously, the nexus between piety and theology. He seems to have thought that herd Scholasticism encouraged a posture before God clearly out of touch with the long tradition of Christian experience.[45] Trent never discussed the nature and function of theology, nor could it. It was blind to the new theological paradigm struggling to be born. For that very reason the rogue Augustinian general's pleas shattered against a wall of incomprehension. Yet not only was there a tension between Catholic consciousness or piety and theology; there were also tensions within Catholic piety and practice. Much piety of the day was irreconcilable with Seripando's theology. And the Scholastic theologies he beat vainly against were felt by many to legitimate and be legitimated by practices that Lutherans considered works-righteousness.[46] Implicit in Seripando's arguments was a critique of attitudes and practices common among Catholics. Trent wanted Church reform, but reform insufficiently radical to accommodate the deeply felt concerns of this prince of the Church.

The Search for a *Via Media* or a *Via Nova*

The issue was to surface again in John Henry Newman's *Lectures on the Doctrine of Justification*, published in 1838.[47] In thirteen lectures delivered at Oxford in 1837 and a long technical appendix which takes up the question of the formal cause of justification, Newman attempts to bridge Roman Catholic and Anglican views. Newman's approach rests upon an analysis of the doctrine of justification associated with Luther, with Catholic theologians such as Bellarmine and Vásquez, and with

45. For another instance of a Counter-Reformation gap between theology and piety, one concerning the question of God in the seventeenth century, cf. Buckley, *At the Origins of Modern Atheism*, esp. 341–63. Buckley underscores the fact that there is an iron logic whereby theological ideas are not without consequences, often unforeseen and unwelcome when they materialize.

46. See, e.g., J. McCue, "Luther and Roman Catholicism on the Mass as Sacrifice," *Journal of Ecumenical Studies* 2 (1965): 45–74.

47. J. H. Newman, *Lectures on the Doctrine of Justification*, 8th impr. (London: Longmans, Green, 1900). See also H. Chadwick, "Justification by Faith: A Perspective," *One in Christ* 20 (1984): 191–225.

the Caroline divines. In the work's third edition, appearing in 1874, after his crossover to Catholicism, Newman asserts: "Unless the author held in substance in 1874 what he published in 1838, he would not at this time be reprinting what he wrote as an Anglican."[48] In this third edition Newman realigns only his position on the formal cause of justification to render it acceptable within Roman Catholicism. Newman the Anglican understood well in 1838 the concession made and the *via media* formula adopted by Contarini, head of the Catholic delegation at the Colloquy of Regensburg, and fought for at Trent by Seripando and Pole.

Newman identifies four main positions on the formal cause of justification: we are justified 1) by the holiness and works wrought in us *through* Christ's merits by the Spirit; 2) by our holiness and works sanctified and completed by Christ's merits; 3) by our faith, which is mercifully taken as the substitute for perfect holiness and thus becomes the acceptable mediating principle between us and God; and 4) by Christ's merits and righteousness imputed to us as our own and made the immediate cause of justification superseding all else in the eyes of God. The first is the high-Roman view, the fourth, the high-Protestant view, and the second and third are intermediate views of high-church Anglicans, resembling the views of Bucer, the Strasbourg reformer, and Pighi.[49] Newman knows there are still other views among Anglican evangelicals. Newman is, however, searching for a broad consensus between high Romanism and high Protestantism. For the former, justification is an inherent righteousness manifest through works springing from the grace of the Spirit in us; for the latter, justification is a faith awareness of the imputation of Christ's merits to us independently of our works.

For Newman, a broad ecumenical consensus that he thought included Roman Catholics, most Anglicans, and many Lutherans would be a *via media* holding that "justification comes *through* the sacraments, is received by faith, *consists* in

48. Newman, *Lectures*, ix.
49. Ibid., 348.

God's presence, and *lives* in obedience."[50] This ties in with the second and third views above, and, according to Newman, it is standard Anglican teaching, the position of Bucer, and of many Catholics. Moreover, it is, Newman thought, at least implicitly taught in the writings of Luther and Melanchthon, and it is the teaching of the Church Fathers. This central thesis is elaborated and analyzed at length in the *Lectures*, which Newman hoped would show little but verbal difference on justification among Catholic and Protestant divines.[51] Newman saw that our inherent righteousness must be supplemented as a formal cause by something he considered essential to the nature of justification, namely, "the cognate presence of Christ in our souls." This would dispel much Anglican criticism of Trent. After much bobbing and weaving to escape Trent's anathematization of a double formal cause, however, Newman finally relinquished his attempt to include the "presence of Christ in our souls" as part of the *unica formalis causa*. Nonetheless, he held to the indwelling of Christ and saw as its necessary and simultaneous consequences the believer's being *counted* righteous (justification) and being *made* righteous (sanctification).

Yet Newman's concerns over justification have rarely been a preoccupation of the mainstream of Catholic theology. Clearly the Catholic theological tradition has awarded an unambiguous primacy to grace, especially since the time of Augustine. But following the emergence of the theorem of the supernatural in the thirteenth century,[52] Catholic theology, if not Catholic piety, has seen grace primarily as *gratia elevans*, as empowerment for participation in the life of the triune God, as healing for the wounds of sin, *gratia sanans*, as well, but only secondarily (though simultaneously) as forgiveness. The concern of Luther, terrified and anxious hearts wrestling with sin and divine wrath and searching for a gracious God, was rarely the concern of the Catholic theological tradition. Luther's problem seems not, as

---

50. Ibid., 278.   51. Ibid., ix.

52. B. Lonergan, *Grace and Freedom*, ed. J. P. Burns (New York: Herder & Herder, 1971), ch. 1. S. Duffy, *The Dynamics of Grace: Perspectives in Theological Anthropology* (Collegeville: Liturgical-Glazier, 1993).

we have noted, to have been widely experienced by Christians in Augustine's day, or even in Thomas's.

Given this theoretical framework, Catholic practice marched off in several directions. Many could blithely engage in a quantitative works-piety leading to a mechanical increase of grace making one a "better" Christian. On the other hand, many could be overwhelmed by the demands of the law, anxious about their salvation, frantically in search of a reconciling God. Or again, others might maintain that the sinner is inherently changed by God's grace but also insist on the incompleteness of the change and hence on the need to rely ultimately on the righteousness of Christ and not on good works. Finally, some might minimize the demands of the law and insist on the solidity of one's own inherent righteousness due to grace so that not much else is required.

All these modalities were present in Catholic piety when Luther arrived on the scene: works-piety, scrupulosity, the modest piety of a Seripando, and the bold and confident reliance on one's inherent righteousness reflected in the bishops of Trent. The Catholic theology of justification did not inculcate works-righteousness, scrupulosity, or self-righteousness. It developed and went its way without an eye to these aberrations of piety as they emerged. Some Protestants, often crediting Catholics with linking their theology, preaching, and piety more closely than is factually so, might tend to attribute to the Catholic theology of justification a causative role in regard to these aberrations. The charge is, however, incomprehensible to Catholic theologians, who see themselves teaching the priority of grace, not works-righteousness, though they may fail to see that their theology may not sufficiently take into account the experience of Catholics.

Many Catholics today, as did many in the Reformation era, sense that their lives, try as they may, are not as Christian as they should be and will not withstand scrutiny. Hence they sense a need for ongoing forgiveness: forgiveness of *sin*, so that divine judgment, yet acceptance, despite persistence in the strategies of sin, stands in the foreground; and *forgiveness* of sin, so that experience of divine mercy is the central reality. Perhaps this experience has been better reflected by spiritual writers than theologians. Perhaps, too, the experience of many Catholics has changed while the Catholic theology of justification has not undergone a critical rearticulation that thematizes the changes in Catholic consciousness. The matrix in which Luther's problematic arose, a legalistic confessional practice and theory that terrified consciences, has dissolved. Without fanfare, private confession and the social control it made possible has, for a host of reasons, all but vanished, a situation fraught with implications yet unregistered. One implication is that, while many Catholics have, like so many of their contemporaries, lost all sense of sin, among many other Catholics there is a new consciousness concerning sin, forgiveness, and hence justification, one closer to Seripando's, and even to Luther's. For this latter group, legalism has declined and growth in Christian life is no longer measured by an accumulation of meritorious deeds.

One of the assertions for which Luther was excommunicated contended that one need not confess all one's mortal sins since it is impossible to be aware of them all.[53] Were one to reword this proposition to the effect that we cannot bring to the light of consciousness all our sins, or much more important, that we cannot plumb the depth of our sinfulness or name the loves that fire our hearts, and hence must continually throw ourselves on the merciful forgiveness of God rather than rely upon the thoroughness of our self-scrutiny and confession, one would probably be voicing the experience of many post-conciliar Catholics. They sense a tragic ambiguity pervading their lives and achievements and are little inclined to fall back on their "good works" or inherent goodness to set them right with their God. Augustine's dicta ring true: what is not of love is sin; there is sin when love is not what it ought to be or is less than it ought to be. Love, the infinite demand of the law, is never wholly meet to our métier. The once clear line between good and evil that made it possible to be sure one was in a state of sin or a state of grace blurs. Small wonder we shield our acts from others and even from ourselves. Seripando and many of

53. *Exsurge Domine*, n. 8, DS 1458.

his contemporaries had a similar feel for the ambiguity and tragedy that haunt human beings. The French poet Baudelaire might write in his *Journal*: "Theory of true civilization: it consists in erasing the effects of original sin."[54] But if so, Seripando and many contemporary Catholics might opine that true civilization does not and cannot exist as long as the greatest saint in our eyes must remain in the eyes of a holy God *simul iustus et peccator*. Acknowledgment of unconscious sin in the justified is a matter of staking out areas for grace to do its work until one attains "to the measure of the full stature of Christ" (Eph. 4:13). To think one's inherent righteousness and small victories are ever sufficient of themselves is a far greater legal fiction than forensic justification by faith. *Hamartia*, missing the mark, suffering the perduring shortfall, is our condition; so too is *agnoēma* (another New Testament word for sin), ignorance of what we ought to have known. Moreover, stress on conscious sin done with due deliberation and full consent to the neglect of unconscious sinfulness hampers recognition of corporate sin and collective guilt or trivializes it because full consent is lacking.[55] It is no kindness to lower the mark of the righteousness of the kingdom to the level of our own sinful righteousness. The *simul* is a far better kindness, inculcating patience with ourselves, compassion towards others, and trust in a prodigal Father who does not hold us under condemnation.

This reawakened sensitivity will hardly send Catholic theologians scurrying to redraft the Catholic theology of justification. It has never been crucial to Catholic theology, drawing attention only when, in ecumenical dialogue, Catholics are forced to define themselves vis-à-vis Lutherans. But perhaps this new sensitivity will deepen our appreciation of the *simul iustus et*

54. Cited by G. Tavard, "The Contemporary Relevance of Justification by Faith," *One in Christ* 21 (1985): 138.

55. Personal justification is not private; the social dimensions of justification by faith cannot be overlooked. See, e.g., R. Niebuhr, "The Relevance of Reformation Doctrine in Our Day," in *The Heritage of the Reformation*, ed. E. Arndt (New York: R. R. Smith, 1950), 249–64; C. Villa-Vincencio, "Protestantism, Modernity, and Justification by Faith," *Scottish Journal of Theology* 38 (1985): 369–82; R. Bertram, "Liberation by Faith: Segundo and Luther in Mutual Criticism," *Dialog* 27 (1988): 268–75; W. Werpehowski, "Justification and Justice in the Theology of Karl Barth," *Thomist* 50 (1986): 623–42; and J. Stumme, "Interpreting the Doctrine of the Two Kingdoms," *Dialog* 27 (1988): 277–84.

peccator, sharpen our awareness of the need at every step of the way for God's forgiveness in Christ, and prod us to confess that even having done all that we should and could, we are in the end unprofitable servants (Luke 17:10). Theological hypotheses and agreements have not been without their impact upon history and the pieties of Christian communities, but so too have shifts in the popular pieties of those communities served to shape theology. Luther's doctrine of justification by faith arose out of a build-up of tensions in Catholic piety in the immediately preceding centuries as he attempted to deal with a growing legalism that begot either complacency or despair. The shift in Catholic piety in the last three decades does not mean that we now find in Catholicism a *Doppelgänger* of sixteenth-century Lutheran piety. On the other hand, it may mean that because of this shift in Catholic piety, many Catholics might now read the Lutheran doctrine of justification and Seripando's double justice as articulations of their own experience. Perhaps the U.S. Lutheran-Catholic "Common Statement" admits as much when it states: "Our entire hope of justification and salvation rests on Christ Jesus and on the Gospel whereby the good news of God's merciful action in Christ is made known; we do not place our trust in anything other than God's promise and saving work in Christ." Ultimately, our reliance is not on our works, virtues, merits, and faith, even though God's grace is at work in them.

Nonetheless, Catholicism today still has little to say about justification. This, to some extent, is due to a perception of ecumenical convergence, but also to a reluctance to equate the gospel for all time with justification by faith. All formulations of the gospel are relative. Yet the Lutheran doctrine of justification by faith is a classic, because through it something perduring in divine-human relations comes into view. Still, no one formula should become the shibboleth of orthodoxy, and thus its profession a works-righteousness, a new, burdensome law, a false security. Not only historical relativity deabsolutizes justification by faith, but the Protestant principle itself does so as well; the critical principle begotten by the doctrine turns back against its parent.

Relativization of the doctrine, however, is one thing; indifference to it, something else altogether. Indifference to the doctrine has arisen because its sixteenth-century matrix and the question that tormented Luther are no longer comprehensible to most of us today. Mindless complacency is a far cry from the terrified conscience. As for those who may be terrified and anxious, what terrifies them today is not sin or divine judgment, but loss of security, sickness, aging, death. On the other hand, for those attuned to the subtleties and ambiguities that color their lives and troubled by the fact that their moral ideals forever outstrip their moral capacities, that "ought" and "can" are disproportioned, Luther and Seripando make eminent good sense, though this latter group finds itself at odds with the anthropology of the day. There are, indeed, subtleties surrounding this doctrine.

Life and theology change; not to recognize this is to attempt to stop the planets. Theologians who deposit all their coin with an era or a formula soon find themselves bankrupt. Paul Tillich was not far from the truth in his contention that justification by faith is not intelligible to people today, at least not to increasing numbers of them.[56] For that reason he tried to move beyond the *Confessio Augustana* and to translate justification by faith into a new, modern idiom. Tillich saw secularized twentieth-century consciousness bedeviled by an anxiety about meaninglessness. Anxiety about guilt may have been rampant in the sixteenth century, but no more. The introspective conscience of the West, articulated by Augustine, deepened by medieval penitential practice, and reformed by Luther, was secularized by Freud and psychotherapeutic practice. Few are the terrified consciences asking for a gracious God or seeking righteousness before a just God as they agonize over eternal damnation. The new, post-conciliar Catholic consciousness noted above is far from being the whole story. Many today feel worthless, because their lives and their world appear ultimately meaningless. But that is quite different from feeling guilty and

56. Cf. P. Tillich, *The Protestant Era* (Chicago: University of Chicago Press, 1948); *The Courage To Be* (New Haven: Yale University Press, 1952).

in need of forgiveness. The problem is uncertainty, hopeless-ness, despair, doubt about God and truth in the face of a dizzy-ing pluralism and relativism, and, we might add, in the face of massive public suffering and the specter of collective death, even after the end of the Cold War. Luther was able to face anxiety and despair over guilt only because of his realization that at a deeper level one is sustained by a basic confidence or faith in God's goodness. Similarly, for Tillich, one can face anx-iety and despair over meaninglessness only if one can some-how presuppose meaning.

Tillich attempted to move beyond Reformation thought in three ways. First, he recognized that today anxiety centers less on sin and more on meaninglessness. Secondly, he argued that just as Luther saw feelings of pervasive guilt and unforgivable-ness as signs of grace, so too hopelessness and despair find in grace their logically necessary presupposition. For Luther, the link was unnecessary, contingent upon God's free decision. God is under no necessity to rescue the despairing. Only God's revealing word tells us that God's grace works through des-pair. But for Tillich, meaninglessness necessarily presupposes meaning. Self-acceptance presupposes acceptance of one's un-conditional acceptance by something or someone, one may not know what.[57] Thirdly, Tillich maintained that justifying faith does not necessarily require a conscious recognition of God. Faith is preconceptual, the transcendent condition of the possi-bility of the courage to be in the face of despair and meaning-lessness.[58]

The Reformers did not think of faith as preconceptual (except perhaps for infants). It involves some kind of conscious refer-ence to the God of Jesus Christ. Thus justification by faith alone does not, in the teaching of the Reformers, argue that despair presupposes faith. Rather, it proclaims the good news that God

57. Tillich's psychotherapeutic analogue came to influence pastoral training in counseling and programs such as CPE, often enough, not without distortion into the placebo "I'm O.K., you're O.K." Too easily justification by grace could become justification by self-induced nice feelings and shallow decisions. Recall that Tillich saw the pietism of the *Schwärmerei* as a betrayal of the classic Reformation doc-trine; *Systematic Theology* II (Chicago: University of Chicago Press, 1957), 177ff.

58. *The Courage To Be*, 164ff.

freely and graciously forgives the unforgivable for Christ's sake. Yet the Reformers neither negate nor affirm Tillich's position; they never considered it. Theirs was not Tillich's matrix. Much of modern theology would argue that God's grace can and does work through despair and that we cannot restrict the gift of faith, basic trust, to those who are consciously Christians.

What Tillich did, then, was to transpose justification by faith from the ethical to the intellectual domain. Not only one in sin, but one in doubt is justified by faith. Doubt need not separate one from God; there is faith in every serious doubt, namely, faith in truth itself, even if the only truth we can express is our lack of truth. If this is expressed in depth and as ultimate concern, God is present and one is justified in one's thinking, in one's questions and doubts about meaning. And so Tillich's paradox: the one who denies God affirms God.[59] Tillich broadened and deepened the doctrine of justification by faith. Much influenced by German idealism, he addressed the question of meaninglessness by awareness of the paradoxical presence of meaning in meaninglessness; he pointed to the universal, unconditional presence of God within all dimensions of life and history without reduction to any particular cultural form. The sinner weighed down with guilt can grasp the good news of justification by faith only if he or she has struggled to measure up to the righteousness that the law demands; so too the doubter is obliged to measure up to the law of truth if he or she is to grasp the good news of justification. The sinner is shattered by the law of righteousness; the doubter, by the law of truth. The doubter is seized by the overwhelming power of the law of truth, yet, unable to meet its demands, sinks into doubt and despair. The sin of the doubter resides in an unwillingness to doubt one's own doubt, while seeking truth in the very doubting. The message of justification, according to Tillich, is a breakthrough, for it brings assurance that truth and meaning are not the goal but the presupposition of the doubt driving one to ultimate concern, much as righteousness and goodness are not so much the goal but the presupposition of the guilt driving one

59. *The Protestant Era*, xiv–xv.

to ultimate concern. In both cases, however, breakthrough and the way home come as a revelation, *sola gratia, sola fide*.

It is important to note that, for Tillich, the unconditional acceptance which justifies is not uncritical acceptance but involves judgment, as Tillich's approach to the Protestant principle makes clear. For a culture of narcissism, self-absolutizing and empty, demanding uncritical approval and permissiveness and viewing human relationships as a means to self-realization and fulfillment, justification by faith is utter nonsense. For Tillich, self-acceptance is not complacency, feeling good about oneself, but nonneurotic acceptance of oneself with one's sense of meaninglessness and guilt. No doubt, we should add that to avoid social Manichaeanism and the privatization of all of this, we must recognize that today the felt meaninglessness of history is, to a large extent, due to the horrors of massive public suffering. Sin is personal, but it is also communal and systemic, and individuals are captive to demonic forces outside themselves, such as socioeconomic and political principalities and powers. A shift in hamartiology effects in turn a shift in soteriology, rendering it more communal, cosmic, and futuristic, more concerned with the Kingdom and not merely with the guilt and anxiety of terrified and despairing individuals hungering for forgiveness and acceptance for themselves. Acceptance for the unacceptable is of concern, but now it is whole peoples who are in need of acceptance. Faith assumes a new modality. It is still trust in Christ for personal forgiveness, hope, and assurance of salvation, but is is also hope *propter Christum solum* for the future of humanity as we begin to fear not God, but ourselves.[60]

A Needed Anthropological Corrective

The new relevance of a doctrine of justification by faith in Catholic consciousness and the priority given to grace as empowerment and healing on the Catholic side and as forgiveness

---

60. See n. 55 on these themes.

and hope on the Protestant side provide us with a much-needed anthropological corrective. Post-Enlightenment anthropologies, marked by the turn to the subject, tend to emphasize the subject's autonomy and capacity for self-making. This emphasis, shared by third-world liberation theologies, raises important questions. Can modern anthropologies do full justice to the inherent goodness of human finitude and materiality and to the interdependence of human beings with one another and the physical world? With the emphasis on persons as actors, creators, authors of personal stories engaged in self-constitution by deliberate choices, are excessive claims made for human agency? Is there a need of grace if one's life is a narrative that one constructs as one will? Has human passivity been defined out of existence? There are severe liabilities in any anthropology that defines personhood in terms of freedom and agency while ignoring the limits of creatureliness and the radical vulnerability of humans to the facticities of internal and external nature and their communal history. To the extent that they portray human agency as immune to the nonvoluntary, to the impingements of other persons and the world around us and in us, modern anthropologies fail to give due weight to the sweeping interpenetration of human subjects and their physical and social worlds.[61]

Expressed more theologically, justification and sanctification are never purely achievements of human striving. The Christian tradition conveys the strong conviction that the transcendent goal of human destiny and the depth of human sin doom all efforts to fulfill any capacity for self-constitution to futility in the absence of God's grace. Grace is needed, however, not merely because the goal outstrips our paltry achievements and the wounds of sin leave us morally incapacitated, but also because we are finite, material entities, living on the edge of nothingness, dependent on God, and interlaced with the rest of creation. Not that humans must be redeemed from creatureliness, but that human dependence on others and on nature within

---

61. Cf. T. Allik, "Narrative Approaches to Human Personhood: Agency, Grace, and Innocent Suffering," *Philosophy and Theology* 1 (1987): 305–33.

and without cannot but affect our relationship with God. The need for grace, even in its appropriation, stems not only from human sinfulness but also from the limitations of humans as finite agents. We can never fully probe our motivations, never fully arrive at togetherness or wholeness through conscious, deliberate choices. Salvific self-appropriation is beyond the pale. The inability to constitute oneself in authoring a narrative is not merely the fallout of sinfulness; it is a perduring trait of creatureliness. Rahner, with his understanding of concupiscence as rooted in human materiality, is here a sure-footed guide.[62] The otherness of the given, the involuntary, the spontaneous, the possibility of moral tragedy, we have with us always. Neither virtue nor sin is ever wholly voluntary, for presence of the nonvoluntary in us makes commitment to any orientation to some extent nonvoluntary. One needs not only forgiveness, but also empowerment. Deliberate choice is not all. Any capacity for self-determination falls prey to destructive violence from within and without. The fragility of the human as self-constituting agent begs divine providential care. Hence our prayer: "Do not put us to the test, but deliver us from evil." Appropriation and maintenance of Christian narratives can only be a grace. And the dynamics of grace do not operate solely at the levels of conscious choice and deliberate action. The pervasiveness of sin, radicated in a preconscious matrix, must be met by a more powerful grace in the deepest depths of human being. Even then, character is never so definitively shaped that one cannot conceive of a situation where the nonvoluntary is so under control that a person will never engage in behavior inconsistent with her or his character. Vulnerability to the nonvoluntary is perduring. An anthropology that precludes conflict, dilemma, and tragedy plays well only in a Pollyanna world.

An anthropology, therefore, will be more adequate to the extent that it can dialectically take into account the labyrinthine interplay of action with passivity and suffering, the

62. K. Rahner, "The Theological Concept of Concupiscence," in *Theological Investigations* I (Baltimore: Helicon, 1961), 347–82. See also T. Allik, "Nature and Spirit: Agency and Concupiscence in Hauerwas and Rahner," *Journal of Religious Ethics* 15 (1987): 14–32.

voluntary with the involuntary, intentions and meanings with energies and forces, the deliberate with the spontaneous, the planned with the unexpected.[63] We are victims as well as agents, mere narrators as well as, or more than, authors. People are often scripted and contribute little to the creation of their story; they may even be unaware they have a story, and hence are unable to tell it. How vital it is to tell the stories of the depersonalized, the losers! The history of suffering wails out for narrative and redress. To the credit of the liberationists, they are telling the stories of history's victims. On the other hand, accrual of the benefits of a story is not wholly dependent on explicit, conscious reaping of the grace that comes through appropriation of one's story. A story's meaning and benefit do not derive solely from the subject's being captain of his or her soul, a free, self-constituting agent. Perhaps, too, inclusion and participation in the larger Christian story of creation, fall, and redemption do not always depend on deliberate agency and conscious awareness.

There is much to learn, then, from the anthropology of classical tragedy.[64] We are caught up in a situation, yet somehow accountable for it. There is a givenness to events, a facticity, yet a complicity too on our part. We are and we aren't responsible. Freudian psychoanalytic theory throws light on these dark corners of existence. Some evils of human existence are traceable to the unconscious in its sheer givenness and obduracy. We are always mortgaged to the past. Yet the unconscious is a tangled web of the historical as well as the "natural." Its story unfolds ineluctably, yet its facticity also bears the prints of personal complicity. Thus again the need for an anthropology of paradox and a dual language: the unconscious displays human activity and passivity, freedom and unfreedom, history and nature. An anthropology of ambiguity and mixed discourse

---

63. Most helpful are the insights of P. Ricoeur's *Freedom and Nature: The Voluntary and the Involuntary* (Evanston: Northwestern University Press, 1966), *Freud and Philosophy: An Essay on Interpretation* (New Haven: Yale University Press, 1970), and *Time and Narrative*, vol. 1 (Chicago: University of Chicago Press, 1984).

64. Cf. the illuminating insights of W. Lowe, *Evil and the Unconscious* (Chico: Scholars Press, 1983).

that is suspicious of crystal-clear distinctions between natural and moral evil is more adequate to experience and the dilemma of unconscious agency. What at first blush seems simply natural turns out to be moral; yet moral evil is part and parcel of the human predicament and summons up and is summoned by elements not of human choosing, hence is a natural evil. Not that the inherent limitations that finitude falls heir to are in themselves evil, sinful, or deterministically conducive to sin. But the limitations of finitude appear inextricably enmeshed as components of the natural evil in what is moral evil and shape the way in which sin embodies itself. Indeed, the enticement to consider finitude, as such, a natural evil is felt only when sin makes its entrance. It was the wisdom of the classical doctrine of original sin that it gave expression to this duality in human sinfulness. Modern anthropologies that neatly reduce human evil to moral evil and dissect it solely in terms of autonomous agency or that facilely reduce human evil to natural evil and dissolve it into a "second nature" beyond control are not true to experience and degenerate into moralism, fatalism, or even utopianism. Simplistic attempts to explain evil without remainder melt down both the mystery of iniquity and the anomaly of grace, so needed for making any sense of it.

Moreover, wrongheaded moralistic and idealistic anthropologies tend to view evil as the unavoidable fellow-traveler of choice and self-awareness. Leaving innocence, unactualized possibility, behind is the nonnegotiable price of progress on the journey to maturity. Inevitably, moral evil results when human agents confront their finitude, now considered a natural evil. The soothing moral imperative of growth and individuation is thought to justify moral evil, yet somehow reduces it to natural evil because of its inevitability as person confronts nature. Thus the distinction between moral and natural evil tends to vanish and the differences between innocence and sin are relativized as all human evil is instrumentalized and voided of its perversity in service of development of the self as an autonomous subject. One must bring good out of evil, but now one is hardly responsible for moral evil. Within the framework of a Christian anthropology, however, finitude is neither evil nor sinful, but a creative limit meant to orient and protect freedom rather than repress it.[65] Hence growth does not demand rebellion against finitude, or the vanquishing of it. Finitude as a dimension of the self is to be befriended, not obliterated. Nor should the distinction between natural and moral evil be permitted to vanish. Though fraught with ambiguity, it is rooted in the ambiguity of human agency itself.

In conclusion, accepting the dialectic between action and passion, agency and suffering, means foregoing attempts to exhaustively rationalize good and evil purely in terms of choice, intention, or some future good. It also means acknowledgment of the creatureliness of all human agency and of the endless need for grace in the pursuit of autonomy and personhood. Only so is it possible to affirm the goodness of human finitude, materiality, and dependence on other humans, the world, and God. Sin and finitude do not equate. Finitude is a goodness, an orienting limit that in itself has nothing to do with sin. Acceptance of finitude as creative limit, however, renders grace as redemptive, less alien to freedom than it might otherwise seem, for grace as humanizing is already ingrained in the relationship of humans to God as creatures who are forever "almosting it." Not only sin, but finitude too, which further complicates involvement in the sinful human situation, calls for grace. The wholeness of human personhood eternally eludes our self-improvements and our how-to gimmicks. Grace is needed to prevent shipwreck and to enable whatever wholeness we achieve. Even so, the finite spirit goes forever unfinished. Not a bad thing. And while it does, sin, rooted in the voluntary and the involuntary, will thrive, and all the more grace as empowerment and forgiveness abound in depths and heights yet undreamt.

65. P. Ricoeur, *The Symbolism of Evil* (New York: Harper & Row, 1967), 250.

~

8

Contrition with Tears

Motivation for Repentance

DAVID N. POWER

In the 1972 *Ordo Paenitentiae*, contrition is described first through use of the Tridentine terms of "sorrow and detestation," and then, borrowing from Paul VI, as a *metanoia* and a new way of seeing, judging, and comporting one's life in the light of the holiness and charity of God which have been made manifest in Jesus Christ.[1] Though the act of contrition which had become traditional after Trent is introduced for the first time into the liturgical text, a number of alternatives have been provided which appeal more to biblical images and paradigms.

The nature of contrition deserves probing. Specifically, what is meant by "dolor," or "sorrow," and how is it related to the remembrance of God's holiness and love? One way of investigating this is to trace the path in medieval sources whereby expressions of contrition for sin were gradually incorporated into sacramental confession. This means looking at devotional and liturgical texts rather than at theologies. It can then be asked what may be learned from such a study when looking for an apt motivation and expression of contrition in current spirituality and in current sacramental practice.

---

1. *Ordo Paenitentiae* 6b. The words are taken from Paul VI, Apostolic Constitution *Paenitemini, Acta Apostolicae Sedis* 58 (1966): 179.

Within the system of private penance the emphasis was placed more and more on complete confession and purpose of amendment. This came over time to take on greater importance than the work of conversion through the apt performance of works of penance that had marked the age of canonical practice. Evidence for this is found both in the system that has come to be called "tariff penance" and in the manuals for confessors that guided the later practice of sacramental confession with immediate absolution.[2] However, just as in the canonical regime works of penance were to be done with contrition of heart, so in the two systems of private penance confession was to be made with similar contrition. One of the qualities attributed to confession was a compunction, whose apt expression was found in tears. The action of the penitent in weeping and lamenting sin, the action of God's grace, and the performance of penances, whether before or after the act of reconciliation, belonged together in constituting the reality of conversion.

By looking at liturgical and devotional literature, this article will show how the notion of compunction came to be formulated in the process of moving from canonical penance to more frequent and more private confessional practice, in order to garner from this some insights into the present requirements of contrition.

Canonical Penance

1. The Old Gelasian Sacramentary

The first piece of evidence considered here takes us back to the period of canonical penance. There are three places in the Gelasian Sacramentary[3] in which some indications are given as

---

2. For a study of these, see Pierre Michaud-Quantin, *Sommes de casuistique et manuels de confession au moyen âge (XII-XVI siècles)*, Analecta Mediaevalia Namurcensia 13 (Louvain: Nauwelaerts, 1962).

3. *Liber Sacramentorum Romanae Ecclesiae Ordinis Anni Circuli (Sacramentarium Gelasianum)*, ed. Leo C. Mohlberg (Rome: Herder, 1960). This will be referred to as *GeV*. See the study by Antoine Chavasse, *Le Sacramentaire Gélasien* (Paris and Tournai: Desclée & Co., 1958), 140–55. The texts take sorting out and their nature

to the quality of contrition necessary to reconciliation. These are: (a) the formula for entrance into the order of penitents on Ash Wednesday; (b) the formula for the reconciliation of penitents on Holy Thursday; and (c) a formula for deathbed reconciliation of those who had not done or had not completed canonical penance.[4]

a. Becoming a penitent: Ash Wednesday service (GeV 78–82). The prayers to be said over the person who is to embark on canonical penance envisage both the confession of sin and due acts of penance. The confession is made in tears and addressed to God's mercy.[5] The confession is compared to that of the publican in Luke 18:13, whereas God's mercy is likened to the action of the shepherd in bringing back the lost sheep on his shoulders. One already sees here, within the dispensation of public penance, attention to the nature of the act of confession of sin and what it expresses.

b. Reconciliation of penitents: Holy Thursday (GeV 352–63). The deacon who requests reconciliation from the bishop makes a nice comparison between the two sacraments of baptism and reconciliation: as the waters of baptism wash away sin, so do the waters of tears.[6] Both belong fittingly within the celebration of the Pasch, when increase is given to the Church through neophytes and restoration of vigor through the return of penitents.

Appealing to Matt. 5:4 ("Blessed are those who mourn, for they shall be consoled"), the deacon's petition to the bishop to receive the penitents describes how they had done their pen-

---

is not adequately expressed by the headings or titles of the sections of the book. From internal evidence, Chavasse shows that there are actually two groups of texts for the public admission and reconciliation of penitents, as well as a short text for deathbed reconciliation.

4. There is also what looks like part of a Mass formula, the prayers of which also turn up in the *Pontificale Romano-Germanicum* of the tenth century in a votive Mass which envisages a commutation for acts of penance. It is better to consider this in the context of the Pontifical.

5. It is called "confessio flebilis." This does not mean a detailed avowal of sins, but rather that avowal which goes with accepting and performing public penance. Unless specifically indicated otherwise, translation of Latin texts in this article are the author's own.

6. "Lavant aquae, lavant lacrimae."

ance with tears. The sinners have eaten the bread of sorrow, in-
undated their beds with tears, afflicted their hearts with lament
and their bodies with fasting—all for the sake of their souls.
Schooled in this penance, they come sorrowing and sighing to
the bishop, asking for reconciliation. The disposition of an afflicted heart is on the one hand needed for an authentic penance and on the other is nurtured by it. It is contrasted with
the joy that comes with forgiveness and with being given a
part in salvation.

In responding to the deacon's appeal in the offering up of
prayer, the bishop asks God to attend to the sighs and tears of
the penitents, and joins his own tears with those of the sinners.
The deliverance of forgiveness is not only a present loosing of
penance and a healing of the wound of sin, but it is more importantly deliverance from future eternal damnation and
eternal sorrow.[7]

c. Deathbed reconciliation (GeV 367–74). This formula is witness to some mitigation of the requirements of canonical practice. The text that seems to be proper to deathbed reconciliation (*GeV* 367) appeals to the tears and sighs of the penitent,[8]
who has not been able to do the normal penance. The ardor of
confession and the petition of the Church must needs prevail
upon the mercy of God, which heals the sinner and restores
the wayward to the unity of the Church.

2. The Romano-Germanic Pontifical

The formula for public penance of the Romano-Germanic
Pontifical[9] of the tenth century (Title XCIX, 224–51) comes at
a time when its practice was on the wane. The text carries a
stress on tears and affliction of heart equal to that of the Gela-

7. The second group of texts (*GeV* 360–66) for the admission and reconciliation of penitents is equally insistent on weeping and lamentation.

8. "Miserere gemituum, miserere lacrimarum."

9. *Le Pontifical Romano-Germanique du Dixième Siècle*, tome 2, ed. Cyrille Vogel
and Reinhard Elze (Città del Vaticano: Biblioteca Apostolica Vaticana, 1963), Title
XCIX, 224–51. Texts for admission to penance on Ash Wednesday (XCIX, 44–66)
as used in the Pontifical relate to tariff penance.

sian. There is, however, a tendency to associate it with God's judgment, with the need for expiation, and with the condition of human life on earth that resulted by way of punishment for sin, when Adam was cast from paradise. In line with this, remission of sin or absolution is related quite explicitly to the power given to priests to bind and loose, or to absolve.[10]

These early medieval texts show that the acknowledgment or confession of sin that was part of the practice of canonical penance had a quality of compunction to it, which is expressed even externally by the shedding of tears. Such compunction is both required for a genuine penance and fostered by the doing of penance. Without it there is no remission of sin. Already in the practice of deathbed reconciliation it is seen to substitute for the doing of penance. It is the accentuation of this disposition of heart which carries over into the private practice of the sacrament, whether in the two-act form of tariff penance or in the later one-act sacramental confession.

Tariff Penance

While the Penitential Books associated with what has come to be called "tariff penance" focus on remedies and penances, it is from certain ritual formularies that we see the nature of the contrition expressed and its association with sighs and tears. There are two rituals that deserve consideration. They are found in the Penitential of Halitgar of Cambrai[11] of the early ninth century and in the Romano-Germanic Pontifical of the tenth.

1. The Pontifical of Halitgar

This rite of tariff penance borrows its prayers from the rites for canonical penance in the Gelasian Sacramentary and to

10. See the formulas not found in the Gelasian but proper to this pontifical: XCIX 238, 241, 243, 244, 246, 247, 248, 249, 250, 251.
11. See the text in F. W. H. Wasserschleben, *Die Bussordnungen der abendländischen Kirche nebst einer rechtsgeschichtlichen Einleitung* (Halle: Graeger, 1851),

these adds the recitation of the seven penitential psalms. Hence, the appeal to weeping and tears is the same as in the Gelasian. What is new is the twist given to this action in the instructions given to confessors who receive penitents. The exordium to the rite can be compared with instructions given to confessors in two other Frankish Penitentials: Fleury[12] and St. Gall.[13] The three texts show the mediating role taken on by the priest-confessor. Their emphasis on the need for the penitent's correct faith and readiness to confess all sins requires the priest-confessor to discern this faith, probe the penitent's state of soul, and help the examination of conscience. However, his role includes leading penitents in prayer and inducing them to the prayer of tears and remorse. The Fleury Penitential instructs the confessor as follows:

[After investigation by the confessor] when the penitent has given the entire confession, the priest himself shall prostrate himself before the altar with the penitent, and confessing they shall repeat the psalms with groaning and if possible with weeping, and both alike prostrate, shall say the passages: "Turn to me, O Lord" (Ps. 6:5), and "Our help is in the name of the Lord" (Ps. 124:8).

The St. Gall Penitential, in pressing the need for confessors to do penance and fasting themselves, states: "No priest or pontiff can treat the wounds of sinners or take away sin from their souls unless in view of the pressing necessity he brings solicitude and prayers and tears." To some extent the move to tears fostered by doing penance is now replaced by the way in which the tears of the priest are made to induce the tears of the penitent. As explained by Lanfranc of Canterbury in an eleventh-century opusculum on penance, placed before God, the priest has to recognize a solidarity in sin with penitents. In the celebration of the sacrament this changes into a solidarity in grace which is likened to the union between the Father and Son.[14]

360–77, and the English translation in John T. McNeill and Helen M. Gamer, *Medieval Handbooks of Penance. A Translation of the Principal Libri Poenitentiales* (reprint, New York: Columbia University Press, 1990), 297–314.

  12. Wasserschleben, 422–25, and McNeil, 280–82.
  13. Wasserschleben, 505–26, and McNeil, 282–85.
  14. Lanfranc, *De Celanda Confessione Libellus*, PL 120, 627.

2. *Romano-Germanic Pontifical*

Besides texts for the practice of canonical penance, this pontifical contains a rite for tariff penance and a Mass formula which serves as a commutation of penance. It thus shows the uncertain and changing state of penance at the time of its composition, in the evidence which it gives for three distinct practices: canonical penance, private tariff penance, and commutation of penances through prayers and Masses.

In the rite for private imposition of penance,[15] the priest carefully examines the penitent on sins committed and on the key articles of faith, completing this by asking whether the penitent is ready to forgive others by whom he or she may have been offended. Before the penance is imposed, the sinner asks with tears for counsel and penance (52–53). Then, prostrate on the ground, the sinner prays with lament, sighs, and tears, thus exciting the heart to proper contrition (54). The priest is to leave the penitent in this position until "fully contrite." After the imposition of penance, the priest and penitent together pray the seven penitential psalms and some of the prayers of the Lenten season.

There is a Mass for the commutation of penance (Title XCIX, 67–70: compare *GeV* 1701–1704) attached to the rite of penance here and when it is inserted into the section of the Pontifical dealing with the sick (Title CXXXVI and following). The gospel (Luke 18:9–14) and prayers of the Mass proffer the example of the humble prayer of the publican, who knows himself a sinner before God and sees himself in contrast with the holiness of God. It is this sense of contrast between sinner and divine holiness which appears to motivate the choice of the publican as an example of contrite confession. Though appeal to the image of the publican is not directly related to tears, it appears to be the same compunction of heart which is in mind both in the exhortation to tears and in the example of his prayer.

---

15. Title XCIX, 44–80. Cf. Title CXXXVI, used for the sick.

Confession to God Alone

The eighth and ninth centuries saw considerable development of the devotion of confession to God alone, that is,
personal prayer. The devotion may have had its roots in monasteries, but as propagated at this time it was intended also for
lay persons who wished to live lives of true devotion. Jonas of
Orleans summarizes the intent of the devotion when he says
that besides confessing to a priest, Christians ought to confess
their sins to God in prayer and wash themselves clean with
sighs and tears.[16] Rather than being proposed as a way to obtain
the forgiveness of sins that is an alternative to confession to a
priest, this compunction was fostered as a normal part of Christian living. As more frequent sacramental confession came into
practice, tearful compunction served as its lifeblood and where
it was missing it had to be induced for the sake of good sacramental practice. The devotional literature on tearful confession
is therefore of interest on the double ground of what it says of
the Christian life and of how it influenced sacramental practice.

The prayer collections, or *libelli precum*,[17] of the Carolingian
era associated with the name of Alcuin provide some of the
principal evidence about the devotion of confessing one's sins
to God during the period of transition from canonical penance
to more private sacramental forms. Allen Frantzen makes this
comment about the confession of sins in these prayer books:

As devotional exercises for the nobility, such prayers were recited with
the psalms; the model for this program of prayer was the psalter, which
included both verses from scripture and private prayers. The confessions were made to God, not to acknowledge specific faults, but to

16. PL 106, 151–52. Specific recognition was given to the practice at the Council of Chalon-sur-Saône (A.D. 813), but all later reference to this canon made sure
that it was not seen to stand in contradiction to the requirements of confession
to priests. On this, see C. Vogel, *Le Pécheur et la Pénitence au Moyen-Age* (Paris:
Cerf, 1969), 202–3.

17. See *Precum Libelli Quattuor Aevi Karolini*, ed. A. Wilmart (Rome:
Ephemerides Liturgicae, 1940); on other manuscript sources, see P. Salmon,
"Livres de prières de l'époque carolingienne," *Revue Bénédictine* 86 (1976): 218–34.

obtain general absolution;[18] their rationale, probably derived by Alcuin and Theodulf [of Orléans] from a common source, is simple: what man remembers, God forgets.[19]

The tendency in these prayers is to accuse oneself globally of various kinds of sin that fall under the categories of the seven capital sins or that are committed through ill use of the various members of the body. This means that in using the prayers one may end up accusing oneself of sins which one may not have in fact committed oneself. The idea appears to have been to generate a general sense of sinfulness, not only in act but in disposition and inclination. The confession or accusation is made with sighs and tears, as in this text, probably composed by Alcuin, in the collection known as the Book of Troye: "Groaning and lamenting,[20] I implore your power, asking that according to the multitude of your mercies I may make a pure confession of all the sins of which my conscience accuses me. . . . "[21]

As the ending of the prayer suggests, Alcuin seems to intend this as a personal and private preparation for confession to a priest and sacramental reconciliation. The style, however, is that of global accusation and so can be compared with the previous prayer in the collection, which has nothing to do with confession to a priest and is taken from the *Synonyma* of Isidore of Seville. Both of these prayers, as well as that attributed (wrongly) to Augustine,[22] follow the procedure of wholesale accusation of sins and vices. Thus the prayer of Isidore includes

18. Frantzen's use of the term "absolution" is rather loose. He means forgiveness of sins, not sacramental or quasi-sacramental absolution.

19. Allen J. Frantzen, *The Literature of Penance in Anglo-Saxon England* (New Brunswick, N.J.: Rutgers University Press, 1983), 114. Frantzen here comments on the fact that the prayers do not represent the devotion of the majority of the laity. However, they are evidence of how a monastic ideal of the Christian life also became an ideal for life in the world.

20. "Totis . . . gemitibus" is the Latin phrase.

21. *Precum Libelli*: 22; *Libellus Trecensis* 18, "Incipit Confessio": " . . . virtutem tuam totis exoro gemitibus, ut secundum multitudinem miserationum tuarum de omnibus peccatis meis de quibus mea me accusat conscientia puram mihi coram te concedas agere confessionem. . . ." The Troye prayer is also in the *Libellus Coloniensis* (Cologne), *Precum Libelli*: 56, where there is also another prayer, "Item de Confessione Peccatorum."

22. *Precum Libelli*: 9.

this self-accusation: "There is no sin with whose stain I have not been blemished, there is no disease on vice by which I have not been polluted."[23]

It is this kind of confession which is associated with tears and weeping. Since so much importance is given in the texts to this expression, it is interesting to note the Mass formula for the gift of tears in the eighth-century Gelasian Sacramentary of Angoulême.[24] The collect of the Mass asks for the tears which will wash away sin and quench the flames of hell.[25] The communion prayer asks for compunction of heart and rivers of tears to lament one's sins in order to merit the consolation of heaven for which the body and blood of Christ prepare the communicant.[26] The preface of the Mass is actually couched not in the form of praise but in the form of a petition for this gift, with reference to Matt. 5:4: "Blessed are those who mourn, for they shall be consoled." Allusion to this beatitude seems quite central to the imagery of compunction. On the one hand, it readily evokes tears and lamentations. On the other, it shows that at root, penance for sin is evoked by the desire to belong to God's kingdom. In some of the prayers, this is concretely expressed as the desire to remain or to belong in the unity of the Church and to take part in its worship, but ultimately of course it is the desire to share eternally in the blessings of the kingdom of God.

Such contrite prayer, expressing compunction through tears and lamentation, obviously carried over into subsequent centuries. One better-known example of this devotion is found in

23. Ibid., 20: "Quia nullum invenitur peccatum cuius sordibus non sim coinquinatus, nullus est vitiorum morbus quo ego miser non sim pollutus."

24. *Liber Sacramentorum Engolismensis*, ed. Patrick Saint-Roch, Corpus Christianorum Latinorum CLIX C (Tournai: Brepols, 1987), 2298–2301. According to the concordance in this volume, the only other eighth-century Gelasian sacramentary in which this Mass is found is the Sacramentary of Monza. See also *Le Sacramentaire Grégorien*, ed. J. Deshusses, Spicilegium Friburgense 16 (Fribourg: Editions Universitaires, 1971), n. 2342.

25. "Omnipotens aeterne Deus, da capiti nostro abundantiam aquae et oculis nostris fontem lacrimarum, ut peccati macula abluti, ultrices paenarum flammas fletus ubertate vincamus."

26. "Corpore et sanguine tuo Domine satiati quaesumus ut pro nostris semper peccatis nobis compunctionem cordis et luctum fluminaque multa lacrimarum largiaris quatenus caelestem in futuris consolationem mereamur."

the eleventh century in the life of Jean de Fécamp.[27] Commenting on this evidence, Jean-Charles Payen remarks that compunction is not only regret for the fault committed, but is the fruit of an ardent love that sees the contrast between the soul with all its propensities and the sweet presence of God. In approaching the soul, God makes it suffer at the sight of its own misery.[28] In a prayer reproduced by André Wilmart,[29] Jean reminds human beings that they are made in the image of God, that God took on flesh for their sake, died, and rose again. In contrast, all on earth is vanity. The prayer excites to remorse by meditation on death and judgment. The day of judgment is indeed the *dies irae* but it is also the day of reward. There is fear attached to this confession, but more importantly there is the contrast felt between being attached to things of earth and the desire for God that the soul experiences.

After the twelfth century there is a certain amount of literature dwelling on the day of judgment as the *dies irae*.[30] The great hymn of the Liturgy for the Dead that goes under that title is within its liturgical context a meditation on death and a prayer for the dead. The main body of this literature, however, in evoking the day of judgment is meant to be an incentive to repentance. Sometimes it speaks of the pains of hell, but more often it evokes the confusion which the sinner must feel on the day of judgment, intending to put the sinner already into such confusion in the mere recollection of sins committed. In this case, it is the meeting with God, or more often with Christ the Judge, rather than the fear of punishment which evokes repentance. This sense of being face-to-face with God or with Christ is more likely to evoke a personal remorse, motivated by love and desire, than anticipation of the pains of hell. This is especially true when it is recalled that Christ the Judge is also the shepherd who goes in search of the lost sheep.

27. See Jean Leclercq, *Un maître de la vie spirituelle au XIe siècle: Jean de Fécamp* (Paris: Vrin, 1946).

28. Jean-Charles Payen, *Le Motif du Repentir dans la Littérature Française Médiévale (Des Origines à 1230)* (Geneva: Librairie Droz, 1967), 37.

29. André Wilmart, *Auteurs spirituels et textes dévots du moyen âge latin: études d'histoire littéraire* (Paris: Bloud & Gay, 1932), 131–34.

30. See J.-C. Payen, "Le Dies Irae dans la Prédication de la Mort et des Fins Dernières au Moyen Age," *Romania* 86 (1965): 48–76.

Frequent Sacramental Confession

Some twelfth-century texts indicate how confession with tears and compunction of heart, first practiced as a private prayer, became attached to the new forms of sacramental confession when confession to a minister became more frequent. This was especially true after the decree of the Lateran Council (A.D. 1215) prescribing annual confession and the promulgation of rules for religious persons and confraternities requiring confession several times a year.

1. The Lay Folks Mass Book

Speaking of how to prepare for sacramental confession, the early thirteenth-century book, *The Lay Folks Mass Book*, written first in French and then translated into English, treats of preparation for reception of the sacrament of the altar. Of the seventh requirement, the text has this to say (rendered here in more contemporary idiom):

The seventh is that he [the penitent] withdraw his mind from all outward things, and gather himself all whole into himself, if he may, so entirely that neither he be scattered by bodily wit nor with vainglory. And then ransack his own conscience, and that what he finds unclean look that he wash them away with tears of compunction. Then it behooves him to go to his confessor and cast out with make schrift all venom of sin.[31]

In this text, one first notes that confession to a priest is expected before receiving the sacrament of communion. Then one notes how tears of compunction, aroused by examination of conscience, precede this confession. Such compunction is associated with the power to recollect oneself, so that it is in looking into one's soul in stillness and withdrawal that sins are noted and the motive for weeping emerges.

31. *The Lay Folks Mass Book*, with Appendix, Notes, and Glossary by Thomas Frederick Simmons, Early English Text Society, Original Series 71 (London: N. Trübner and Co., 1879), 11.

2. *The Ancrene Riwle*

Another thirteenth-century work, *The Ancrene Riwle*, excites to frequent confession. Though the rule is for anchorites, in listing the qualities required for a good confession it is influenced by the manuals on confession of that epoch put into the hands of confessors who had to deal with the new affluence of penitents.[32] Even for these pious women the rule requires a confession that is "accusatory, bitter with sorrow, complete, naked, frequent, speedy, humble, ashamed, made with fear, hopeful, prudent, true, voluntary, of one's sins, made with firm purpose of amendment, and long-considered beforehand.[33] For the bitterness of confession, which is to be expressed in weeping, the rule gives four reasons. First, the sinner has lost God, and not only God but the "dear mother St. Mary" and "Mother Holy Church," and the company of the angels and saints besides. Second, the sinner enters into a pact with the devil and becomes a child of the devil, instead of a child of God. Third, the sinner loses the kingdom of heaven. Fourth, the sinner betrays the trust which God has bestowed and has turned as a child from a loving Father. Though this is not listed as a separate reason, the rule obviously also sees sin as poor recompense to Christ who has given his blood for sinners. It marvels at the fact that all that he asks in exchange for this is the sinner's tears: "Our Lord accepts our tears from us in exchange for His blood, and is well pleased."

These are sample texts from the period when frequent sacramental confession was on the rise, and which have their more immediate roots in the prayers for confession to God alone already quoted. In reading them, we would be mistaken to attend too much to the motive of fear. If fear has a place, it is only to lead to proper compunction, prompted by love and desire. True, it is a contemplation of God and of union with God that

32. On the sixteen conditions for a good confession, see Thomas N. Tentler, *Sin and Confession on the Eve of the Reformation* (Princeton: Princeton University Press, 1977), 106ff.

33. See the version of the rule put into modern English, *The Ancrene Riwle*, trans. M. B. Salu (Notre Dame: University of Notre Dame Press, 1956), 135–36.

is based on contrast between God and the sinful creature, between heaven and this earth. If, however, a culture of fear took hold in any measure,[34] it may be because the ideal was too high and perhaps more radically there was an underestimation of the things of life and of earth in Christian spirituality.

Nature and Sources of the Devotion

To better understand the motives for compunction and the reasons why it moves to tears, it is helpful to look back to some of the spiritual writings that were assimilated into the devotion and spirituality of this epoch marked by increased confession of sin in all walks of life. There are four western authors who seem to be important in this regard, and they in turn may have been influenced by eastern customs. These are John Cassian, Caesarius of Arles, Isidore of Seville, and Gregory the Great.[35]

For Cassian, who is writing for monks, the tearful prayer of compunction and contrite avowal of sin before God is a step on the road to contemplation. Caesarius developed the notion that what the sinner remembers, God forgets, and that this then leads to the possibility of forgetting one's sins oneself.[36] Within the conscience the human person finds both the presence of God and the remembrance of sins. Sins destroy the communion which the presence of God offers and their remembrance causes the kind of confusion which one must feel in face of a judge who represents righteousness. In this sense, the judgment of conscience upon oneself and the judgment of

34. This is the thesis of Jean Delumeau, *Sin and Fear. The Emergence of a Western Guilt Culture. 13th–18th Centuries*, trans. Eric Nicholson (New York: St. Martin's Press, 1990).

35. See William Lori, "Confessio Soli Deo. Antecedents and Development of the Notion" (Ph.D. diss., The Catholic University of America, 1982). Lori analyzes the texts of Cassian, Caesarius, and Isidore on the avowal of sin which is part of the spiritual life.

36. A typical lapidary formula reads as follows: "Peccatum tuum si tu agnoscis, deus ignoscit; nam quomodo potest fieri, ut illi peccato deus dignetur ignoscere, quod in se homo dedignatur agnoscere." *Sermo* 189, in *Caesarius Arlenatensis. Sermones*, ed. G. Morin, Corpus Christianorum Latinorum 104 (Tournai: Brepols, 1952).

God of which the Scriptures speak coincide. If one remembers one's sins and confesses them contritely and with tears, God will forget them. This then allows the sinner also to forget these sins in the light of God's mercy and enjoy the sweetness of the divine presence.

Isidore in turn gives graphic expression to the remorse of conscience and to the affliction of a troubled soul. His is a prayer which both aids self-knowledge and makes one mindful of the presence of God in the soul. Rather than simply confessing sins which one has actually committed, however, Isidore seems prone to augur a confession of sins of which one sees oneself capable, highlighting the contrast between the meanness of the human soul and the holiness of God. It is the soul's utmost unworthiness before God which seems to be the spiritual motivation of Isidore's confession of sin.[37]

The tearful and contrite avowal of sin which these authors counsel is part and parcel of the contemplation of the divine majesty and holiness. It accompanies or prepares a prayer of contemplation which rejoices in the condescension of God in inhabiting and communing with the soul. Fear of God is not the end of the fear and groaning expressed in confession, but rather a deeper communion with God is the end and purpose of the fear of God or of the loss of God. Giving lively expression to the fear of punishment is but one way of driving home what has been lost in failing to accept the gift of divine presence through sin.

It is Gregory the Great in his *Moralia in Job* who gave what became the classical expression of the four kinds of compunction of heart that belong in the spiritual life, leading from the dominance of fear to the dominance of love.[38] The first kind of compunction is that expressed by the publican in the parable of Luke 18 (hence no doubt his popularity in medieval Latin prayers). It is the remembrance of sins committed which, according to the Rule of Benedict, ought to lead to a daily con-

37. The prayer of Isidore in the Book of Troye, quoted above, is a good example.
38. This is summarized in the presentation by R. Gillet in *Grégoire le Grand. Morales sur Job*, Livres I et II, introduction et notes de R. Gillet, Sources Chrétiennes 32bis (Paris: Cerf, 1975), 72–81.

fession with tears and groanings. The second kind is the fear of
the chastisement for sin and is fostered by daily meditation on
death, on the day of judgment, and on the fires of hell. In the
third kind of compunction, according to Gregory, one turns to
dwell on the evils and afflictions of this present life, to a vision
of life suggested by the reading of Job as a time of trial, affliction, and darkness. Our very presence on this earth keeps us in
darkness and away from God. Thus one comes to the fourth
and highest kind of compunction, that of the desire for God
and of the pain at not possessing the fullness of divine communion. This is the kind of compunction expressed by Mary
Magdalene when she washed the feet of Jesus with her tears.

Viewed in this light, one sees how the tears of compunction
appropriate to the confession of sin, and in time seen as necessary to the sacrament, belong ultimately to a prayer of desire
for God and for the love of God. One also sees how this has to
be nourished carefully and gradually. Without the remembrance and confession of sins committed, and even without
the fear of the consequences to oneself of sin, it is deemed impossible to ascend to true contrition or to a perfect love of God.
There is a discipline here which perfects the heart and one can
see how even the practice of frequent confession can be part of
this discipline.

This is then the kind of contrition and compunction which
found expression in the medieval confession to God alone and
later in the more frequent practice of sacramental confession.
If later practice suggests a stronger accent on the motivation of
fear, this is because not all were schooled to a compunction
moved by the desire for God.

Where frequent sacramental confession became part of the
devout life as practiced by persons advancing in the spiritual
life, compunction was closely allied with the discipline that
prepares one for the prayer of contemplation. Compunction included remorse for sins and fear of pain and loss, inasmuch as
these were thought necessary for realizing the holiness of God
and what it meant for human beings to be called to communion with God.

Otherwise, however, as indicated by the literature of manuals for confessors, yearly confession became a way of dealing

with wayward faith and with what were deemed mortal sins. Though this literature is more intent on assuring a complete confession of sins and the resolve to give up sin, in some of the attendant literature it appears that even in this case the contrition of compunction, which centers on the desire for God, was deemed the appropriate internal act of the penitent. Since, however, there was no life-long discipline of prayer to lead up to this, admonitions tended to emphasize that part of compunction which is motivated by the fear of punishment and by meditation on death and judgment.

When compared to practice during the period of canonical penance, the frequency of sacramental confession and sacramental confession's appropriation of the prayer of compunction is a significant development which changes the place of the sacrament in the life of the Christian and of the body of the Church. It became something other than the reconciliation with God and with the Church after a period of penance which the Holy Thursday reconciliation had once been. Confession itself, with the careful accusation of sins and the prayer of compunction, took on the value of two previously distinct though related practices. For serious sinners, forgiveness and readiness for reconciliation were attributed largely to the performance of penances and the prayers which gave them form or context. For every Christian, the practice of confession to God alone was a way of attuning the heart to the awesomeness of divine grace and to the need for conversion and forgiveness. Now sacramental confession, with contrite accusation of sin and priestly absolution, had become a regular practice for all Christians so that priestly absolution took on a significance rather different from that of sacramental reconciliation in the days of canonical penance. To say merely that sacramental confession and absolution is the normal or ordinary way to obtain forgiveness of sins is to forget how it was used, not only to prompt the annual confession of serious sins, but also to foster the communion of a contrite heart with God, that is, of a heart absorbed in the awe of the contrast between the holiness of God which calls and the sinfulness of the creature who is called.

The problem with the kind of compunction which would have been expected is not really the fear of which at one level

it is an expression, since this was seen as but a step on the way
to desire for God and a sorrow moved by love. What is more
difficult to appropriate is the disregard for this world and for
life in this world that was thought necessary to prompt true
desire for God. This we may well find disconcerting. In other
words, the problem is really whether contrition needs to imply
the contempt for the world which appears to have been integral to the motivation for contrition underlying the whole
practice of frequent confession since the turning point between
the first and second millennia.

To stress only the shortcomings of this tradition of contrition
would unfortunately be to ignore its lessons. Elements worth
recalling from expressions of compunction are the biblical
images of the publican and the humility which he expresses
in face of God, and of the sinner who combined such ardor
of love with her repentance, as well as the central place of
the beatitude offered to those who mourn and the role of the
psalms in giving an interpersonal expression to sorrow. In the
interpretation given to these texts in medieval literature, they
are associated with a sorrow which is inspired by awe in face of
God's holiness and which leads to a greater desire for God and
a yearning for a part in the divine kingdom. While these motifs
are too often, as far as we are concerned, connected with disregard for the things of the world, they can be retrieved into a
different vision of how life on earth and the ultimate reality of
God's kingdom are related.

Compunction for Sin in Contemporary Life

1. The new Ordo Paenitentiae

While retaining the word "satisfaction" as used in Trent's
decree on the sacrament of penance, the new order of penance
stresses that acts of penance are meant to aid a conversion of
heart and of action. It also offers the definition of contrition
mentioned earlier. Despite the description offered in the order,
not much seems to have been done in recent writing to exam-

ine what today motivates contrition and whether there is room for a heartfelt and tearful sorrow comparable to that of the early days of frequent confession. The formulas offered to express contrition avoid any mention of the fear of punishment, since this may in fact have taken on too much vigor in confessional practice.

There is a need in current penitential and confessional practice to develop an appropriate theology and catechesis of contrition for sin, both for the well-being of the Christian life and for a good implementation of sacramental penance in the different forms approved in the 1972 order. Not only do we need a new order of penance in the sense of the rite, but a new order in the sense in which the virtue of compunction can be fostered in the Christian life as an authentically Christian sorrow for sins committed and acknowledged. But on what is this to be based? In other words, can an apt contemporary sense of God's holiness inspire a contrition which takes the affairs of this life seriously, but misses nothing of the awesome contrast between the God of holiness and the human being ever prone to sin and waywardness?

A starting point is to ask whether the new prayers of contrition[39] offer a basis for sorrow that is both genuine and not at odds with a sensitivity to the good of this life and of the things of this earth. Some scriptural sources have been employed in the composition of these prayers. Two psalms are used, namely, Psalm 24 [25]:6–7 and Psalm 50 [51]:4–5. The biblical paradigms evoked are those of the prodigal son returning to his father, of the thief on the cross imploring entry into the kingdom of God, and of the repentant Peter making up for betrayal with the ardor of his love. There is also a rather general recall of God's mercy as shown to sinners and to the sick, and of the mystery of Christ's death and resurrection. No use is made of the figure of the publican, nor is there any reference to the second of the beatitudes.

The intention behind the actual choice of biblical figures probably comes from the desire to stress the offer of God's mercy made to the one who has fully confessed sin. The

---

39. See the prayers, *Ordo Paenitentiae* 85–92.

prayers are more an appeal to this mercy than expressions of contrition. While appealing strongly enough to God's mercy, they do nothing to evoke the holiness of God which belongs within the description of contrition borrowed from Paul VI. Perhaps it is thought that the preceding liturgy, inclusive of God's word, will have allowed the sinner to express sorrow and resolve and that the proper attitude in receiving absolution is to throw oneself on God's mercy. This itself is a corrective to the understanding of the priestly act as a legal judgment and loosing, allowing it to take on more of the dimensions of an offer of mercy and forgiveness in remembrance of the death and resurrection of Christ.

The issue of how to express contrition is not therefore resolved in the new prayers that precede or accompany the prayer of absolution, and so heartfelt contrition needs to be evoked in other parts of the liturgy. Both the words of Paul VI and the tradition which has been examined above would lead one to say that the key issue in contrition is a proper appreciation of the holiness of God. Only on that basis can one really grasp what is the charity or love of God for humanity and for the world.

2. Moved by God's holiness

As expressed in biblical images and stories, the holiness of God has to do with the divine presence in the world and with the awe inspired by the covenant.[40] The great image of God's holiness in Isaiah 6:1–13 has to do with God's manifestation and covenant, with the marks of divine presence that accompany the choice of a messenger, and the call of the people to live by covenant. As the chant of the "Holy" was incorporated into the Byzantine liturgy, it came to express how the holiness of God enveloped the world through the gracious action of the Word and the Spirit. A sense of the holiness of God as it changes the life of a people may be recovered through the biblical images

40. Inspiration has been drawn for this section from Walter Brueggemann, *The Creative Word. Canon as a Model for Biblical Education* (Philadelphia: Fortress Press, 1986), 67–117.

and concepts of wisdom and justice. It is in the doing of justice and the living by wisdom that God is known as holy, both near to humans and yet ineffable. Divine justice is grounded in God's covenant freedom and fidelity. God's coming is pure gift, an act of divine freedom, and at the same time a commitment to the future of humanity. To live by the covenant is to respond in freedom to this freedom, and to act towards others with the same devotion to the poor, to the stranger, to the enhancement of life for all, as is found in God's own liberating action. This is justice, and sin is to live by other standards, by another set of hopes whereon to build the future or the present.

To practice wisdom is to be attentive to God's nearness in all things and to discern this presence faithfully. It is to live life as a gift and a responsibility that is ultimately in God's hands, not in ours. It is to be sensitive to God's special nearness to the poor and the suffering, as well as sensitive to the earth and to the heavens as God's dwelling place. We are given to the earth and are to live in harmony with it, respecting that the divine wisdom which shapes the earth also shapes our lives. There is no need to explain disasters and tragedies as ordinance of providence, but there is an urgency about being attentive to God's presence and gift of life at the center of the universe and in the being of the smallest of creatures. To be wise is to know the potential of human action in living by the harmony of created things, and it is also to know the limits on human action and the limits on the human discernment of the ineffable.

While wisdom is a matter of daily life, a discernment of God in the ordinary, a readiness to live in the simplicity of the daily task, prophetic justice constantly breaks into the running of human affairs. God's covenant calls for reversals, it changes our judgment about things. The parable of the Pharisee and the Publican has to do just with that reversal, as well as with the wisdom of knowing the limits of human discernment. In God's judgment it is not the doer of the law who is just, but the sinner who humbles himself before God. The humility of the publican is a humility of wisdom. Faced with the issue of how to live a rather ambiguous métier in keeping with the covenant, the publican knows the limits of human wisdom and human judgment and falls back on commending himself to God's mercy. On the other hand, no wise person can live by the covenant without knowing that its call to befriend the poor must change the way in which everything is done and life is ordered.

Since all life is received and lived in God's freedom, since God comes and rules by gift, the life of holiness is a life lived in eschatological hope. This does not simply embrace a future beyond history wherein all are united in the communion of God's love, but it looks to an earthly future when God's rule prevails, when human societies live by the sense of God's nearness and in obedience to the imperatives of covenant justice. It is to know that the unveiling of this rule is tied to God's free interventions, to the divine manifestation in the witness of chosen servants and messengers, or of the just who even in suffering for justice retain trust in God and hope for the future. In covenant wisdom and justice, where the ineffable freedom of God is accepted as the ultimate criterion of holiness and good, sin is seen as a lack of discernment of God's presence, a violation of covenant justice, a breaking of the limits of human freedom.

The remembrance of Jesus Christ is celebrated in penance as the offer and invitation of God's mercy and of God's power to overcome and forgive sin. It is also, however, a memory that expresses the covenant ethic and inspires sorrow for the failure to live by God's covenant justice. Images of the suffering Christ can incorporate wisdom and justice. Christ is remembered in the enactment of his mysteries as the Just One who suffered for the unfree, who mourned the absence of God's rule, who let justice break through in counteraction to human judgments. In his preaching, we are hearers of the wisdom of his parabolic embrace of that which is most human and most earthly, of the nearness and gift of God in all living things.

The beatitude, "Blessed are those who mourn, for they shall be consoled," may still serve as the integrating idiom of all the phases of true Christian repentance. Contemporary exegesis shows a double meaning in this beatitude as it progressed from an original form to the present form which it has in Matthew's gospel. On the one hand, this is God's blessing on those who suffer, on those who are poor, downtrodden, and unfree, in short, on those for whom the rule of God is promised as a liberating force. On the other hand, it is a blessing on those who perceive the absence of God's rule and yet desire it, who lament the order of things in which God's holiness is not the vital force, and who desire the coming of God's rule in Christ.

To live by this blessing can embrace a three-step movement in the perfecting of sorrow for sin. First, it expresses the regret at being excluded from God's covenant, of not being a sharer in the promises of the future, and so of being reduced to a shattered and incomplete existence, because of one's failure to live by that covenant. Second, it expresses the movement to a regret over impeding the advent of God's rule, of having submitted one's own life, the life of others, perhaps the earth itself, to another rule that only brings unhappiness and injustice. Third, since at its core it is the expression of desire, it can awaken the desire for God and for the rule of God, both now and in the future, a yearning which is alert to the ineffable holiness of God and the freedom of God's gift, and which counts the self as nothing in the hope of this holiness for all of creation. While the note of eschatological ultimacy will always remain in repentance, it embraces the desire for a present time of earthly fulfillment which is ordered according to divine justice. It escapes the disregard for earth which crept into a medieval repentance inspired by a certain kind of monastic ideal, even while it recognizes that the limits of earthly existence necessarily fall short of a full communion in the ineffable holiness of God.

The holiness of God expresses both distance and nearness and absorbs the wisdom of living in earthly life by an awareness of nearness and mystery at one and the same time. The God who is creator approaches in divine freedom, proclaiming the name "I am who I am," and inviting humans to an address which says "thou art." This is both nearness and distance, freedom and commitment, mystery and communion. The justice of God shines forth in the way in which it comes about among a people, where the stranger is neighbor and the debtor gets back his cloak for the night. Justice cannot be constructed by precepts alone but has to be discerned by the discernment of God's ineffable action in creation and in the lives and even suffering of the poor and the just. There is always the fear of not being able to discern, of discernment moved by desires other than the desire for God, whether in the performance of justice, in the gift of one's bodiliness, or in the covenant with earth. The prayer of the psalms is a reminder that the covenant is lived out in the relation with the God who allows the people to use the address "thou," so that saving action and holiness are lived within the relationship of mutual fidelity and communion.

To arouse this kind of compunction, more reflection may be needed on the contrast between an order in which God's rule and justice prevail and orders where less disinterested motivations hold sway. A better appreciation of all the beatitudes would surely open the way to this. Meditation on the passion of Christ as the judgment of human courts on the Just One, and in reverse as God's judgment on human judgments, could ground contrition in the remembrance of Christ's saving mystery. Some appreciative retrieval of the use of the psalms may provide formulas that penitents can use, both as accusation and as confident trust in God's mercy, with the hope of a greater share in divine love.

In Psalm 25,[41] for example, the sinner turns to God in trust, recognizing that all justice, truth, and compassion come from God. There is a recalling of God's ways with people, an imagery of what makes for divine justice—forgiveness, gentleness, care of the poor, compassion. There is a frank recognition of sinfulness that goes to the roots of sin in oneself, without however indulging the broad kind of accusation found in medieval sources. The misery of sin is expressed, the being alone and without purpose, far from the companionship of God and of the companions of God. Finally, the prayer ends with a plea for all the people to whom the sinner belongs and among whom salvation, justice, and freedom from sin are to be found as God's own gift.

41. See the contemporary rendering of the psalm in Francis Patrick Sullivan, *Tragic Psalms* (Washington, D.C.: Pastoral Press, 1987), 30–31.

The prayer as it stands may be too poetic and too formally biblical for popular appeal today. However, any prayer must touch the imagination and the heart, and effect the sense of contrast between a world of sin and a world in which God dwells and guides. It has to get beyond the acknowledgment of deeds of wrongdoing to a more fundamental sense of sin. It has to express desire, desire both for the self and for the people to whom one belongs. Given the necessity of these elements, penitential psalm texts can at least serve as a model for the composition of more popular prayers, which include an anamnesis of Christ's ministry and of his paschal mystery. By way of example, the following composition tries to capture the sense of repentance inspired by the psalm formulas and the remembrance of Christ:

God, I turn to you in trust, knowing myself a sinner. Be mindful of the mercy and compassion which you showed in giving your child, Jesus Christ, for our redemption and in raising him from the dead, as in your power you overcome sin and death. Be mindful of this compassion and not of my sins. I thirst, O God, for your justice, for a world ruled by your justice, your gentle kindness, your care for the sinner, the poor and the suffering. I long for a world in which your presence is known and felt by all. My sins keep me from living in your presence and by your justice. Restore me, O God, to your rule and to your communion. Renew within my heart your Spirit of justice, truth, and obedience. Restore your Church as a witness to your justice. Restore the world as a place where your loving presence is light and guide. Bring all people to the fullness of life, which you have promised to us in Jesus Christ and the Holy Spirit. Amen.[42]

This kind of prayer could be used in personal and daily devotion, as a contemporary form of confession to God alone. It could also be used within the sacramental action. Actually, the ideal solution to the way in which to express contrition within the sacrament would be the revision of the final prayer-declaration-absolution[43] of the minister. In fidelity to the best of what tradition tells us of liturgical forms in sacramental celebration, this prayer would best be a prayer of blessing. In it

42. The composition is the author's own.
43. As the text stands, it is a hybrid, suggesting something of each of these forms.

God would be blessed for the gift of compassionate mercy and the sinner blessed by the action of this mercy here and now, requested and assured in the prayer of the Church. As a blessing, it would be a prayer of solidarity, of minister and penitent(s) together. It would include the anamnesis of Christ's mystery and the invocation of the Spirit. As the format of blessing allows, it could include an embolism which expresses the recall of sin and contrition for sin. In this way, contrition becomes part of blessing and indeed sorrow for sin would thus lead to that perfect expression of the desire for God and for God's rule, which is doxology. Perhaps such revision will come in time, the more Christian communities retrieve the full potential of liturgical traditions. In the meantime, within the liturgy of the sacrament repentant sinners and minister can learn to pray together along the lines suggested by the prayer.

9

~

Eschatology

Contemporary Context and
Disputed Questions

PETER C. PHAN

Carl Peter's interest in eschatology—the study of the last things—was deep and long-lasting. His doctoral dissertation in theology investigates the nature of participated eternity of the blessed in their vision of God as expounded by St. Thomas Aquinas and his commentators.[1] His dissertation in philosophy studies a related theme, namely, the evitermity of the soul and separated substances according to Thomas Aquinas. Throughout his academic career, he returned to eschatology in several of his writings[2] and repeatedly taught two courses on

1. See *Participated Eternity in the Vision of God: A Study of the Opinion of Thomas Aquinas and His Commentators on the Duration of the Acts of Glory,* Analecta Gregoriana 142, Series Facultatis Theologicae, sect. B, no. 45 (Rome: Gregorian University Press, 1964).

2. See *Encyclopedia Americana,* 17th ed., s. v. "Limbo"; *The New Catholic Encyclopedia,* 5th ed., s. v. "Eternity of God"; "Christian Eschatology and a Theology of Exceptions: Part 1," in *Transcendence and Immanence: Reconstruction in the Light of Process Thinking: Festschrift in Honor of Joseph Papin,* ed. Joseph Armenti (Saint Meinrad, Ind.: Abbey Press, 1972), 141–50; "Why Catholic Theology Needs Future Talk Today," *Proceedings of the Catholic Theological Society of America* 27 (1972): 142–67; "Metaphysical Finalism or Christian Eschatology?" *The Thomist* 37 (1974): 125–45; "A Roman Catholic Contribution to the Quest of a Credible Eschatology," *Proceedings of the Catholic Theological Society of America* 29 (1974): 255–71; "Christian Eschatology and a Theology of Exceptions: Part 2," in *Wisdom and Knowledge: Festschrift for Joseph Papin,* ed. Joseph Armenti (St. Meinrad, Ind.: St. Meinrad Press, 1976), 283–92; "The Last Things and *Lumen Gentium,*" *Chicago*

eschatology at The Catholic University of America.[3]

Carl Peter's interest in eschatology was not merely an intellectual affair. It also touched him deeply on a personal level. In a letter written to his family on June 13, 1962, he reported on the defense of his doctoral dissertation in theology at the Gregorian University; after thanking them for their support and prayers, he wrote:

I had my defense yesterday afternoon at 4:15 and it went well. It makes you feel very good after so much work when a man like Father Bernard Lonergan, who, in my opinion, is the greatest living theologian, can find no point of theology to disagree with and who says so in conclusion and then says he feels the thesis will be of decided use to theologians.

In a P.S. to that letter he added:

I thought of this many times yesterday after the defense. St. Thomas writes that souls in heaven see in God everything that is happening to those they loved while on earth. Dad was always so interested in advancing intellectual values for his sons and daughter that, though he is not now on earth, I am sure he saw the events of yesterday and was happy over it. Thomas says that this is an accidental joy—over and above that which comes from seeing God as the Supreme Good face-to-face. But it is still a real joy, nonetheless.[4]

Given Carl Peter's life-long interest in eschatology, it is appropriate that one of the essays in his honor should deal with this theological theme. It is also fitting that the starting point of our reflections is a recent document of the International Theological Commission, of which Peter was a member until his death. The document, entitled "Some Current Questions in Eschatology," was prepared by a subcommittee of the Commission that included Carl Peter among its members.[5] In this

---

Studies 24 (1985): 225–37; "The Church's Treasures (*Thesauri Ecclesiae*) Then and Now," *Theological Studies* 47 (1986): 251–72; "Indulgences," in *The New Dictionary of Theology*, ed. Joseph Komonchak, Mary Collins, and Dermot Lane (Wilmington, Del.: Michael Glazier, 1987), 513–15.

3. The two courses are entitled "Christian Eschatology" and "Eschatology of Thomas Aquinas."

4. The letter was quoted in the funeral homily by Carl Peter's brother, Monsignor Val Peter, at the Mass of the Resurrection at Christ the King Church in Omaha on Friday, August 23, 1991.

5. The English text was published in the *Irish Theological Quarterly* 58 (1992–93): 209–43. The Latin original is available in *Gregorianum* 73, no. 3 (1992):

essay I will first of all give a brief summary of the document. Secondly, I will highlight for critical reflection some of the most significant issues raised by the document. Finally, in light of my critique I will make some suggestions as to how eschatology should be approached today.

I. Eschatology: Current Context and Issues

In many ways the recent document of the International Theological Commission is a continuation and confirmation of an earlier and much shorter document issued by the Sacred Congregation for the Doctrine of the Faith on May 11, 1979, entitled *Recentiores episcoporum synodi*.[6] CQE takes up again each and every eschatological issue mentioned in *RES* and reaffirms *in globo* all the doctrinal teachings contained therein.[7] On the other hand, in view of theological developments that took place in the intervening decade, *CQE* elaborates at much greater length upon the theological context in which contemporary eschatology is being formulated. It also singles out for extensive discussion certain aspects it considers as essential to an orthodox doctrine of the last things.

395–435. This document was prepared under the leadership of Rev. Candido Pozo. The members of the subcommittee included, besides Carl Peter, J. Ambaum, G. Gnilka, J. Ibañez Langlois, M. Ledwith, S. Nagy, and Bishops B. Kloppenburg, J. Medina Estevez, and C. Schönborn. The document was debated in the plenary session of December 1991, approved by written vote *in forma specifica*, and published with the approval of Cardinal Joseph Ratzinger, President of the Commission. It will be referred to as *CQE*, followed by page numbers.

6. For an English translation by the Vatican Press office, see *The Reality After Death*, in *Vatican Council II: More Post-Conciliar Documents*, ed. Austin Flannery (Collegeville: The Liturgical Press, 1982), 500–504. The Latin original is found in *Acta Apostolicae Sedis* 71 (1979): 939–43. The document will be referred to as *RES*, followed by page numbers.

7. *RES* affirms eight eschatological realities: the resurrection of the dead; the resurrection as the raising up of the whole person; the survival of the soul after death; the validity of the Church's funeral rites and practices of praying for the dead; the *parousia* of Christ as distinct and deferred with respect to the situation of people immediately after death; the unique meaning of Mary's Assumption as anticipation of the glorification that is the destiny of all the other elect; the existence of heaven, hell, and purgatory; and the fundamental continuity as well as the radical break between our present life in Christ and the future life. See *RES*, 501–2.

Like *RES*, the document of the International Theological Commission begins by affirming the centrality of the article of the Creed regarding the resurrection and future life. Unfortunately, it points out, the Christian faith in life everlasting is being seriously threatened by the contemporary cultural and theological context. Three factors of this context are identified: secularism, "theological darkness," and temporal messianism. Secularism, with its autonomous vision of humanity and the world, removes the sense of mystery, and hence of the life beyond. By "theological darkness" the Commission refers to what it regards as novel interpretations of dogmas, especially in christology (e.g., Jesus' divinity and resurrection), that throw doubt on articles of faith regarding eschatology and hence perturb the faithful, particularly when these interpretations seep into catechesis and preaching. Finally, temporal messianism is detected in "some theologians of liberation" who emphasize political and economic liberation to the detriment if not denial of transcendental salvation.[8]

After these introductory reflections, *CQE* passes in review the major elements of Christian eschatology and contemporary theological interpretations of them. Its positions can be summarized as follows:

1. The resurrection of Jesus is the cause and model of our resurrection. Since the risen Jesus' body is identical with his earthly body (albeit transformed), our resurrection will also be bodily. Our risen bodies will not be some spiritualized or ethereal bodies created *ex novo* by God, but will be really identical with our earthly bodies, though transformed like that of Jesus. Nevertheless, the resurrection is not a return to the conditions of earthly existence. In other words, it is not reanimation. Rather, "[t]his body which is now shaped by the soul (*psyche*) will be shaped in the glorious resurrection by the spirit (*pneuma*)."[9]

---

8. See *CQE*, 209–13. The document has the irritating tendency of referring to "some" theologians without mentioning their names or writings so that readers are not provided with the opportunity to double-check the accuracy of its claims. It does this again when speaking of "some" theologians who question the reality of bodily resurrection (215) and "some" who explain the theory of resurrection in death by means of "atemporalism" (217).

9. *CQE*, 215. The document repeatedly refers to the eleventh Council of Toledo

To defend the identity between the earthly body and its risen form, *CQE* appeals to a series of hermeneutical principles.[10] Since eschatological assertions do not refer merely to the future but also to realities that have already occurred in Christ, made evident in his resurrection, the first principle of hermeneutics of eschatological assertions requires that we fully accept truths which God, who has knowledge of the future, has revealed to us. Secondly, our interpretation of the resurrection of the dead must be based on our knowledge of the resurrection of Christ. Thirdly, our eternal life must be understood as life of communion with God in Christ. Lastly, our interpretation of the resurrection must take into account the teachings of the Creeds and those of the Fathers, both of which emphasize the bodily dimension of the resurrection and the identity between the earthly body and the risen one.[11]

2. *CQE* strongly rejects the recent theory of the resurrection at the moment of death. While sympathetic to its aversion to Platonic dualism, it argues that the theory does not do justice to the *future* character of Christ's *parousia* with which the resurrection is professed to occur simultaneously. Violence is done, the document maintains, to the New Testament texts if Christ's

---

(675) which asserts in its creed that "Hoc ergo exemplo Capitis nostri confitemur veram fieri resurrectionem carnis omnium mortuorum. Nec in aerea vel qualibet alia carne (ut quidam delirant) surrecturos nos credimus, sed in ista, qua vivimus, consistimus, et movemur." See H. Denzinger and A. Schönmetzer, eds., *Enchiridion Symbolorum*, 36th ed. (Freiburg: Herder, 1976) 540 (hereinafter cited as DS).

10. The Commission invokes its own document, "The Interpretation of Dogma" (1988). The English text can be found in *Origins* 20, no. 1 (1990): 1–14. The translation from the German original was done by Carl Peter.

11. *CQE*, 215–16. With regard to the third principle, the document quotes the terse formulation of eschatology by Hans Urs von Balthasar: "God is 'the last thing' for the creature. Gained, he is heaven; lost, hell; testing, judgment; purifying, purgatory. He himself is that in which the finite dies and through which it rises again in him and to him. He himself is such that he turns himself to the world, namely, in his Son *Jesus Christ* who is the manifestation of God and therefore also the sum of the 'last things'." Balthasar's text is from his "Eschatologie," in *Fragen der Theologie Heute* (Einsiedeln: Benziger Verlag, 1958), 407–8.

Concerning the teachings of the Creeds and the Fathers, *CQE* quotes the *Fides Damasi*, which affirms that the resurrection will take place "in this flesh, in which we now live" (DS 72) and St. Irenaeus's statement that the resurrection occurs "in the very same bodies in which they had died: for if (the resurrection were) not in these very same (scl. bodies), neither would those who had died be the same as those who would rise" (*Adversus haereses* 5, 13, 1).

parousia is interpreted as a permanent event consisting in the individual's encounter with the Lord in his or her death. Moreover, *CQE* claims that the atemporalism theory (which holds that since after death time no longer exists, each person who dies rises in death, and his or her resurrection coincides with a simultaneous collective resurrection) does not conform to the biblical notion of time.[12]

3. As a result of its view of the resurrection as a future event connected with Christ's *parousia, CQE* emphatically affirms the existence of the intermediate state. It argues that such a state is implied in the Old Testament's concept of *sheol* and in such New Testament texts as Luke 23:43, John 14:1–3, and Phil. 1:21–24. Such a state is transitory; it looks forward to the future *parousia* of Christ who will conform our lowly bodies with his glorified body.[13]

4. Another consequence of the view of the resurrection as a future event, and not something that occurs in death, is the affirmation of what the Commission calls the "eschatology of souls." Between a person's death and his or her resurrection something that is conscious perdures and can be called "soul." The survival of the conscious soul prior to the resurrection is, according to the Commission, the guarantee of "the continuity and identity between the person who lived and the person who will rise, inasmuch as in virtue of such a survival the concrete individual never totally ceases to exist."[14]

12. See *CQE*, 217–18. The document's argument against the atemporalism theory is threefold: 1) The New Testament texts regarding the souls of the martyrs (e.g., Rev. 6:9–11) seem to imply temporal succession; 2) In 1 Thess. 4:16 Paul uses the future tense in speaking about the resurrection (*anastesontai*); 3) A radical denial of any meaning for time in the resurrection does not take into account its truly corporeal dimension.

13. See *CQE*, 219–20.

14. *CQE*, 221. According to the Commission, there are four denials of the immortality of the soul: 1) certain second-century Christians who, under the influence of Gnosticism, held that the resurrection is only a mere survival of the soul endowed with a kind of corporeity. (It is to be noted in passing that these Christians can hardly be regarded, as the Commission does, as denying the immortality of the soul; rather, what they rejected is the resurrection of the flesh.); 2) Tatian and some Arabian heretics who thought the entire person dies, including the soul, and that the resurrection is a new creation of the dead person from nothing (*thnetopsychism*); 3) some twentieth-century Protestant theologians who,

5. *CQE* rejects the charge that its "two-stage" eschatology is derived from Platonic dualism. Rather it is based, so the Commission argues, on Vatican II's anthropology recognizing the *duality* of the human person, constituted by body and soul. Furthermore, such an anthropology is implicit in the Bible, and *CQE* cites among other texts Wis. 16:13–14 and Mt 10:28 to support it.[15]

6. For *CQE* death is both an evil and a good thing. Insofar as death tears the human person asunder, it is an evil, and a sense of repugnance and sadness over one's impending death or the death of others is quite legitimate. On the other hand, since the resurrection is not possible without death, and if death is a "death in the Lord," death becomes a good thing. This fact explains, the Commission says, the hope for death found among saints and mystics. The Commission also points out that, though the Church no longer forbids the cremation of corpses, this practice would be wrong if it expresses a denial of the resurrection of the body.[16]

---

in line with their theological anthropology and like the second group, proposed the *Ganztod* theory according to which the soul perishes at death; for these there is only the resurrection, and not the resurrection *and* the immortality of the soul; and 4) some contemporary Catholic theologians who, uncomfortable with the theory of the resurrection alone, overcame it with the theory of the resurrection in death already mentioned above.

The Commission claims that the denial of the immortality of the soul causes difficulty in ecumenical dialogue since both the Lutheran tradition (as well as Luther himself) and the Orthodox Church strongly affirm the immortality of the soul. Furthermore, "eschatology of the soul" is also said to be helpful in interreligious dialogue, since many religions affirm the existence of souls after death. See *CQE*, 221–22.

15. See *CQE*, 223–25. The Commission also goes to great length to show certain texts by Thomas Aquinas cannot be used to reject the "duality" of body and soul. For example, in *Super primam epistolam ad Corinthios*, c. 15, lect. 2, n. 924, Thomas says that "my soul is not I." This statement, however, cannot be construed as a denial of the soul being an essential element of the human person. What Thomas means, the Commission points out, is that inasmuch as it is not the entire person, the human soul can be said not to be the "I" or the person. In fact, from this Thomas deduces in the separated soul an appetite for the body or the resurrection. On the other hand, it must be said that "my soul is I" insofar as the human "I," the Commission contends, subsists in the separated soul because only in this way the identity and continuity of the risen person with the person that lived can be maintained. See *CQE*, 225–26.

16. See *CQE*, 226–29.

7. On the basis of the doctrine of the communion of saints, *CQE* reaffirms the validity and necessity of the invocation of saints. It carefully distinguishes this practice from that of evoking spirits, which is designed to obtain hidden information from the dead. *CQE* also reiterates the validity and necessity of praying for the dead.[17]

8. The practice of praying for the dead as well as the burial liturgy implies the existence of a "post mortem purificatory phase." *CQE* warns that too close a parallel between the purificatory process and the process of damnation (hell) should be avoided, as if the difference between the two lies merely in that the former is temporary while the latter is eternal. In fact, the former is characterized by love, the latter, by hate.[18]

9. *CQE* categorically repudiates the doctrine of reincarnation: "This is a child of paganism in direct opposition to Scripture and Church tradition, and has been always rejected by Christian faith and theology."[19] It charges that this doctrine denies three central Christian dogmas: the possibility of eternal damnation, redemption by God's grace rather than by human efforts, and the resurrection of the body. In opposition to the doctrine of reincarnation, *CQE* affirms that "we have only a single life on earth."[20]

10. *CQE* interprets eternal life and beatific vision in terms of friendship with God: "The theme of the vision of God 'face to face' (1 Cor 13:12; cf. 1 Jn 3:2) is to be understood as an expression of intimate friendship."[21] But since friendship cannot be forced and its offer may be rejected, *CQE* warns that the possibility of hell must be seriously taken into account, though one should be sober in its description and should "avoid attempts to grasp in concrete detail how to reconcile God's infinite goodness and human liberty."[22]

17. See *CQE*, 229–31.
18. See *CQE*, 231–32.
19. *CQE*, 232–33. To support this statement, the Commission refers to L. Scheffczyk, *Der Reinkarnationsgedanke in der altchristlichen Literatur* (Munich: Bayerische Akademie der Wissenschaften, 1985).
20. *CQE*, 234. The document finds the biblical basis of this teaching in Heb. 9:27: "It is appointed to humans to die once and after that the judgment."
21. *CQE*, 235.
22. *CQE*, 236. The document helpfully notes that "the Church has never once

11. *CQE* concludes by applying the principle that "the law of prayer is the law of belief" to the doctrine of the last things. From the liturgy for the dead, the Commission derives the following doctrines. First, the resurrection of Christ is the ultimate reality which throws light on every other eschatological truth. Second, our resurrection will take place at the end of the world. Third, there is an "eschatology of souls," that is, an intermediate state which in turn implies the immortality of the soul. Fourth, there is a post-mortem purification. Finally, the eschatology of souls is ordered towards the resurrection of the body. In the words of *CQE*, "the liturgy serves to strike a balance between the individual and collective elements in eschatology and to bring forth the christological meaning of the ultimate realities, without which eschatology would be reduced to mere human speculation."[23]

II. Eschatology: Disputed Questions

My intention in this section is to highlight certain issues broached by *CQE* for critical discussion. For clarity's sake I will divide the eleven points made by the Commission into three groups: those that should command universal agreement without reservation; those that would elicit consent, but *iuxta modum*; and those that call for critical evaluation. Attention will be focused on the second and third groups.

A. *Universally Agreeable Statements*

To the first group belong such affirmations as:

1. The resurrection of Jesus is the cause and model of our resurrection and therefore must be the starting point for Christian eschatology.[24]

---

declared the damnation of a single person as a concrete fact. But, since hell is a genuine possibility for every person, it is not right—although today this is something which is forgotten in the preaching at exequies—to treat salvation as a kind of quasi-automatic consequence" (236–37).

23. *CQE*, 238–39.

24. See, for instance, the statement by Ted Peters in his *God—the World's*

2. The resurrection is not a return to this life or reanimation.[25]

3. The resurrection concerns the whole individual and not only the body or the disembodied soul.[26]

4. The resurrection is not only an event happening to the individual but also an ecclesial and cosmic event.[27]

5. There are both radical continuity and radical discontinuity between the present life and the future.[28]

6. The theological principle *lex orandi, lex credendi* holds for eschatology so that the Church's liturgy for the dead and the

---

Future: Systematic Theology for a Postmodern Era (Minneapolis: Fortress, 1993), 306: "Eschatology begins at Easter. At Easter the end appeared ahead of time. It appeared proleptically. Thus, the resurrection of Jesus Christ is the foundation upon which we must build our constructive thoughts regarding the future." The christologization of eschatology is also vigorously championed by Giorgio Gozzelino who speaks of the "christology of the last ends." See his "Problemi e compiti dell'escatologia contemporanea: Come parlare dell'escatologia oggi," *Salesianum* 54 (1992): 93, where he insists that this christological concentration demands that the resurrection of human beings "venga rigorosamente ricalcata, essendone il prolungamento, sulla risurrezione di Cristo; non restringendosi, come se la risurrezione di Gesù si riducesse all'esito del sepolcro vuoto, alla sola ripresa della materia, ma aprendosi invece al corrispettivo antropologico degli eventi cristologici dell'ascensione, sessione alla destra del Padre, acquisizione della signoria sul mondo e sulla storia, ed effusione dello Spirito Santo."

25. The German Catholic Adult Catechism rejects a "primitive materialism" which holds that "we would reassume in resurrection the same matter, the same flesh and the same bones, as in this life." See *The Church's Confession of Faith: A Catholic Catechism for Adults*, trans. Stephen Arndt and ed. Mark Jordan (San Francisco: Ignatius Books, 1987), 338. See also Hans Küng, *Eternal Life? Life After Death as a Medical, Philosophical, and Theological Problem*, trans. Edward Quinn (Garden City, N.Y.: Doubleday & Co., 1984), 112–13, where Küng affirms that the resurrection is neither "return to the life in space and time" nor "continuation of this life in space and time."

26. See Karl Rahner, "The Resurrection of the Body," in *Theological Investigations*, trans. Karl-H. Kruger, vol. 2 (New York: The Seabury Press, 1963), 210–11: "'Body' [*Fleisch*] means the whole man in his proper embodied reality. 'Resurrection' means, therefore, the termination and perfection of the *whole* man before God, which gives him 'eternal life'."

27. See Daniel Migliore, *Faith Seeking Understanding: An Introduction to Christian Theology* (Grand Rapids, Mich.: Wm. B. Eerdmans Publishing Co., 1991), 244: "If God's promise includes the body, then it also embraces society, the body politic, and indeed the entire cosmos with which our bodies are so intimately bound up." Zachary Hayes, writing from a Roman Catholic perspective, adds the ecclesial dimension: "The social nature of humanity finds its historical fulfillment in the mystery of the church, and its final fulfillment in the sharing of life with all others who together share the life of God." See *Visions of a Future: A Study of Christian Eschatology* (Wilmington, Del.: Michael Glazier, 1989), 196.

28. See Dermot Lane, "Eschatology," in *The New Dictionary of Theology*, 342: "A new and creative tension between the present and the future, between the al-

practice of interceding for the deceased by prayer, alms, good works, and, most importantly, the offering of the Eucharist constitute an indispensable *locus theologicus* for a theology of the life beyond.[29]

B. Points Agreed upon Iuxta Modum

Besides these by and large uncontroverted statements there is another series of affirmations and theological elaborations contained in *CQE* which, in my judgment, would meet with a sympathetic hearing from many contemporary Catholic theologians, though they would require further nuancing and expansion.

1. With regard to the hermeneutics of eschatological assertions, there can be no disagreement with the four principles formulated by *CQE* (see point 1 in Section I above). However, it is rather strange that in dealing with this theme the Commission quoted a text from von Balthasar (see note 11) and ignored one of the most influential essays on the hermeneutics of eschatological statements in the history of Roman Catholic theology. I refer to Karl Rahner's 1960 article entitled "Theologische Prinzipien der Hermeneutik eschatologischer Aussagen."[30] There are several points of agreement between the Commission's principles and Rahner's.[31] But there are other principles espoused by Rahner that, had the Commission taken them into account, would have enriched its document considerably. I will mention only four. First, Rahner strongly insists that "knowledge of the future will be knowledge of the futurity of the present: escha-

ready and the not yet, between the known and the unknown, between the present life and eternal life, must be maintained in eschatology."

29. See *The Church's Confession of Faith*, 347. Speaking of purgatory the German Catechism says: " . . . the real foundation for this doctrine is the *Church's practice of prayer and penance.*"

30. See the English translation in *Theological Investigations*, trans. Kevin Smyth, vol. 4 (New York: Crossroad, 1982), 323–46. For an exposition of Rahner's hermeneutics, see Peter C. Phan, *Eternity in Time: A Study of Karl Rahner's Eschatology* (Selinsgrove: Susquehanna University Press, 1988), 64–76.

31. For example, both Rahner and the Commission require that the future dimension of the eschatological realities be maintained (Rahner's theses 1, 2, 3 and 5), and the contents of eschatology be determined by the Christ event (Rahner's thesis 6, parts d and e).

tological knowledge is knowledge of the eschatological present. An eschatological assertion is not an additional, supplementary statement appended to an assertion about the present and the past of the human person but an inner moment of this person's self-understanding."[32] Two corollaries follow from this principle. (1) A balance is preserved between presentist and existentialist eschatology (that of C. H. Dodd and R. Bultmann) on the one hand and eschatology as prolepsis and hope (that of W. Pannenberg and J. Moltmann) on the other.[33] In this way, the insights of these potentially opposing eschatologies are preserved to enrich each other. (2) A criterion is provided for distinguishing between genuine Christian eschatology and popular predictive millenarianism (which Rahner infelicitously calls "apocalyptic"), a distinction left unclear in *CQE*. To read from the present forward into the future (*aussagen*) is eschatology, to read from the future back into the present (*einsagen*) is apocalyptic. Eschatology is not an advance report of the end-time events about which many Christians are curious and search for information in the Bible. Rather, just as protology is an aetiological account from the present situation of sin and salvation back into the origins and not a historical report of what transpired at the beginning of the world, so too eschatology is an aetiological account from the present situation of sin and grace forward into its future stage of final fulfillment and not an anticipatory description of what will happen at the end of time and beyond. Eschatology is anthropology conjugated in the future tense on the basis of christology.

Secondly, Rahner clearly distinguishes between the logical status of statements about salvation (heaven) and that of statements about damnation (hell). The former is a statement of fact, the latter a statement of possibility. This principle, only adumbrated in *CQE*, provides the correct framework for preaching and catechizing about eschatological realities: "Hence on principle only *one* predestination will be spoken of in a Christian eschatology. And it contains only *one* theme which is there on its

---

32. *Theological Investigations*, 4:329.
33. For an interpretation of various models of contemporary eschatology, see Phan, *Eternity in Time*, 26–31.

behalf: the victory of grace in redemption consummated. Possible damnation can only be spoken of, but must be spoken of, insofar as, and only insofar as it is forbidden to us to make the sure triumph of grace in the world as providing us with already fixed and acquired points in our estimation of an existence which is still to be lived out in the boldness of freedom."[34] This principle, too, supplies a context for a discussion of the vexing problem of *apocatastasis*, as will be discussed later on in this essay.

Thirdly, Rahner's emphasis on the unity of the human person serves as a necessary counterpoint to the Commission's stress on the duality of the human person, and hence is a necessary corrective to the Commission's "eschatology of souls" and teaching on the intermediate state. "All eschatological assertions," says Rahner, "have the *one* totality of the human person in mind, which cannot be neatly *divided* into two parts, body and soul."[35] It follows that statements about body and soul, about individual and collective eschatologies, cannot be read as two sets of affirmations about two different things but as being concerned "in a different way with the *whole* man."[36] Obviously, this principle has implications for the doctrines of the intermediate state and purgatory.

Fourthly, Rahner points out the need for remythologizing or transmythologizing the language of biblical eschatology. He rejects Bultmann's demythologizing program insofar as it implies a stripping away of biblical mythical images. Indeed, for Rahner, no thinking is possible without images, as Thomas Aquinas's doctrine of *conversio ad phantasma* shows. For a systematic theology of the last things Rahner suggest four concrete steps. First, interpreters must submit their sources and

---

34. *Theological Investigations*, 4:340. CQE does state that the Church has never once declared the damnation of a single person as a concrete fact (236–37), but it does not clearly contrast the logical status of statements about salvation with that of statements about hell. Perhaps due to this lack it is unable to discuss the theme of *apocatastasis* in a genuinely illuminating way. As a consequence, it warns that, because hell is a "genuine possibility," sermons at exequies should refrain from referring to the deceased as "quasi-automatically" saved.
35. *Theological Investigations*, 4:340.
36. Ibid.

methods to a strict, critical examination. This they often do by relying on the researches of their biblical colleagues, who employ the appropriate tools of literary and historical criticism to discover the meanings intended by the historical texts. Secondly, they then raise the question of what assertions are binding in eschatology by distinguishing the intended meanings from their cultural amalgams. Thirdly, they must see if and how they can reduce these assertions to a small number of basic assertions from which their eschatology can be derived. Lastly, they must ask whether these basic assertions are elements of christology and anthropology transposed into their mode of fulfillment, distinguishing between authentic eschatology and false apocalyptic.[37]

In sum, had the Commission deployed a fuller hermeneutics of eschatological assertions in developing its eschatology, *CQE* would have been more organically structured, more complete in its exposition, and more receptive to insights of contemporary eschatology even when these do not coincide with its point of view.

2. There is no quarrel with the Commission's description of death as both an evil (insofar as it is a consequence of sin) and good thing (insofar as death is "the very condition of and way to a future glorious resurrection"[38]). Equally acceptable is its explanation of the "death in the Lord." However, there is missing here the whole theology of death which relates *human* death to freedom and which sees it not only as something to be undergone in a spirit of penance,[39] but also as a moment of active final and definitive self-determination. One certainly needs not accept Ladislaus Boros's *Endentscheidungshypothese*[40] to

37. See *Theological Investigations*, 4:345–46.
38. *CQE*, 227. The document cites with approval a passage from Gregory of Nyssa's *Oratio consolatoria in Pulcheriam* in which he says that death becomes a good thing because unless it precedes there is no resurrection. See *Gregorii Nysseni opera*, ed. W. Jaeger and H. Langerbeck (Leiden: Brill, 1967) 9:472.
39. *CQE*, 226: "Death must be accepted by Christians with a certain sense of penance, for Christians have before their eyes the words of Paul: 'the wages of sin is death' (Rom. 6:23)."
40. See his *The Mystery of Death*, trans. Gregory Bainbridge (New York: Herder and Herder, 1965). Boros's hypothesis of a final decision in death holds that "death gives man the opportunity of posing his first completely personal act;

appreciate the fact that in dying one can actively dispose of
oneself in freedom and that death can be, to use the words of
Rahner, action (*Tat*), fulfillment (*Vollendung*), and self-possession
(*Sich-in-Besitz*).[41]

Furthermore, the Commission, perhaps because of its overriding concern to defend the immortality of the soul, fails to
emphasize adequately that death affects the *whole* person.[42]
Death, as Rahner has pointed out, affects humans not only in
their bodies but in their souls as well, not only "at the level of
the material and the biological, but on the plane of self-
awareness, personhood, freedom, responsibility, love and faithfulness. . . ."[43] True, *CQE* does affirm that "indeed, since the
person is not the soul alone, but the body and soul essentially
united, death affects the person."[44] However, it fails to elaborate

death is, therefore, by reason of its very being, the moment above all others for
the awakening of consciousness, for freedom, for the encounter with God, for the
final decision about his eternal destiny" (ix). The same thesis is repeated with
slight variations on pp. 84 and 165.

41. It is well known that Rahner has developed a distinctive theology of death.
See his *On the Theology of Death*, trans. C. H. Henkey (New York: Herder and
Herder, 1961). For a detailed exposition and critique of the theologies of death of
both Boros and Rahner see Phan, *Eternity in Time*, 79–115. It is curious that
Joseph Ratzinger did not mention Rahner's theology of death either in his 1977
volume on eschatology or in the 1988 English edition of the same work to which
he appends an afterword, save an exceedingly brief allusion to Rahner's theory of
pancosmicity. See *Dogmatic Theology: Eschatology: Death and Eternal Life*, trans.
Michael Waldstein and Aidan Nichols (Washington, D.C.: The Catholic University of America Press, 1988). The allusion to Rahner is on p. 191.

42. Recall that *CQE* stresses the *duality* of the human person, though it carefully notes that duality is not dualism. Joseph Ratzinger discerns in contemporary
theology a fear, "reaching almost panic proportions, of any accusation of dualism. To see a man as a being compounded of body and soul, to believe in a continued existence for the soul between the death of the body and its resurrection,
seemed like a betrayal of the biblical and modern recognition of the unity of
man, the unity of the creation" (*Eschatology*, 250). It is symptomatic that he
speaks of "the death of the body" rather than the death of the human person.

43. "Theological Considerations Concerning the Moment of Death," in *Theological Investigations*, trans. David Bourke, vol. 11 (New York: Crossroad, 1982),
317. Rahner goes on to say: "It [death] affects man as one and whole. For we of
today find it even less possible than those of former times to reduce man either
to spirit or to matter. Nor can we conceive of him as a union of both these principles *in such a way that* the destruction of this unity entails no further difficulty
either in reality or in our own minds. The death of man consists in the immediate confrontation of man, together with the whole of his history as a free person
now consummated and complete, with the absolute mystery, with God" (318).

44. *CQE*, 226.

how the soul is truly affected by death, short of ceasing to exist. It would seem that the Commission is still operating with the understanding of death as separation of the soul from the body and appears to be unaware that such a description of death, though legitimate in its emphasis on the immortality of the soul, is seriously inadequate in describing death as a *human* event.[45]

3. Another eschatological doctrine as expounded by *CQE* with which there is perhaps a large agreement but which calls for expansion is purgatory. *CQE* deserves commendation for warning against associating purgatory too closely with hell, since there is an essential difference between them, the former centered on love, the latter on hate. However, the Commission's exposition of purgatory remains unsatisfactory, at least on two counts. First, it lacks an anthropology to account for the necessity of "purification." Its language is still impersonal and objectivistic. It speaks of "stains" resulting from sins that need to be removed.[46] Missing is an understanding of the human person as a multileveled being whose innermost center requires a process of integration and transformation to be fully united with God, even though guilt has been forgiven. In this way, the "temporal punishments" can be understood, not as something imposed from without upon the sinner, but as a required maturing process, more or less intense and painful, whereby the person comes to a full decision for God.[47]

Secondly, *CQE* remains ambiguous on how the process of purification is carried out beyond death. On the one hand, in defense of the intermediate state and the resurrection of the dead as a future event, it argues that "[e]ven the souls of the blessed, since they are in communion with the Christ who has

45. For a critique of this notion of death as separation of the soul from the body, see Phan, *Eternity in Time*, 84–85.

46. *CQE*, 231.

47. For an elaboration of this anthropology in connection with purgatory, see Karl Rahner, "Remarks on the Theology of Indulgences," in *Theological Investigations*, 2:175–201; idem, "A Brief Theological Study on Indulgences," in *Theological Investigations*, trans. David Bourke, vol. 10 (New York: The Seabury Press, 1973), 150–65; idem, "Purgatory," in *Theological Investigations*, trans. Edward Quinn, vol. 19 (New York: Crossroad, 1983), 181–93. For an exposition of Rahner's view on purgatory, see Phan, *Eternity in Time*, 122–31.

been raised in a bodily way, cannot be thought of without any connection with time,"[48] though it never explains how this temporal connection is to be understood and how it affects the separated soul. On the other hand, when it comes to explain post-mortem purification, it falls back on St. John of the Cross's exposition on how the Holy Spirit acts as "the flame of living love" purifying the soul to enable it to reach the perfect love of God.[49] In this explanation, the "duration" of purgatory is apparently understood not in terms of length of "time" but in terms of the depth and intensity of love.[50] Logical consistency seems to dictate that an understanding of post-mortem purification as a process of *personal encounter* with God jettisons the concept of an intermediate state. This leads us into the third series of affirmations of *CQE*, which will provoke critical questioning.

C. Points for Critical Questioning

Two issues raised by *CQE* will be subjected to analysis, namely, the intermediate state and reincarnation. Another issue, not treated at length by the document but deserving more nuanced reflections, is the possibility of universal restoration.

1. The main burden of *CQE* is the affirmation of the intermediate state. Intimately connected with it are the document's

48. *CQE*, 218.
49. See *CQE*, 232.
50. It seems that Ratzinger suffers from the same ambiguity in his exposition of purgatory as an encounter with Christ the Judge. On the one hand he affirms that "[m]an does not have to strip away his temporality in order thereby to become 'eternal'," and on the other hand he goes on to say that "[t]he transforming 'moment' of this encounter cannot be quantified by the measurements of earthly time. It is, indeed, not eternal but a transition, and yet trying to qualify it as of 'short' or 'long' duration on the basis of temporal measurements derived from physics would be naive and unproductive" (*Eschatology*, 230). It is a clear instance of trying to have one's cake and eat it too. In the same volume, Ratzinger argues that time must be understood not only physically, but also anthropologically. He calls this time "*memoria*-time," which, he claims, separates itself from physical time, yet does not for all that become eternity (see p. 184). Granted that this time exists (and I think it does), still the question remains whether there is a difference *within* this time before and after death (and I think there is, otherwise death causes no rupture at all). Ratzinger does not seem to be aware of this ques-

emphasis on Christ's *parousia* and the resurrection as future events, its categorical rejection of the hypotheses of *Ganztod* and resurrection in death (which it regards as "incompatible with a legitimate theological pluralism"[51]), its elaboration of what is idiosyncratically termed "the eschatology of souls," its insistence on the immortality of the soul and the "duality" of the human person, and its explication of purgatory as a temporal process. The Commission falls short of declaring unambiguously that the doctrine of the intermediate state is a dogma of faith, but the whole tenor of *CQE* tends toward that view, especially in its interpretation of Scripture, the creeds (e.g., the *Fides Damasi*), councils (e.g., the eleventh council of Toledo), papal documents (e.g., Benedict XII's *Benedictus Deus* and Paul VI's *Credo of the People of God*), and recent Vatican statements (e.g., *RES*).

The basic question then is: Is the intermediate state a doctrine of faith? The answer to this question can be approached in two ways: by examining *CQE's* arguments in defense of the intermediate state and by offering a plausible alternative understanding of it.

It is of course impossible to evaluate all the arguments the Commission advances in support of the existence of the intermediate state.[52] Here I will focus on two aspects, one methodological, the other substantive.

a) The first remark concerns *CQE's* appeal to authoritative sources, whether biblical or traditional. In interpreting these sources, it is important to distinguish between what is said and what is meant, or to use the language of Rahner mentioned

---

tion and only speaks of this time as different from physical time and eternity.

Zachary Hayes is more consistent when he writes: " . . . it seems that once the shift has been made from the concept of purgatory as a place to the concept of personal encounter, the question of any sort of temporal duration may be an inappropriate understanding of the symbol. . . . Purgatory is neither long nor short in temporal categories. It is intense in proportion to the need of purgation in the individual person." See his *Visions of a Future*, 114. It is interesting to note that Hayes cites Ratzinger to support his view without mentioning the latter's insistence on the fact that the dead have "time."

51. *CQE*, 222.

52. By and large these arguments correspond to those Joseph Ratzinger brings forward in his book *Eschatology*.

above, to identify what assertions are binding by distinguishing their intended meanings from their cultural amalgams. For instance, in stressing the identity between the earthly body and the risen one, *CQE* cites the eleventh council of Toledo's formula that we will rise "in the very same flesh in which we live, in which we subsist, and in which we move."[53] Again it appeals to *Fides Damasi*'s affirmation that the resurrection will take place "in this flesh, in which we now live."[54] Finally, it summarizes patristic teaching as affirming that "personal identity cannot be defended in the absence of bodily identity."[55] The question still remaining for discussion is what is meant by "the very *same* flesh," "in *this* flesh," and "*bodily* identity." At the very least, of course, it must be said that these sources maintain the *reality* of the risen body, but it is not yet decided a priori what counts for the reality of the body. What makes the body real? Blood and bones? Matter-energy? The individual's history of self-determination in freedom in and through the body? Can and should a distinction be drawn between body and bodiliness?[56] Is "bodiliness" sufficient ground for the identity of the person before death and after death? Or does relatedness to history and matter suffice? The answers to these questions cannot be derived simply from texts of Scripture and Tradition. Formulated on the basis of these authoritative sources, these answers should be enriched by contemporary scientific, psychological, philosophical, and theological insights on anthropology. Further, even if it is determined that biblical, patristic, and conciliar authors do intend by body the physiological entity as such, it still remains to be settled whether this intended sense necessarily belongs to

53. *CQE*, 214.   54. *CQE*, 216.

55. *CQE*, 216.

56. *CQE* claims that the conceptual distinction between a "body" and a "corpse" and that between the two senses of body (represented by the German words *Leib* and *Körper*) are scarcely understood outside academic circles (217). With regard to the first distinction, it must be said that the Commission seriously underestimates the intelligence of the proverbial person on the street. Regarding the second, Ratzinger concedes that H. E. Hengstenberg's distinction between "body" (the physical reality) and "bodiliness" (the metaphysical principle) is justified, even though, in his view, it does not resolve the problem of the identity of the risen body; see *Eschatology*, 288, n. 4. At any rate, it seems odd that intelligibility "outside academic circles" should be used as a criterion for the validity of a theological distinction.

the revealed message, since it may be part of a more naive and prescientific worldview in which the message was formulated, and not the message itself.

Similarly, when *CQE* argues that time must still continue somehow after death, since otherwise it would be difficult to understand Paul's use of the future tense when speaking of the resurrection (*anastesontai*),[57] it too quickly assumes that because we cannot speak about the beyond (or God for that matter) except in temporal categories, time must therefore exist in the afterlife. Further, even if it is agreed that Paul did intend the resurrection as a future event, it is still to be settled whether Paul would reject the view that the dead, or more precisely those who die in Christ, are already somehow risen in and through the risen body of Christ.[58] It would seem that the hermeneutics of eschatological assertions is far more complex than *CQE* appears to assume.

b) Turning to more substantive issues, one can raise the question of whether *CQE*'s arguments for the existence of the intermediate state are compelling. This is tantamount to asking whether its arguments against the hypotheses of *Ganztod* and the resurrection in death are convincing. More positively, are its proofs for a two-phase eschatology and the "eschatology of souls" (the immortality of the soul) persuasive?

With regard to *CQE*'s use of Scripture (e.g., the concept of *sheol*: Dan. 12:2, Isa. 26:19, Luke 23:43, John 14:1–3, and Phil. 1:21–24), what has been said above applies. The most that can be said about the scriptural references is that they do seem to *suggest* the existence of the interim state, but no more than that. Whether in fact they explicitly and unambiguously assert that there is a temporal period between the death of a person and the general resurrection during which a bodiless soul awaits the reunion with its body cannot simply be assumed from their modes of expression.

57. *CQE*, 218.

58. At least one exegete, Pierre Benoit, thinks that on the basis of 2 Cor. 5:1–10, Phil. 3:20–21; Col. 2:12, and Eph. 2:6 one can say that according to Paul those who die in Christ are immediately "risen" by being united to the risen body of Christ. See his "Resurrection at the End of Time or Immediately after Death?" in *Immortality & Resurrection* (New York: Herder and Herder, 1970).

CQE's arguments against the hypothesis of *Ganztod* are two-fold: that it is rooted in a Protestant anthropology, and that it cannot account for the continuity between the person who dies and the person who rises.[59] The *Ganztod* hypothesis holds that the whole human person dies in death and that he or she is re-created by God only at the end of time. It must be admitted that *CQE* is right on both of its charges, especially in the second charge. It is indeed difficult to see how in this hypothesis the identity of the person can be preserved in this and the future life. However, the mere fact that the hypothesis is theologically rooted in a Protestant anthropology does not make it ipso facto suspect. Indeed, there is an insight in it that must, in my judgment, be retrieved for an integral eschatology, namely, that death does affect the *whole* person, including the soul. It is this insight that is brought to the fore in the hypothesis of the resurrection in death.[60]

CQE's arguments against the theory of immediate resurrection in death are also twofold: that it is unknown to the New Testament which speaks of the resurrection at the *parousia* and never at a person's death, and that it is contrary to the teaching of the Congregation for the Doctrine of the Faith as expounded in *RES*. With regard to the alleged lack of biblical basis, it must be said that it is too simplistic to identify the time of the resurrection of the individual with the *parousia tout court*. True, the *parousia* was referred to as a future event, but no fixed date was given it. Furthermore, though Paul associates the resurrection with Christ's *parousia* (cf. 1 Cor. 15), he does speak of the resurrection as something already occurring in the life of the Christian (cf. Col. 2:12f.; Eph. 2:5f.).[61] Lastly, one should bear in mind the realized eschatology of John in which Christ's resurrection

59. See *CQE*, 221–22.
60. The major proponents of this theory include Joseph M. Shaw, Russell Aldwinkle, Ladislaus Boros, and more recently Gilbert Greshake. It is well known that there has been a long-running debate between Greshake and Ratzinger on the merit of this theory.
61. This is not to say that there is no future bodily resurrection or eternal glory to come. See the error of Hymenaeus and Philetus in 2 Tim. 2:18. The question is whether one may speak of the resurrection other than at the moment of the *parousia*, however this "moment" is interpreted.

and *epiphaneia* have merged into a single event and in which the believer by virtue of faith *"has* eternal life and does not come into judgment, but has passed from death to life" (John 5:24; cf. 3:18, 36; 6:47).[62] Thus, while it is true that the New Testament does not speak explicitly of the resurrection in death, and that it does refer to the *parousia* as a future event, it cannot be apodictically proved that the hypothesis of the resurrection in death is totally and absolutely contradictory to the teaching of the New Testament.

Concerning the second argument, it is to be noted that *CQE* overstates its case when it affirms that the hypothesis of the resurrection in death contradicts the teaching of *RES*. In fact, there is a significant difference between the official text in the *Acta Apostolicae Sedis* (19 May 1979, p. 939) and the text published in *Osservatore Romano* (23 July 1979, pp. 7–8). The latter text says that "a spiritual element survives and subsists after death, an element endowed with consciousness and will, so that the 'human self' subsists" (no. 3), whereas in the former text, there is an added phrase "though deprived for the present of the complement of its body" (*interim tamen complemento sui corporis carens*). This variance may indicate that there exists an uncertainty on the part of the magisterium regarding the dogmatic value of the doctrine of the intermediate state and therefore suggests indirectly that the doctrine of the intermediate state is not a dogma of faith and that it is not impossible to think of individual resurrection in death.

The question, then, is whether a plausible interpretation of the intermediate state can be proffered in such a way that no dogmas and practices of faith are thereby denied. Perhaps Rahner's statement on the intermediate state can be taken as paradigmatic:

I should only like to point out that it (i.e., the doctrine of the intermediate state) is not a dogma, and can therefore remain open to the free discussions of theologians. We shall leave the question open,

---

62. In tension with these texts stand others which speak of a future resurrection and universal judgment on the basis of deeds, over which Jesus will preside (cf. 6:39, 40, 44, 54; 5:27–29).

whether in our time the doctrine of the intermediate state does not perhaps enjoy a certain merit on kerygmatic or didactical grounds, or for reasons connected with religious instruction, or with the history of thought. Where this intellectual framework is still alive and undisputed, and where it can without difficulty make clear to people what is really meant—the blessedness of their souls and the glorification of their bodies—no objection can be levied against it, even today. . . . Basically, I should like to postulate the following: it is by no means certain that the doctrine about the intermediate state is *anything more* than an intellectual framework, or way of thinking. So whatever it has to tell us (apart from statements about the commencement through death of the final form of man's history of freedom, and about the inclusion of the body in this final form) does not necessarily have to be part of Christian eschatology itself. We might put the matter differently and say: no one is in danger of defending a heresy if he maintains the view that the single and total perfecting of man in 'body' and 'soul' takes place immediately after death, that the resurrection of the flesh and the general judgement take place 'parallel' to the temporal history of the world; and that both coincide with the sum of the particular judgements of individual men and women. As long as he can produce good reasons for his view he can go on maintaining his opinion, always provided that he does not mean that the time scheme of world history itself can also be eliminated from his theological statement.[63]

It is impossible to present a detailed defense of this thesis here.[64] Suffice it to mention a few points. Pope Benedict XII's constitution *Benedictus Deus*, to which *CQE* repeatedly appeals to defend its view on the intermediate state, should be regarded not as dogmatically teaching the existence of the intermediate state but as using it *only* as a framework or cultural assumption to affirm the perfecting or condemnation of the person immediately after death and the glorification of the body.

Rahner acknowledges that there are two series of biblical statements, one affirming the future resurrection of the dead and the other the immediate vision of God after death. To reconcile these two apparently conflicting series of affirmations,

---

63. "The Intermediate State," in *Theological Investigations*, trans. Margaret Kohl, vol. 17 (New York: Crossroad, 1981), 114–15.

64. For a detailed exposition of Rahner's view, see Phan, *Eternity in Time*, 116–22.

later theological tradition employed the twin notions of the intermediate state and the *anima separata*. But these are only cultural amalgams to harmonize the individual and collective eschatologies, and therefore to deny the existence of the intermediate state is not tantamount to dismissing collective or cosmic eschatology, since it is still possible to conceive of the individual eschatology as an intrinsic element of a progressive transformation of world history and of the cosmos in general.

Without postulating the intermediate state, Rahner believes that the enduring relation between spirit and matter can be expressed in Scholastic language by saying that the glorified body is permanently informed by the perfected spirit soul. The identity between the earthly self and the glorified one does not come from the identity of the body or parts of it but from the identity of the free, spiritual subject who has achieved himself or herself in a definitive way through acts of freedom. These acts are performed, of course, always and only in and through the body.

The philosophical distinction of body and soul (in the language of *CQE*, the "duality" of the human person) is a valid element of anthropology. However, even with such a valid distinction the human person must count empirically and ontologically, first and last as being *one*, so that one need not conceive of the soul as separated from the body after death and existing in an intermediate state waiting for an eventual reunion with its body. Furthermore, the immortality of the soul may mean no more than that the human person, as a being of self-transcendence and freedom, is one who through his or her history of freedom can achieve final and definitive validity before God, and need not imply the doctrine of the intermediate state.

Finally, the dogma of the Assumption of Mary need not be seen as excluding the possibility of other human beings enjoying the same "privilege." Rahner concedes that it is quite possible that theologians involved in the drawing up of the Apostolic Constitution *Munificentissimus Deus* might have entertained the notion that the bodily assumption is unique to Mary, but nowhere in the definition is it explicitly declared that it is exclusive of Mary.

In light of all these considerations Rahner wonders whether it is not possible to hold the hypothesis of the resurrection in death. At any rate, he suggests that "the idea of the intermediate state contains a little harmless mythology, which is not dangerous as long as we do not take the idea too seriously and do not view it as binding on faith."[65]

Is Rahner's view consistent with the Church's practice of offering suffrages for the dead? Rahner suggests that the prayers for the dead in "purgatory" can be regarded as intercessions for their blessed death. One may object that these prayers are offered for those who are already dead, and not for their eventual "holy" deaths. Rahner replies that if in the traditional idea of purgatory we still regard suffrages offered for a particular soul in purgatory as appropriate even though we do not know whether that deceased person needs them or not, it would not be absurd to apply our intercessions for a particular "holy" death, no matter when precisely in our earthly time these prayers are said. After all, Jesus' prayers on the cross were valid even for those who had died before him.[66]

2. The second issue to be considered is reincarnation. The judgment of *CQE* is peremptory: the doctrine of reincarnation is "a child of paganism in direct opposition to Scripture and Church tradition."[67] There is no doubt that this aspect of escha-

---

65. *Theological Investigations*, 17:123. For Rahner's further reflections on the body and its relation to the soul, see "The Body in the Order of Salvation," ibid., 71–89.

In view of the foregoing reflections, I cannot but regard Ratzinger's evaluation of the hypothesis of resurrection in death and the intermediate state as excessively sweeping and laboring under non sequiturs: "The thesis of resurrection in death dematerializes the resurrection. It entails that real matter has no part in the event of the consummation. This theory reduces Christian hope to the level of the individual. If individual men and women *qua* individuals can, through death, enter upon the End, then history as such remains outside salvation and cannot receive its own fulfillment. . . . Denial of the soul and affirmation of the resurrection in death mean a spiritualistic theory of immortality, which regards as impossible true resurrection and the salvation of the world as a whole." See *Eschatology*, 267.

66. See "Purgatory," in *Theological Investigations*, 19:186–87.

67. *CQE*, 231. The same unequivocal condemnation is found in the German Catechism, *The Church's Confession of Faith*, 335: "The assumption of a *re-embodiment* or a *reincarnation* of the soul after death in a new worldly life completely contradicts Holy Scripture and the Church's Tradition of faith." The catechism gives three reasons for its rejection of reincarnation: no number of earthly

tology has attracted much attention recently, not only in popular circles such as the New Age movement, but also in scholarly ambiances.[68] It goes without saying that if the doctrine of reincarnation denies the possibility of hell, redemption, and resurrection, as

---

lives suffices for the purification and fulfillment of humans; the identity of the person cannot be preserved; and, this life cannot be taken seriously if it is not the only chance that humans have for deciding for or against God. It seems to me that reincarnationists have ready answers for all these three objections. See, for instance, Geddes MacGregor, *Images of Afterlife: Beliefs from Antiquity to Modern Times* (New York: Paragon House, 1992), 207-17.

68. Theological literature on reincarnation in the last decade includes the following: Geddes MacGregor, *Reincarnation as a Christian Hope* (Totawa, N.J.: Barnes & Noble, 1982); A. Couture, "Réincarnation ou résurrection? Revue d'un débat et amorce d'une recherche," *Sciences ecclésiastiques* 36 (1984): 351-74; idem, "Réincarnation ou résurrection? Revue d'un débat et amorce d'une recherche," *Sciences ecclésiastiques* 37 (1985): 75-96; A. Schmied, "Die Reinkarnationsidee als Ansatzpunkt eines Vermittlungsversuch zwischen christlichem und hinduistichem Denken," *Theologie der Gegenwart* 27 (1984): 241-48; M. von Bruck, "Reincarnation or Continuous Manifestation?" *Indian Theological Studies* 22 (1985): 234-65; K. Douven, "Reïncarnatie: pastorale ervaringen," *Ons Geestelijk Leven* 63 (1986): 213-21; W. Logister, "Reïncarnatie—een christelijke onmogelijkheid?" *Ons Geestelijk Leven* 63 (1986): 178-86; H. Waldenfels, "Auferstehung, Reinkarnation, Nichts? Der Mensch auf der Suche nach seiner Zukunft," *Lebendiges Zeugnis* 41, no. 4 (1986): 39-50; C.-A. Keller, ed., *La Réincarnation* (Bern: Peter Lang, 1986); D. Muller, *Réincarnation et foi chrétienne* (Geneva: Labor et Fides, 1986); P. Thomas, *La Réincarnation: oui ou non?* (Paris: Le Centurion, 1987); L. V. Thomas, J. M. Sévrin, and J. Sheuer, eds., *Réincarnation, immortalité, résurrection* (Bruxelles: Publications des Facultés universitaires Saint Louis, 1988); G. Greshake, *Tod—und dann? Ende—Reinkarnation—Auferstehung. Der Streit der Hoffnungen* (Freiburg: Herder, 1988); J. K. Keller, "Christian Reincarnationist Thought as Presented by Its Major 20th Century Proponents" (Ph.D. diss., Northwestern University, 1987); A. Schmied, "Der Christ vor der Reinkarnationsidee," *Theologie der Gegenwart* 31 (1988): 37-49; H. Beck, *Reinkarnation oder Auferstehung: ein Widerspruch?* (Innsbruck: Resch, 1988); H. Frohnhofen, "Reinkarnation und frühe Kirche," *Stimmen der Zeit* 207 (1989): 236-44; R. Kraneborg, *Reïncarnatie en christelijk geloof* (Kampen: J. H. Kok, 1989); J. J. MacIntosh, "Reincarnation and Relativized Identity," *Religious Studies* 25 (1989): 153-65; C. B. Daniels, "In Defence of Reincarnation," *Religious Studies* 26 (1990): 501-4; B. K. Grayson, "Is Reincarnation Compatible with Christianity? A Historical, Biblical, and Theological Evaluation" (Ph.D. diss., Southwestern Baptist Theological Seminary, 1989); M. Kehl, "Wiedergeburt—Häresie oder Hoffnung?" *Geist und Leben* 63 (1990): 445-57; R. Leuze, "Das Ziel der Geschichte–Reinkarnationslehre und christlicher Glaube," in *Von Wittenberg nach Memphis: Festschrift für Reinhard Schwarz*, ed. W. Homolka and O. Ziegelmeier (Göttingen: Vandenhoeck & Ruprecht, 1989), 190-203; H. W. Noonan, "The Possibility of Reincarnation," *Religious Studies* 26 (1990): 483-91; various authors, "Résurrection et réincarnations. Foi et croyances," *Lumière et Vie* 38, no. 195 (1989): 2-97; M. Stoeber, "Personal Identity and Rebirth," *Religious Studies* 26 (1990): 493-500; E. Vanden Berghe, "Reïnkarnatie—hoeft het vel?" *Col-*

CQE construes it to do, then it is incompatible with the Christian faith. There are also other aspects of reincarnation that are not morally acceptable, such as its connection with the caste system (as in Hinduism) or the possibility of rebirth in forms of life higher or lower than human (as in Buddhism). The question, however, is whether all doctrines of reincarnation cannot be reconciled with the basic tenets of the Christian faith.

Before we go further with our discussion on reincarnation, a word of caution should be said about its pastoral dimension. One should take care that theological hypotheses remain just that, that is, provisional attempts at making sense of religious experience. They must not be immediately communicated in catechesis or preaching, much less translated into pastoral directives. In this case, the task of reflecting on the possibility of understanding reincarnation in Christian terms is made more urgent by the need for interreligious dialogue. To characterize this belief, which is almost universal in other world religions, as "the child of paganism" is not only historically incorrect but interreligiously counterproductive.

With this need for interfaith dialogue in mind, let us proceed cautiously to see if certain aspects of reincarnation are not so directly opposed to Christian faith as to make this belief at least theologically nonheretical. The doctrine, we may note, is conceived as an answer to the philosophical and religious question of justice in a world in which human lots are so unequally and unjustly assigned. It seeks to provide both an explanation for human beings about themselves, their origin, and their future as well as a justification for God. If, however, instead of viewing reincarnation as a solution to the theodicy problem, we place it in the context of death as the termination of the

lationes 20 (1990): 399–416; K. Vanhoutte, "Reïncarnatieleer: een eerste terreinverkenning," *Collationes* 20 (1990) 357–78; J. Vernette, *Réincarnation, résurrection. Communiquer avec l'au-delà. Les mystères de la vie après la vie* (Mulhouse: Salvator, 1989); D. Cockburn, "The Evidence for Reincarnation," *Religious Studies* 27 (1991): 199–207; A. Feder, *Reinkarnationshypothese in der New-Age-Bewegung* (Nettetal: Steyler, 1991); R. Friedli, "La réincarnation. Une approche en anthropologie culturelle comparée," *Zeitschrift für Missionswissenschaft und Religionswissenchaft* 75 (1991): 97–116; H. W. House, "Resurrection, Reincarnation, and Humanness," *Bibiotheca Sacra* 148 (1991): 131–50; J. Thomas, "Réincarnation ou resurrection?" *Etudes* 374 (1991): 235–43.

human person's history of freedom, that is, as a process of definitive and final self-determination, then it might be adopted as a plausible theory in those cases in which the physical death of a person does not necessarily coincide with the definitive end of his or her history of freedom.

A hint can be taken from Rahner's reflections on purgatory. In this context Rahner asks whether the Christian eschatological doctrines apply in a binding way as statements of faith to all human beings, that is, all those who belong to the human species. Or do they refer *only* to those who have disposed of themselves in a definitive way through their free decisions? Traditional eschatology has of course always assumed the first alternative. But is this obvious and certain? Is it theologically plausible to maintain that there are people whose eternal destiny God has refused for all eternity to permit to be also the finality of their act of freedom through no fault of theirs?

Does this mean that one can accept the doctrine of reincarnation? Rahner himself has little sympathy for this belief. He finds it impossible to accept that version of the reincarnation doctrine in which reincarnation is represented as a continuous and endless repetition of temporal existence. Such endless metempsychosis by which a person can never arrive at final self-determination would be equivalent to damnation itself. He also rejects any doctrine of reincarnation that presupposes that the human soul is understood as a substance independent of the body, surviving the decay of the human bodies which it successively inhabits, even though not unendingly. Finally, Rahner also rejects a reincarnation in subhuman creatures as unnecessary and unworthy of the human person.

But Rahner wonders whether a *modified* version of the doctrine of reincarnation from the standpoint of a realistic anthropology might not be acceptable to the Christian faith. In line with his understanding of freedom as the capacity for definitive and final self-determination, Rahner tentatively suggests that the doctrine of reincarnation is not implausible in the cases of those whose clinical death is not identical with the end of their history of freedom. One can think of infants who are stillborn or who die before they reach the age of reason. Other cases may include people who because of psychological impairments are incapable of responsible decision. Lastly, even "adults" in the general sense of the word may not always be capable of making *that* decision which engages the depths of the person and is rendered final by death. Of course, Christian faith *must* continue to presume, and rightly so, that such a definitive personal decision can certainly be made in the normal course of *one* human life. On the other hand it *may* accept the theory of reincarnation at least for those individuals whose lives do not possess a genuine history of freedom.[69]

3. The last issue to which *CQE* briefly refers concerns universalism, or the theory of universal redemption (*apocatastasis*). To judge from recent literature, it is a theme that, like reincarnation, has recently provoked much theological reflection.[70] It is regrettable that the Commission has not given it a more extensive consideration. On the contrary, the remarks it makes in this regard tend to be oblique and rather negative in tone. It emphasizes the seriousness of human decisions and the eternity of hell.

69. See "Purgatory," in *Theological Investigations* 19:189–93. Note the extremely tentative and exploratory character of Rahner's speculation on reincarnation. The essay is written in the form of dialogue between two theologians, one of a conservative bent, the other somewhat more progressive. For an exposition of Rahner's reflections on reincarnation, see Phan, *Eternity in Time*, 128–31.

70. See, for instance, Jerry L. Walls, *Hell: The Logic of Damnation* (Notre Dame: The University of Notre Dame Press, 1992); John R. Sachs, "Current Eschatology: Universal Salvation and the Problem of Hell," *Theological Studies* 52 (1991): 227–54; Hans Urs von Balthasar, *Dare We Hope "That All Men Be Saved"?* with *A Short Discourse on Hell* and *Apokatastasis: Universal Reconciliation* (San Francisco: Ignatius, 1988); G. Blandino, "A Hypothesis on the Eternity of Hell," *Miscellanea Franciscana* 91 (1991): 226–31; H. O. J. Brown, "Will the Lost Suffer Forever?" *Criswell Theological Review* 4 (1990): 261–78; S. T. Davis, "Universalism, Hell, and the Fate of the Ignorant," *Modern Theology* 6 (1989–90): 173–86; T. Talbott, "The Doctrine of Everlasting Punishment," *Faith and Philosophy* 7 (1990): 19–42; M. Wheeler, "The Limit of Hell: Lodge, Murdoch, Burgess, Golding," *Literature & Theology* 4 (1990): 72–83; C. E. Rabinowitz, "*Apokatastasis* and *Synteleia*: Eschatological and Soteriological Speculation in Origen" (Ph.D. diss., Fordham University, 1989); C. Gunton, "When the Gates of Hell Fall Down: Towards a Modern Theology of the Justice of God," *New Blackfriars* 69 (1988): 488–96; Wilhelm Breuning, "Zur Lehre von der Apokatastasis," *Internationale katholische Zeitschrift* 10 (1981): 19–31; Esteban Deak, "Apokatastasis: The Problem of Universal Salvation in Twentieth-Century Theology" (Ph.D. diss., University of St. Michael's College, 1979). For an extensive bibliography on this theme, see G. Müller, *Apokatastasis pantōn: A Bibliography* (Basel: Missionsbuchhandlung, 1969).

Contrary to reincarnation, *apocatastasis*—the doctrine that ultimately all rational creatures, including angels, humans, and devils, will share in the grace of salvation—cannot be shown to be absent from biblical and traditional teaching.[71] It does not, however, lack fierce opponents such as Augustine. In its Origenist formulation, which includes the conversion of demons, it was condemned by the Provincial Council of Constantinople in 543. However, theologians from the Fathers such as Clement of Alexandria and Gregory of Nyssa to contemporary theologians such as Hans Urs von Balthasar and Karl Rahner have attempted to formulate a version of *apocatastasis* that is consonant with the Christian faith.

This is not the place to elaborate such a theology of universal restoration. Briefly, four considerations lie at its foundation. First, as has been argued above in the section on the hermeneutics of eschatological assertions, statements on heaven and those on hell are not logically parallel. There is a fundamental "asymmetry" (von Balthasar's expression) between them: the former are about reality, the latter, possibility. Though the possibility of hell is real (first of all for me, then maybe for others), neither Scripture nor Church tradition has claimed that anyone in fact has been or will be forever lost. Secondly, reflections on Christ's descent into hell (von Balthasar's theology of "the mystery of Holy Saturday") show that in Jesus God has demonstrated his radical unwillingness to abandon sinners, even where God is by definition excluded. Thirdly, reflections on human freedom as the capacity for final and definitive self-determination (Karl Rahner's concept of "transcendental freedom") seem to suggest that human freedom will not attain its finality except in God. Fourthly, a renewed theology of hope, based on God's universal will to save and on grace as a triumphant reality of human history, argues that we not only may but *must* hope for the salvation of all. Such a hope is not an idle posture but constitutes a moral imperative to act in such a way that all will be saved.

While *CQE's* emphasis on the real possibility of hell is certainly legitimate, its message would have been "good news"

---

71. See, for instance, Brian E. Daley, *The Hope of the Early Church: A Handbook of Patristic Eschatology* (Cambridge: Cambridge University Press, 1991).

had it taken into consideration contemporary reflections on the possibility of universal restoration.[72]

III. Eschatology: New Approaches and Directions

In this concluding part I will summarize what seems to be secure data in Christian eschatology and briefly indicate newer approaches that it must consider.

Giorgio Gozzelino, in his survey of contemporary eschatology, derives five lessons from his historical analysis: 1) Despite the reticence of many theologians and preachers to speak about eschatological realities, eschatology *must* be spoken of, without which the "good news" cannot be integrally proclaimed. 2) Despite a tendency of many theologians to speak only of the *eschaton*, eschatology must refer to both the *eschaton* and the *eschata* on the basis of the Scripture. 3) To avoid fragmentation in such an eschatology, the various eschatological realities must be based on christology and the various themes coordinated with and related to Jesus' resurrection and the resurrection of the dead. 4) To avoid irrelevance, such an eschatology must show the import of all eschatological realities for the *present* life of Christians and highlight their *salvific* significance. 5) Such an eschatology must create, by means of witness of life, favorable existential conditions for an understanding and acceptance of eschatological truths.[73]

I fully subscribe to these directives; to them I would, however, add another one. Such an eschatology must be done in the context of interreligious dialogue. It is well known that images of afterlife are not the exclusive preserve of Christianity, nor has Christian eschatology been innocent of images and ideas of eschatology found in other world religions. It is imperative, therefore, that a discourse on Christian eschatology be informed and enriched by a genuine conversation with escha-

72. For reflections on *apocatastasis* as an object of hope, see Phan, *Eternity in Time*, 152–56.
73. See "Problemi e compiti dell'escatologia contemporanea," *Salesianum* 54 (1992): 91–98.

tological beliefs of other faiths. I have explored possibilities of this kind in such issues as reincarnation and apocatastasis.[74]

Beyond these general directives there are more specific approaches to eschatology that must be taken into account. Given limited space, I will merely mention them without attempting even a cursory exposition of each of them. The first approach is liberationist.[75] Christian eschatology must enfold the implications of the belief in the afterlife not only for the individual's eternal destiny but also for the promotion of justice and peace and for the transformation of society.[76] Though this strand of eschatology runs the risk of horizontalism, which focuses exclusively on innerworldly realities (what *CQE* refers to as "temporal messianism"[77]), it can contribute, when elaborated by such theologians as Gustavo Gutiérrez and by the documents of Medellín and Puebla, to the renewal of the theology of hope as active anticipation of God as the Absolute Future of history, of utopia as denunciation of the existing order and proclamation of what is not yet, of Christian spirituality in which salvation and liberation, faith and political activism, worship and solidarity with the oppressed are seen as two sides of the same coin.[78]

Connected with liberationist eschatology is the second approach, namely, feminist eschatology. Rosemary Radford Ruether critiques traditional eschatology for its typically male focus on the survival and immortality of the individual rather than on that of the whole of humanity. Furthermore, she chastises it for its ambiguity toward the female risen body which, according to some theologians (e.g., Gregory of Nyssa and Au-

74. An important attempt to reflect on Christian eschatology in the context of interreligious dialogue is John Hick's *Death and Eternal Life* (San Francisco: Harper & Row, 1976).

75. *CQE* briefly mentions liberationist eschatology only to warn readers of the danger of "temporal messianism" (211–12).

76. See Gustavo Gutiérrez, *A Theology of Liberation*, trans. Caridad Inda and John Eagleson (Maryknoll: Orbis, 1988), 121–40. This chapter is entitled "Eschatology and Politics." See also J. B. Libanio and María Clara Bingemer, *Escatologia Crista* (Petropolis: Vozes, 1985).

77. *CQE*, 211.

78. For a discussion of this linkage between these two sets of realities in liberation theology, see Peter C. Phan, "Peacemaking in Latin American Liberation Theology," *Eglise et Théologie* 24 (1993): 25–41.

gustine), will be transformed in some mysterious way so that it no longer excites lust and is fit for childbearing. Finally, she suggests that eschatology abandon the once-and-for-all linear model of historical progression and adopt a different model of hope and change based on conversion. This conversion is a person's movement toward the center, conversion to other human beings and to the earth, rather than a flight into an unrealizable future to the neglect of the present life.[79]

The mention of conversion to the earth hints at the third approach to eschatology, namely, ecological theology. It has been argued that western Christian theology, with its heritage of classical Neoplatonism and Jewish apocalypticism, its anthropocentric bias, and its emphasis on the domination of nature by means of technology, has been hostile to the environment.[80] Whatever the truth of this charge may be, it is imperative that in our nuclear age eschatology must reflect on the place and role of humans in the cosmos and the fate of the universe in the endtime, given our unprecedented ability to obliterate life itself.[81] Sallie McFague concludes her most recent book, *The Body of God: An Ecological Theology*,[82] with a chapter on eschatology in which she argues that we humans have been *decentered* as the point and goal of creation and *recentered* as God's partners in helping creation grow and prosper in our tiny part as

79. See *Sexism and God-Talk: Toward a Feminist Theology* (Boston: Beacon Press, 1983), 235–58; idem, "Eschatology and Feminism," in *Lift Every Voice: Constructing Christian Theologies from the Underside*, ed. Susan Brooks Thistlethwaite and Mary Potter Engel (San Francisco: HarperSanFrancisco, 1990), 111–24.

80. See, for instance, Lynn White, Jr., "The Historical Roots of Our Ecological Crisis," *Science* 155 (1967): 1207; Rosemary Radford Ruether, *Liberation Theology: Human Hope Confronts Christian History and American Power* (New York: Paulist Press, 1972). A more nuanced view is offered by H. Paul Santmire, *The Travail of Nature: The Ambiguous Ecological Promise of Christian Theology* (Minneapolis: Fortress Press, 1992). Santmire notes the coexistence of two motifs in the history of theology, which he calls the "spiritual motif" and the "ecological motif." The former emphasizes the human person's transcendence over nature, whereas the latter, his or her rootedness and embodiment in the world.

81. See Gordon Kaufman, "Nuclear Eschatology," in his *Theology for a Nuclear Age* (Manchester: Manchester University Press, 1985), 1–15, and John B. Cobb, Jr., *Is It Too Late? A Theology of Ecology* (New York: Bruce, 1972). For reflections on theology and the ecological crisis as a moral problem, see Peter C. Phan, "Pope John Paul II and the Ecological Crisis," forthcoming in *Irish Theological Quarterly*.

82. Minneapolis: Fortress Press, 1993.

God's body. She outlines five principles of this ecological eschatology to replace the "dualistic, hierarchical, consumer-
oriented, individualistic, anthropocentric, modern paradigm":[83]
radical interdependence and independence of each on and
from all and unity in diversity of all with and from all; appropriate living within this scheme of things in which "ecological
sin"—wanting to have all for oneself and one's kind—is
avoided; solidarity with the oppressed; and seeing human
beings as called to be stewards of life on this planet and to side
with the oppressed life-forms on earth.[84]

Lastly, underlying and supporting both feminist and ecological eschatologies is process eschatology based on the thought
of Alfred North Whitehead and Charles Hartshorne. Such eschatology highlights the relational and evolving nature of all
reality, including the divine. It emphasizes the radical openness
of human history and the essential connection between
humans and the environment.[85] It lifts up three themes of
Christian eschatology, namely, that in the reign of God there is
forgiveness of sins, reversal of oppressive structures, and renewal of the earth.[86]

In conclusion, it is clear that Christian eschatology has entered a new era in which a new framework is required for re-
interpreting the *eschaton* and the *eschata*. Interreligious dialogue, liberation theology, feminist thought, ecology as well as
the new physics, and process philosophy impel the theologian

83. Ibid., 202.

84. See ibid., 198–202. McFague elaborates upon the kind of ethical behavior
appropriate to this ecological eschatology and the role of the church as sign of
the new creation in bringing about this organic vision of the world as the body
of God.

85. See John B. Cobb, Jr., and David Ray Griffin, *Process Theology: An Introductory Exposition* (Philadelphia: Westminster Press, 1976), chap. 7, "Eschatology."
The authors summarize the main features of process eschatology as follows:
"There is agreement that human life is more than a succession of events between
birth and death, that God aims at personal life as the condition of intensities of
experience, that God saves what can be saved. There is assurance that death and
perpetual perishing are not the last word. But there remains a profound mystery
which even Whitehead's intuition could not penetrate" (124).

86. See Marjorie Hewitt Suchocki, *God Christ Church: A Practical Guide to Process
Theology* (New York: Crossroad, 1989), 183–98. See also her work which deals with
evil in process eschatology, *The End of Evil: Process Eschatology in Historical Context*
(Albany: State University of New York Press, 1988).

to take up once again the never-ending task of *cogitatio fidei*, in eschatology as well as in other areas of theology. Carl Peter, in whose honor this essay is written, might not agree with many of the hypotheses expounded therein, but would, I believe, heartily support such a task.

Notes on Contributors

RICHARD J. DILLON is a priest of the Archdiocese of New York and associate professor of theology at Fordham University in New York City. He was awarded a doctorate in Sacred Scripture by the Pontifical Biblical Institute, *summa cum laude*, in 1978, and his dissertation, directed by Carlo M. Martini, S.J., was selected for publication in the monograph series of the institute, *Analecta Biblica* (no. 82). His other publications include the commentary on the Acts of the Apostles in the *New Jerome Biblical Commentary*, and articles in *Catholic Biblical Quarterly*, *New Testament Studies*, and *Worship*. He served a total of seven years as chairperson of the Theology Department at Fordham, and has also taught Scripture at St. Joseph's Seminary, Dunwoodie, and St. John's University in Collegeville, Minnesota. It was at St. John's that Father Dillon often shared the summer-session faculty roster with Carl Peter.

STEPHEN J. DUFFY is professor of systematic theology at Loyola University in New Orleans. He is the author of *The Graced Horizon: Nature and Grace in Modern Catholic Thought* and *The Dynamics of Grace: Perspectives in Theological Anthropology*. He was one of Carl Peter's many doctoral students.

JOHN T. FORD, C.S.C., is professor of systematic theology at The Catholic University of America. A graduate of the University of Notre Dame, he received a master's degree from Holy Cross College in Washington, D.C., and earned a licentiate and doctorate in theology at the Gregorian University in Rome. He has served as president of the North American Academy of Ecumenists, a member of the United Methodist-Roman Catholic Dialogue, a consultant to the Reformed-Roman Catholic International Dialogue, an observer-consultant for the Consultation on Church Union, and a member of the Faith and Order Commission of the National Council of Churches.

PATRICK GRANFIELD is professor of systematic theology at The Catholic University of America. He holds a Ph.D. from the Pontifical Institute of St. Anselm, Rome, and an S.T.D. from The Catholic University of America. His latest book is *The Limits of the Papacy: Authority and Autonomy in the Church.* He is also the editor of the recently published *The Church and Communication.*

ERIC W. GRITSCH is the Maryland Synod Professor of Church History at Gettysburg Lutheran Seminary and the director of the Institute for Luther Studies. He has authored, edited, or translated some fifteen books. Since 1971 he has been a member of the U.S. Lutheran-Roman Catholic Dialogue, which occasioned a close working relationship with Carl Peter.

WALTER KASPER is bishop of the diocese of Rottenburg-Stuttgart. A world-renowned theologian, he taught at the University of Tübingen. Among his many publications, *Jesus the Christ* and *The God of Jesus Christ* have been widely used as textbooks.

JOSEPH A. KOMONCHAK is professor of theology in the Department of Religion and Religious Education at The Catholic University of America. He holds a Ph.D. from Union Theological Seminary in New York City. He is the editor of *The New Dictionary of Theology* and *The Reception of Vatican II.* He has published extensively in the field of ecclesiology and Vatican II.

PETER C. PHAN is professor of systematic theology and chairperson of the Department of Theology at The Catholic University of America. He holds an S.T.D. from the Salesian Pontifical University, Rome, and a Ph.D. from the University of London. His publications include *Social Thought, Culture and Eschatology, Grace and the Human Condition,* and *Eternity in Time.* He has also edited several books on interreligious dialogue.

DAVID N. POWER is a professed member of the congregation of the Missionary Oblates of Mary Immaculate. Born in Ireland, where he taught theology from 1957 to 1971, he holds an S.T.D. from the Pontifical Liturgical Institute, San Anselmo, Rome. Having taught between 1971 and 1977 at the Gregorian University and at the University of St. Thomas Aquinas, Rome, he has taught in the Department of Theology at The Catholic University of America since 1977. From 1986 to 1989 he was chair of the department, and is currently Shakespeare Caldwell-Duval Distinguished Professor. He served on the general editorial board of the international theological review *Concilium* from 1969 to 1992, and is at present editorial consultant for *Theological Studies*. He is a past president of the North American Academy of Liturgy and recipient of the academy's annual Berakah award. Among his recent major publications are *The Sacrifice We Offer: The Tridentine Dogma and Its Reinterpretation, The Eucharistic Mystery: Revitalizing the Tradition*, and a volume of previously published articles, *Worship: Culture and Theology*.

ROBERT TRISCO is professor of church history at The Catholic University of America. He holds a doctorate in church history from the Pontifical Gregorian University. He has been editor of *Catholic Historical Review* since 1963 and a member of the Pontifical Committee for Historical Sciences since 1982. A fellow seminarian with Carl Peter at the North American College from 1951 to 1955, and a colleague of Carl Peter at The Catholic University of America from 1963 to 1991, he is a consultant to several committees of the National Conference of Catholic Bishops.

Bibliography of Carl J. Peter

"Instrumentalism and the Philosophy of John Dewey." Ph.L. thesis, Pontifical Gregorian University, 1954.

"Instrumentalism, the Logic of John Dewey: An Exposition and Appraisal." In *Roman Echoes of the North American College*, 135–40. Rome, 1954.

The Doctrine of Thomas Aquinas Regarding Eviternity in the Rational Soul and Separated Substances. Ph.D. diss. Rome, 1964.

Participated Eternity in the Vision of God: A Study of the Opinion of Thomas Aquinas and His Commentators on the Duration of the Acts of Glory, S.T.D. diss. Analecta Gregoriana 142, Series Facultatis Theologicae, sect. B, no. 45. Rome: Gregorian University Press, 1964.

"The Position of Karl Rahner Regarding the Supernatural." *Proceedings of the Catholic Theological Society of America* 20 (1965): 81–94.

"Auricular Confession and the Council of Trent." *Proceedings of the Catholic Theological Society of America* 22 (1967): 185–200. Reprinted in *The Jurist* 28 (1968): 280–97.

Encyclopedia Americana, 17th ed. (1967), s.v. "Limbo."

The New Catholic Encyclopedia, s.vv. "Eternity of God," "Generation of the Word" "Jesus Christ, Messianic Consciousness of," "Jesus Christ, Psychological Unity of," "Logos, Theology of," "Original Justice," "Original Sin," "Son, God the," "Word, the."

"Statement during Catholic University of America Strike." In *Beyond One Man*, edited by Albert C. Pierce, 41–43.

"Catholicism and the Presence of the Living God." *American Ecclesiastical Review* 158 (1968): 325–38.

"The Ministry of the Church." *Journal of Ecumenical Studies* 5 (1968): 462–65. (Joint authorship of statement approved by national dialogue whose members were appointed by Catholic Bishops' Committee for Ecumenical and Interreligious Affairs and the North American Area Council of the World Alliance of Reformed Churches.)

"The Problem of God and the Unity of Christians." *Journal of the Lutheran School of Theology at Chicago* 1 (1968): 27–35.

"Culture and the Vocation Crisis." *Review for Religious* 28 (1969): 186–95.

"Divine Necessity and Contingency, a Note on R. W. Hepburn." *The Thomist* 33 (1969): 150–61.

"Renewal of Penance and the Problem of God." *Theological Studies* 30 (1969): 489–97.

"Catholic Belief and Human Values." *The Lamp* 68 (1970): 9, 28–29.
"Does Faith Call for the Church?" *Proceedings of the Catholic Theological Society of America* 25 (1970): 188–96, 212–18.
"Faith, Ministry, and the Role of Philosophy in the Training of Future Priests." *Proceedings of the American Catholic Philosophical Association* 44 (1970): 249–60.
"The Eucharist and Christianity as the Way in the Future." *American Ecclesiastical Review* 164 (1971): 395–403.
"Integral Confession and the Council of Trent." *Concilium* 61 (1971): 99–109.
"Original Sin: A Test Case in Theology." *Concilium* 70 (1971): 106–112.
"The Role of the Bible in Roman Catholic Theology." *Interpretation* 25 (1971): 87–94. Translated into German in *Theologie der Gegenwart* 14 (1967): 128–34.
"Christian Eschatology and a Theology of Exceptions: Part I." In *Transcendence and Immanence: Reconstruction in the Light of Process Thinking: Festschrift in Honor of Joseph Papin*, 141–50. St. Meinrad: Abbey Press, 1972.
"A Theological Component of Priestly Spirituality." *Annual Report of the North American College in Rome* (1972): 7–14.
"Why Catholic Theology Needs Future Talk Today." *Proceedings of the Catholic Theological Society of America* 27 (1972): 142–67. (Presidential Address for 1972.)
"Dimensions of *Jus Divinum* in Roman Catholic Theology." *Theological Studies* 34 (1973): 227–50.
"Metaphysical Finalism or Christian Eschatology?" *The Thomist* 38 (1974): 125–45.
"A New Challenge from an Old Creed." *Worship* 47 (1973): 150–54.
"The New Norms for Communal Penance—Will They Help?" *Worship* 47 (1973): 2–10.
"A Word on Behalf of *Method in Theology*." *The Thomist* 37 (1973): 602–10.
"Integrity Today?" *Communio* 1 (1974): 60–82.
"Ministry and the Church Universal: Differing Attitudes Toward Papal Primacy." *Origins* 3, no. 38, (1974): 585–600. Joint statement of the Bilateral Ecumenical Consultation of Lutherans and Roman Catholics in U.S.A. Also in *Papal Primacy and the Universal Church: Lutherans and Catholics in Dialogue V*, edited by Paul C. Empie and T. Austin Murphy; 9–38, 254. Minneapolis: Augsburg, 1974.
"A Roman Catholic Contribution to the Quest of a Credible Eschatology." *Proceedings of the Catholic Theological Society of America* 29 (1974): 255–71.
"The Church—Can It Help Man Move Forward?" In *The Church and Human Society at the Threshold of the Third Millennium*, 135–57. The Villanova University Symposium, vol. 6. Villanova, 1975.
"The Hartford Statement: An Appeal for Theological Affirmation." *Origins* 4, no. 33 (1975): 552–53; and *Worldview* 18, no. 4 (1975): 39–41. (Joint authorship.)

"I Stand in Debt to Them." In *Roman Echoes of the North American College*, 22–3. Rome, 1975.

The New Catholic Encyclopedia, Supplement 16 (1975), s.vv. "Communal Penance," "Confession," "Penance, Sacrament of."

"A Case Study Approach to the Forgiveness of Sins." In *Christian Theology: A Case Approach*, edited by R. A. Evans and T. D. Parker, 229–33. New York: Harper-Row, 1976.

"Christian Eschatology and a Theology of Exceptions: Part 2." In *Wisdom and Knowledge: Festschrift for Joseph Papin*, edited by Joseph Armenti. 283–92. St. Meinrad: St. Meinrad Press, 1976.

"A Creative Alienation: *Hartford* and the Future of Roman Catholic Thought." In *Against the World for the World: The Hartford Appeal and the Future of American Religion*, edited by Peter L. Berger and Richard J. Neuhaus, 78–98. New York: Seabury, 1976.

"Ecumenism and Denominational Conversion: Reflections of a Roman Catholic." *Communio* 3 (1976): 188–89.

"Eucharistic Congress in Bicentennial Year of American Revolution." *Communio* 3 (1976): 373–76.

"Papal Primacy: Ecumenical Developments." *Proceedings of the Catholic Theological Society of America* 31 (1976): 137–41.

"Ambiguity, Criticism, and Promise." *The New Catholic World* (July-August 1977): 181–90.

"Address to the Ninth General Convention of the American Lutheran Church." In *1978 Reports and Actions of the Ninth General Convention of the American Lutheran Church*, edited by Arnold R. Mickelson; 3:1176–79. Minneapolis: Office of the General Secretary of The American Lutheran Church, 1978.

"Doctrine and the Future: Some Suggestions." In *Toward Vatican III: The Work That Needs to be Done*, edited by D. Tracy, J. B. Metz, and Hans Küng, 45–54. New York: Seabury, 1978.

"Rendering an Account of Hope: A Joint Task of Theologians and Bishops." *Chicago Studies* 17 (1978): 159–67.

"Tired Dogma and General Absolution." In *General Absolution: Toward A Deeper Understanding*, 11–14. Chicago: Federation of Diocesan Liturgical Commissions, 1978.

"Hopeful Stewards of Tradition: The Open Christian and History's Potential." *Origins* 9 (1979): 25–28. Reprinted in *The Catholic Mind* 78 (1979): 26–33.

"Searching for Transcendence with Dupré." *The Journal of Religion* 59 (1979) 335–39.

"A Shift to the Human Subject in Roman Catholic Theology." *Communio* 6 (1979): 56–72.

"Teaching Authority and Infallibility in the Church." *Theological Studies* 40 (1979): 113–66. (Paper co-authored with members of Lutheran-Roman Roman Catholic Bilateral Ecumenical Consultation in the U.S.A.)

"Unfinished Business and Opportunities of the Present: The Lutheran-Roman Catholic Dialogue—U.S.A." *The Catholic Mind* 77 (1979): 27–32.

"A Rahner-Küng Debate and Ecumenical Possibilities." *Teaching Authority and Infallibility in the Church: Lutherans and Catholics in Dialogue VI*, edited by Paul Empie, T. Austin Murphy, and Joseph Burgess, 159–62, 325–26. Minneapolis: Augsburg, 1980.

"Rome and the Ministry of Other Churches." *Ecumenical Trends* 9 (January 1980): 5–7.

"Justification and the Catholic Principle." *Lutheran Theological Seminary Bulletin* (The Martin Luther Colloquium) 61 (1981): 16–25.

"Memory, Celebration, and Credibility: A Paper Prepared for the Fiftieth Anniversary of the Priestly Ordination of His Eminence John Cardinal Dearden: December 8, 1982." Detroit, 1982.

"Intervention of the N.C.C.B. Synod Delegation on General Absolution." *Origins* 13 (1983): 328–30. (Principal Drafter.)

"Justification by Faith." Consensus Statement of the U.S. Lutheran-Roman Catholic Dialogue. *Origins* 13 (1983): 277, 279–304. (Joint authorship.)

"Dialog der Kirchen in den U.S.A." *Evangelische Kommentare* 17 (1984): 139–40.

Encyclopedia Americana (1984), s.vv. "Original Sin," "Pelagianism."

"Evaluation of the Angelican–Roman Catholic Final Report." *Origins* 14 (1984): 409–13. (Principal drafter of this first NCCB response to an ecumenical document.)

"Penance and Reconciliation: International Theological Commission's Report." *Origins* 13 (1984): 513–24. (Member of subcommittee that prepared text.)

"Wisdom and the Josephinum." *The Josephinum Journal of Theology* 3 (1984): 7–11.

"The Decree on Justification in the Council of Trent." In *Justification by Faith: Lutherans and Catholics in Dialogue VII*, edited by H. G. Anderson, T. Austin Murphy, and J. A. Burgess, 218–29, 361–65. Minneapolis: Augsburg, 1985.

"From *Sermo* to *Anathema*: A Dispute about the Confession of Mortal Sins." In *Studies in Catholic History in Honor of John Tracy Ellis,* edited by N. H. Minnich, R. B. Eno, and R. F. Trisco, 566–88. Wilmington: Glazier, 1985.

"Justification by Faith and the Need of Another Critical Principle." In *Justification by Faith*, 304–15, 376–78.

"The Last Things and *Lumen Gentium*." *Chicago Studies* 24 (1985): 225–37.

"The Church's Treasures (*Thesauri Ecclesiae*) Then and Now." *Theological Studies* 47 (1986): 251–72.

"Dialogo tra luterani e cattolici negli Stati Uniti: il contributo della teologia all' unità cristiana in tutto il mondo." *Teologia: Rivista della Facoltà teologica dell'Italia Settentrionale* 11 (1986): 168–80.

"Justification and the Catholic Principle." In *Encounters with Luther,* edited by E. W. Gritsch, 19–35. Gettysburg: Institute for Luther Studies, 1986. Reprint.

"The Lutheran-Catholic Dialogue." *Creighton University Window* 2 (1986): 4–9.

"Sin and Atonement in the Roman Catholic Tradition." In *The Human Condition in the Jewish and Christian Traditions*, edited by F. E. Greenspahn, 129–46. Hoboken: Ktav Publishing House, 1986.

"Jesus Christ and Dogma: Karl Rahner and Chalcedon." *Chicago Studies* 26 (1987): 315–29.

"The Office of Bishop and the *Jus Divinum*: Trent and the Lutheran Confessions: A Rereading with Ecumenical Possibilities." *Cristianesimo nella Storia* 8 (1987): 93–113.

"Polarization, Ecumenism, and Memories." *Worship* 61 (1987): 425–29.

"Mediation as a Moment of Truth for Lutheran-Catholic Dialogue." *Origins* 17 (1988): 537–41. Reprinted as "A Moment of Truth for Lutheran-Catholic Dialogue." *One in Christ* 24 (1988): 142–51.

The New Dictionary of Theology (1988), s.vv. "Good Works," "Indulgences," "Justification," "Merit," "Relics," "Sanctification."

"Theological Notes or Hierarchy of Truths?" *Proceedings of the Catholic Theological Society of America* 43 (1988): 98–101.

"Amid Shadows and Delays: Anglican/Roman Catholic Dialogue." *Ecumenical Trends* 18 (1989): 129–32.

"The Ecumenical Unburdening of the Mariological Problem: A Roman Catholic Response." *Journal of Ecumenical Studies* 26, no. 4 (1989): 697–703.

"Justification by Faith Alone, the Article by Which the Church Stands or Falls?" *Dialog* 28 (1989): 129–32.

New Catholic Encyclopedia (1989), s.vv. "Christian Anthropology," "International Theological Commission," "Synod of Bishops—Sixth General Assembly, 1983."

"Theses on Christian Memory, Hope, and Assent: The Current Theological Debate about Dissent." *Communio* 16 (1989): 233–43.

"St. Thomas Aquinas and Theology Today." *Origins* 18 (1989): 604–6.

"Canon Law and Communion." *Dialog* 29 (1990): 104–6.

"On the Interpretation of Dogmas." English translation of German original with Latin title "De Interpretatione Dogmatum," work of the International Theological Commission. *Origins* 20 (1990): 3–14.

"Roman Catholic Theologian Responds to Lutheran Plans for Ministry." *Ecumenical Trends* 19 (1990): 133–37.

"The Many Faces of Academic Freedom." *Origins* 20 (1991): 520–24.

"Mountains Moved by Faith That Hopes," *Word and World* 11, no. 3 (1991): 293–96.

"The Communion of Saints in the Final Days of the Council of Trent." In *The One Mediator, the Saints, and Mary: Lutherans and Catholics in Dialogue VIII*, edited by H. G. Anderson et al., 219–33, 377–79. Minneapolis: Augsburg, 1992.

"A Role Model in an Ecumenical Winter." *Worship* 66 (1992): 2–10.

Doctoral Students of Carl J. Peter

The following is a list of doctoral students advised by
Carl Peter at The Catholic University of America.

BURKE, DENNIS J. "The Prophetic Mission of Henri de Lubac: A Study
of His Theological Anthropology and Its Function in the Renewal of
Theology." Ph.D. diss., 1968.

MCMORROW, KEVIN F. "A Re-evaluation of Christ's Special Religious
Knowledge (*Beata*): An Historical Investigation of Thomas Aquinas
and His Commentators." S.T.D. diss., 1969.

SCANLON, MICHAEL J. "The Christian Anthropology of John
Wesley." S.T.D. diss., 1969.

DUFFY, STEPHEN J. "The Gratuity of Grace: A Critical Analysis of a
Contemporary Theological Development." S.T.D. diss., 1970.

NEWMAN, WILLIAM A. "*Jus Divinum* in Two Tridentine Theologians:
Melchior Cano and Ruard Tapper." S.T.D. diss., 1970.

MAHAR, PAUL J. "A Critical Exposition of the Notion of Commitment
in the Works of Henry Nelson Wieman." S.T.D. diss., 1971.

BEER, PETER J. "The Theological Notions of Satisfaction Operative in
the Tridentine Debates and Decrees." S.T.D. diss., 1972.

DETERS, FREDERICK J. "The Meaning and Role of the Trinity in the
Radical Monotheism of H. Richard Niebuhr." S.T.D. diss., 1973.

MINELLA, MARY J. "The Eschatological Dimension in Henry Nelson
Wieman's Empirical Theology of Creativity." S.T.D. diss., 1974.

POPIVCHAK, RONALD P. "Peter Mohila, Metropolitan of Kiev
(1632–47): Critical Translation and Evaluation of His 'Orthodox Confession of Faith.'" S.T.D. diss., 1975.

DALLEN, JAMES "A Decade of Discussion on the Reform of Penance:
Theological Analysis and Critique." S.T.D. diss., 1976.

BEGGERT, WILLIAM F. "The Christologies of Karl Rahner, S.J., and
Hans Küng: Comparison and Evaluation." S.T.D. diss., 1979.

JOHNSON, ELIZABETH. "Analogy/Doxology and Their Connection with
Christology in the Thought of Wolfhart Pannenberg." Ph.D. diss.,
1981.

SWANN, WILLIAM S. "The Relationship Between Penance, Reconciliation with the Church, and Admission to the Eucharist in the Letters
and *De Lapsis* of Cyprian of Carthage." S.T.D. diss., 1981 (co-directed
with R. Eno).

MCKENNA, THOMAS F. "Conversion and Growth: The Theological Interpretation by Henry Nelson Wieman and the Doctrine of the
Council of Trent." S.T.D. diss., 1982.

MERKT, JOSEPH T. "Sacra Doctrina and Eschatology: A Test Case for the Study of Method and Content in the Writings of Thomas Aquinas." S.T.D. diss., 1983.

KALITA, THOMAS M. "The Influence of Nicholas of Lyra on Martin Luther's Commentary on Genesis." S.T.D. diss., 1985.

EVANS, GEORGE P. "The Cult of the Saints in the Early Lutheran Reformation and in the Second Vatican Council: A Comparison." S.T.D. diss., 1987.

Tabula Gratulatoria

Diocese of Albany
Reverend Edward C. Arnold
Archdiocese of Baltimore
Most Reverend Robert J. Banks
Mr. and Mrs. George B. Begg, Jr.
Mr. Joseph J. Beisel
Diocese of Boise
Reverend Monsignor Myles M.
 Bourke
Reverend Monsignor Lawrence
 K. Breslin
Diocese of Bridgeport
Reverend David R. Bruning
Mr. and Mrs. Dennis J. Burke
Reverend Monsignor Angelo M.
 Caligiuri
Reverend Monsignor Anthony L.
 Capitani
Archdiocese of Chicago
Reverend Monsignor Edward J.
 Ciuba
Reverend Raymond F. Collins
Reverend Monsignor Thomas E.
 Crane
Reverend Blase Joseph Cupich
Reverend Christopher
 De Giovine
Most Reverend Ambrose
 De Paoli
Diocese of Dodge City
Reverend Timothy M. Dolan
Reverend Frank S. Donio
Reverend Monsignor T. David
 Dougherty

Reverend Monsignor Philip J.
 Dowling
Reverend Monsignor Thomas M.
 Duffy
Reverend Monsignor Edward J.
 Duncan
Reverend Monsignor Walter
 Edyvean
Reverend Georges Y. El-Khalli
Diocese of Erie
Mr. and Mrs. James B. Estes
Evangelical Lutheran Church
 in America, Southeastern
 Synod
Reverend J. Thomas Finucan
Most Reverend Bernard J.
 Flanagan
Reverend Monsignor James J.
 Flood
Reverend Robert M. Garrity
Diocese of Gary
Reverend Monsignor Bernard C.
 Gerhardt
Diocese of Grand Island
Diocese of Great Falls-Billings
Reverend Eugene L. Gunning
Reverend Stephen P. Happel
Diocese of Helena
Reverend Monsignor J. Warren
 Holleran
Diocese of Joliet
Reverend Richard E. Jozwiak
Reverend Thomas M. Kalita
Reverend James A. Kastner

His Eminence William Cardinal Keeler

Reverend Monsignor Charles B. King

Reverend Thomas E. Kramer

Reverend Raymond J. Kupke

Reverend Ralph J. Lawrence

Most Reverend William J. Levada

Most Reverend Oscar H. Lipscomb

Reverend Monsignor Roy Edward Literski

His Eminence Adam Cardinal Maida

Reverend Thaddeus S. Maida

Reverend Richard C. Meredith

Missionaries of La Salette

Reverend Monsignor James M. Moynihan

Reverend Monsignor James J. Mulligan

Dr. Carmen Marie Nanko

Archdiocese of New York

Reverend Joseph A. O'Brien

Reverend Raymond O'Brien

Archdiocese of Omaha

Paulist Fathers

Dr. and Mrs. James B. Peter

Reverend Paul F. Peter

Reverend Val J. Peter

Reverend Monsignor Joseph W. Pokusa

Reverend John F. Porter

Diocese of Raleigh

Reverend Monsignor Joseph Ranieri

Reverend Monsignor Roger G. Roensch

Dr. and Mrs. Paul and Sara Russell

St. Vincent De Paul Village

Reverend Gary Schexnayder

Most Reverend Stanley G. Schlarman

Reverend Walter J. Schmitz [deceased]

Diocese of Scranton

Reverend Monsignor Paul W. Sheridan

Reverend Monsignor Edward A. Synan

Reverend Monsignor Herbert K. Tillyer

Most Reverend James Timlin

Reverend Monsignor Robert Trisco

Reverend Christopher J. Walsh

Dr. Clarence C. Walton

Reverend Monsignor John F. Wippel

Index

Anthropology: and justification, 209–14

Collegiality: effective and affective, 94–97; present context, 89–91
Compunction: and contemporary life, 232–40; and God's holiness, 234–40; and the *Ordo Paenitentiae*, 232–34; and tears, 228–32

Death, 254–56

Ecological eschatology, 273–74
Episcopal conferences: characteristics of, 108–10; criticisms of, 102–3; history, 100–102; theological authority, 105–8; theological status, 103–5
Eschatology: agreeable statements of, 249–51; *apocatastasis*, 269–71; and Carl Peter, 35–48, 241–43; current context, 244–49; and death, 254–56; ecological eschatology, 273–74; "eschatological reservation," 36–39; feminist eschatology, 272–73; hermeneutics of, 249–51; intermediate state, 257–65; and the international Theological Commission, 243–49; liberational eschatology, 272; process eschatology, 274; purgatory, 256–57; reincarnation, 265–69

Feminist eschatology, 272–73

Hermeneutics: of eschatological statements, 251–54

Infallibility: and Luis Bermejo, 146–49; biblical basis of, 131–33; and Peter Chirico, 153–56; and Patrick Granfield, 149–51; and Isaac Hecker, 145–46; and Hans Küng, 114; and Bernard Lonergan, 156–68; and Martin Luther, 112; and Lutheran/Roman Catholic convergence, 123–31; and John Henry Newman, 141–45; and James O' Connor, 140; and Margaret O'Gara, 136–38; and Carl Peter, 115–22; and Francis Sullivan, 152–54; and Gustave Thils, 138–40; tradition of, 133–35; and Vatican I, 135–41; and Vatican II, 127–28
Intermediate state, 257–65
International Theological Commission: and eschatology, 243–49; and Carl Peter, 17

Jus Divinum: and Carl Peter, 18–20
Justification: and Augustine, 164–65; contemporary experience of, 202–7; and the Council of Trent, 189–93; as criterion of all church life, 49–50; and Franciscan theologians, 166–67; and liturgical sharing, 178–81; and Luther, 167–69, 183–89; and Lutheran Churches, 169–70; and Lutheran-Catholic dialogue, 173–78; and John Henry Newman, 199–201; post-Reformation theology of, 170–73; and Girolamo Seripando, 190–99; and Thomas

Church and Theology: Essays in Memory of Carl J. Peter was composed in Stone Serif
by Books International, Norcross, Georgia; printed on 60-pound Booktext
Natural and bound by BookCrafters, Inc., of Chelsea, Michigan; and designed
and produced by Kachergis Book Design, Pittsboro, North Carolina.